# ESSENTIAL EDINBURGH

♣♣♣

Alan Hamilton

# ESSENTIAL EDINBURGH

♣♣♣

ANDRE DEUTSCH

First published 1978 by
André Deutsch Limited
105 Great Russell Street London WC1

Copyright © 1978 by Alan Hamilton
All rights reserved

Printed in Great Britain by
Cox & Wyman Ltd
London, Fakenham and Reading

ISBN 0 233 96984 5

For Duncan

# Contents

♣♣♣

# List of Plates

♣ ♣ ♣

*Photographs by J. Thomson*

# Acknowledgements

✦✦✦

A great many people have provided information for this book. I owe particular thanks to the Historic Buildings Council of the Scottish Development Department, to whose records I was given free access, and whose anonymous inspectors have been constantly at my elbow. I had invaluable assistance from the National Trust for Scotland, especially from Philip Sked and John Batty. I received endless patience and help from officials of Lothian Regional and Edinburgh District councils, notably their press departments. The Edinburgh Room of the Central Public Library was, as always, invaluable and its staff accommodating, as were the staff of the Edinburgh New Town Conservation Committee. Many other organizations and individuals answered my inquiries willingly and patiently, and I offer them all my thanks. I am also grateful to Christopher Stafford, who suggested this book, Christopher Wheeler, who encouraged it, the Editor of *The Times*, who gave it his blessing, Stephen Harrison, who got me around the city, and Rosalind Bartlett, who prepared the final manuscript. My thanks to them all.

# Author's Note

♣ ♣ ♣

Although this book attempts to be reasonably comprehensive, it makes no claims to be an exhaustive catalogue of items of interest in the City of Edinburgh District. I hope, however, that it describes sufficient places of note – historic, architectural, literary, scenic and plain odd – to satisfy the curiosity of visitor and resident alike. Inclusion of an item in this book is no guarantee of public access, and although the great majority may be seen and enjoyed without difficulty, there are some where the privacy of the owners should be respected at all times.

# CHAPTER I

# The Edinburghers

♣♣♣

'I have been trying all my life,' said the essayist Charles Lamb, 'to like Scotchmen, and am obliged to desist from the experiment in despair.'

Lamb was articulating what a good many Englishmen and other more distant foreigners have felt before and since, that a Scotsman's motives are impenetrable and his finer qualities are, to say the least, elusive. The Scottish race has been variously and plentifully accused of being dour, mean, venal, sly, narrow, slothful, sluttish, nasty, dirty, immoderately drunken, embarrassingly sentimental, masterfully hypocritical, and a blueprint for disaster when eleven of them are together on a football field.

Sydney Smith, 19th-century man of letters, believed that it required a surgical operation to get a joke into a Scotsman's brain. But, on the other hand, Dr Samuel Johnson grudgingly admitted that much might be made of a Scotchman if he were caught young, and some years ago an American professor discovered, after exhaustive research, that next to the Jews the Scots exhibited a higher incidence of genius per head of population than any other race on earth. Others have supported this assertion by observing that the Scots must be an intelligent race, as so many of them leave their native land at the earliest opportunity.

Those who know us better will appreciate that we display these vices only in moderation. We are sentimental because we are intensely proud of our history, our nationhood and our ancestors, but we do not admire open displays of sentiment in others. We are not dour, rather we need an occasional small dose of Calvinist rigour to temper our naturally high spirits. And we are certainly not mean; we may sometimes be cautious, for we have long memories of poverty, but we are just as often generous to a fault.

We are not hypocritical, at least not very. We are imbued with a strong streak of common sense, and we are masters of the art of the possible. We love nothing better than logical argument, so much so that, in Edinburgh at least, we are sometimes suspected of even making love on a metaphysical level, which may account for the relatively static population. We are far from humourless; our humour is often sardonic or de-bunking, because we do not wish to make ourselves vulnerable, or it is dry and intellectual, making a sharp political point, because we are political animals with a long and strong democratic tradition which we wish to preserve.

We are, above all, independent in character and original in thought, which may explain why we have spent so much of our history fighting amongst ourselves, and why present-day Scottish politics are so fragmented; if two Scotsmen form a political party, one of them will immediately form a splinter group. It may also explain why, while we produce so many top-class individual footballers, they can sometimes invite calamity when they play together as a team.

That the Scottish character is a double-sided phenomenon is not in doubt, when in one breath it can sing laments for the return of a long-dead prince of a minority religion who brought ruin to the land, and in the next seriously propose to turn itself into an oil-rich autonomous republic with its own army, navy and air force. This happy ability to make the conflicting and the illogical live side by side is a national trait which characterizes Scotland's spectacular capital city of Edinburgh.

Edinburgh boasts one of the finest and best-preserved neo-classical town planning developments anywhere; yet not many years ago she also boasted the nastiest slums in Europe outside Naples. The medical men of Edinburgh have led the world in transplantation surgery and the eradication of tuberculosis, yet until 1977 the city pumped all her sewage, raw and untreated, into the sea just off her shore. We have teaching hospitals and a medical school that are amongst the finest in the world, yet we propel ourselves to an early grave on an unhealthy diet of bread, cakes, biscuits and soft water.

And it is entirely characteristic that her best-known brothel should have been housed in a Grade A historic building.

Like Rome, Edinburgh is built on seven hills. From the rich Lothian coastal plain skirting the Forth estuary she spreads upwards, over the rumps of ancient volcanoes, into the Pentland Hills, and comes to rest at a 1,600-foot summit in the midst of a grouse moor. Her geographical location is her prime asset, and fine use she has made of it. But unlike Rome, Edinburgh has a climate which Robert Louis Stevenson regarded as one of the vilest under heaven.

Stevenson was forced to escape with his delicate constitution to the kinder climes of the South Pacific, where he was free from the *haar*, the chilling sea mist that creeps quietly in from the Forth propelled by an icy east wind to blanket the city and turn a bright, clear afternoon into a dripping blanket of freezing, penetrating cotton wool. The east wind need not be accompanied by the mist; it can slip its chilly fingers inside the warmest clothing entirely on its own.

But there are compensations. These are northern latitudes, the same distance from the equator as Perryville, Alaska, Moscow, Tyndinskiy, Siberia, and Nain, Labrador. In summer, the days are long, the air is crisp and invigorating, there are a surprising number of sunshine hours, and temperatures in the eighties are perfectly common. The annual rainfall is a drop or two above twenty-five inches. Sir Edward Appleton, a distinguished physicist and former principal of the University, held that Edinburgh's fecundity in producing great men had not a little to do with the climate: cool enough to stimulate the brain, but not cold enough to sap all one's imaginative powers in working out how to keep warm.

Upon her high and windy ridge old Edinburgh has watched the march of Scottish history, and every ebb and flow of that often stormy tide has left its mark on the ancient stones. For 646 years, from the granting of its first charter by King Robert Bruce in 1329, the city itself had a long and proud history of independent government, the provost and town council were masters in their own home and, by and large, imaginative, efficient and good housekeepers. For centuries they protected their town against fire, sword, English raiders and incompetent

Scottish kings; but they were powerless against the encroachments of modern bureaucracy.

In 1975, in the first major reconstruction of Scottish local government since 1929, the Town Council of Edinburgh was abolished by Act of Parliament, and in its place came a two-tier structure of local government which has yet to prove its superiority. Edinburgh is now ruled by two masters.

The Lothian Regional Council, which governs the ancient province of Lothian from Dunbar to Linlithgow, now controls the major functions of local government, and is responsible for collecting rates, and providing from them the services of education, main drainage, highways, planning, transport, water supply, industrial development, police and fire services, social welfare and the care of young offenders.

What was once Edinburgh Town Council is now the City of Edinburgh District Council, and although its members and staff are in many cases the same people as before, their former power has been stripped away, leaving housing as their main responsibility, with some other menial tasks thrown in, like looking after public baths, burial grounds, refuse collection, slaughterhouses, museums, libraries and public golf courses. The chairman was allowed to keep the title of Lord Provost, an office which has been in continuous occupation since 1296, but he had to fend off a mean attempt to deprive him of his robes and chain of office.

The two-tier system has the effect of making the governors even more remote from the governed, and it does not appear to make for speedy and decisive action. The district council may want to build a few houses, but first it has to ask Lothian region if it can have some drains.

But let us be fair to the city's new masters; hardly was the Queen's signature dry on the Act of Parliament when they were launching ambitious projects of undoubted benefit to Edinburgh. In 1977, in the Megget valley far to the south in the Border hills, they began work on a vast new reservoir which will bring an extra 45 million gallons of water a day to the region. And at the same time, to their great credit, they have begun to do something sensible about the roads.

Edinburgh is a museum as well as a metropolis, and with

some 2,500 preserved buildings within its boundaries, it is not an easy place to tamper with – thank heaven. Since a major study was carried out on the problem in 1949, there have been numerous schemes, some more lunatic and environmentally disastrous than others, for a variety of ring roads, relief roads and other sacrificial offerings to the motor car. All would have caused harm, in greater or lesser degree, to the city. Now they have been abandoned in favour of the only sane solution, a bypass which will avoid the city entirely.

But some damage has already been done. The alternative road schemes, which would have cut great swathes through the urban area, were on the drawing board and in the mouths of councillors for long enough to create ribbons of planning blight along their proposed routes. Edinburgh has lost much good building unnecessarily.

Another commendable decision by the new kings of Lothian has been to eradicate the worst scars of the area's industrial past. To the west of the city is a mountain range of huge orange spoil tips, remnants of the world's first commercial oilfield, which the regional council is bent upon removing. James 'Paraffin' Young, a Glasgow chemist, was producing oil from the West Lothian shales in 1853, six years before the first American oil well was drilled. Production reached a peak of 25 million gallons per year in the late 19th century, but the last mine closed in 1962, leaving only the vast piles of waste that makes excellent foundations for motorways. To the south and east of the city a number of large colliery waste tips, many still burning and producing noxious gases, are being removed or landscaped.

Such manifestations of heavy industry are untypical of the city itself. Lothian coal goes mostly to the power stations, and evidence of the new oil industry, this time from the North Sea, will be found in the board rooms of the banks and investment houses of Edinburgh rather than on the ground. Edinburgh is not, nor ever has been, a major centre of manufacturing. It is a city of white-collar workers, and of all big British cities it is the most predominantly middle-class.

The picture emerges in a few simple statistics. The city has a working population of about 195,000, and an unemployment pool which tends to be one or two per cent below the Scottish average. Of those in work, only some 25,000 are engaged in manufacturing industry, while almost as many – 21,000 – work in public administration, in the offices of local and national government. Another 55,000 work in banks, insurance offices, finance houses, assorted businesses, and professional, scientific and educational establishments. Almost three-quarters of the city's workforce is engaged in a service industry of one kind or another, be it financing an oil platform or delivering bread.

The same picture is shown in the way that the city draws its revenue. Edinburgh has a total rateable value of £38.7 million; of that total, only £2 million is accounted for by industrial premises, while commercial premises contribute £12 million, and housing a substantial £16 million. It is a city of offices and houses, and good houses too.

But even Edinburgh has to earn its living from something more productive than paperwork. It is one of the major brewing centres of the United Kingdom, and its two distilleries, both among the largest in Scotland, produce bulk grain whisky for blending with the finer Highland malts; blending is itself a major industry, although the entire whisky industry produces colossal sums for the British Treasury with only a handful of workers. Printing, one of the city's traditional industries, is still a major employer, although another traditional industry, fine paper production, has all but died out.

There are heavy industrial plants making electronic equipment, electrical generators, paper mill machinery and fertilizers, and little factories making food flavourings, bagpipes, socks, printing ink, rusks, wire, wooden legs and a hundred other items. Because her industrial workforce is relatively small and diverse, Edinburgh lacks the immensely rich and warm store of working-class humour and folklore, born of oppression and hard times, that is one of Glasgow's greatest gifts to the world.

By its very nature as a capital, Edinburgh is bound to be a city of bureaucrats and other sundry office workers. But there has been no monarch in permanent residence since 1603, and no parliament since 1707, so what, in heaven's name, do they all *do*?

Devolution of Scottish affairs has gone further than is often realized. As well as the principal Scottish government departments at St Andrew's House under the control of the Secretary of State for Scotland, covering agriculture, fisheries, prisons, health and education, almost every Government ministry now has a Scottish branch office in Edinburgh. And many public bodies have their headquarters here, for the North of Scotland Hydro-Electric Board to the White Fish Authority.

When Scotland lost her own parliament in 1707, she could very well have lost her sense of nationhood altogether had she not been able to hang on to two of her own peculiar institutions, her church and her law courts. Both still exist today in a spirit of healthy independence from their English counterparts, and both have their headquarters in Edinburgh.

The Church of Scotland – the 'Kirk' – is the established church of the nation, and the largest, with 1,900 ministers and rather more than one million communicants. It is a Presbyterian church, and has in its time been held up as the most democratic body of men in the world. The individual congregations elect their ministers, and there is no hierarchy, all ministers being equal, and no head of the church, at least not on this earth. Even the Sovereign is a mere member of the Kirk, and much of its time since the Reformation of 1560 has been spent in fighting off the introduction of bishops. Like most organizations which claim impeccable democratic credentials, it is in fact ruled and run by committees, the highest being the General Assembly, of which all ministers are members, and which sits in Edinburgh in May of each year, providing a fine pageant of clerical grey.

Otherwise the Kirk shows little outward sign of its organization, except for a handsome Italianate office building in George Street. But unlike some other established churches, it takes an active interest in affairs of state, and its church and nation committee will usually make a contribution to any national debate. What is more, people occasionally pay attention to it.

The Kirk was shaken to its foundations in 1843. During its General Assembly in Edinburgh that year, 470 ministers walked out in protest that the Kirk had 'gone soft', losing its evangelical spirit and accepting patronage of ministries; this was called 'the Disruption'. They formed their own Free Church of Scotland, which existed until a reunification in 1929. Even then, not all ministers chose to return to the fold, and a rump of the Disruption still exists in the present-day Free Church, a small organization drawing its support chiefly from the Highlands and Islands, and which rather cheekily holds its General Assembly concurrently with the Kirk, in a hall just across the street.

The Free Church maintains a strong streak of undiluted Calvinism, and its assembly will quite readily despatch a telegram to the Royal Family rebuking them for playing polo or some such frolic on the Sabbath Day. The Roman Catholic church has some 800,000 members in Scotland, enjoys generally good relations with the Kirk, also plays an active part in public life, and is stronger in the west of Scotland than in Edinburgh.

But there is one body of men in the city more powerful, more influential, more involved, than any other, and that is the legal profession. Look at any Edinburgh man holding public office, be he sitting on a committee, administering a charity, campaigning for the preservation of a monument, or selling your house, and you will find a Scots lawyer underneath.

During the city's golden age of art and letters in the early 19th century, almost all the eminent men, from Sir Walter Scott downwards, were lawyers. Today they operate a legal machine which is unique, and in many ways superior to other European models.

Scots law is unusual in being derived from both of the principal legal systems of Europe, English law and Roman law, although it inclines towards the Roman model and differs from contemporary English legal practice in several important respects. A crime is a crime on both sides of the border, with one or two minor technical exceptions, but we have different ways of dealing with it up here. Scots lawyers themselves would claim that their system is more compassionate, more logical, more concerned with the individual than with property, with justice rather than technicality, and based more on principle than on precedent. They may exaggerate a little, but it is noteworthy that England has adopted, or is considering the adoption of, several important Scottish legal practices.

The senior court for criminal offences is the High Court of Justiciary in Edinburgh, from which there is appeal only to the Scottish Court of Criminal Appeal, and not to the House of Lords. The principal civil court is the Court of Session, also in Edinburgh, which does allow appeal to the Lords. This is, of course, all quite academic to the law-abiding visitor, but he will nonetheless run into the peculiarities of Scots civil law if he wishes to buy a house. There are no Dutch auctions in front gardens, no 'gazumping', and no last minute changes of mind; if you wish to buy a house, you make a written offer to a lawyer, and if your offer is accepted, you are deemed to have entered a binding contract. It is an excellent system for the seller, but it can be trying for the buyer.

The Scottish legal bench has for centuries provided Edinburgh with some of its most colourful characters, from the charming and the eccentric to the downright unbearable. From their number, for example, came one of the world-class bores of the 18th century. Lord Hermand was fond of illustrating obscure legal points from the bench by reading aloud entire chapters of Scott's *Guy Mannering*; as bores go, his friends would say, Hermand is artesian. There is no bore of his class sitting in the High Court today, but there are still characters, like the erudite and charming Lord Birsay, who takes his unique Scottish Land Court to the remotest corners of the kingdom, with all the powers of the High Court and the informality, completed by his perpetual kilt, of a Sunday-school picnic.

Scots lawyers are less isolated from the rest of the world than they used to be. Not only are the Scottish and English systems being gradually brought into line, but membership of the European Community has provided another outlet for the Scots tradition of Roman law.

At the time of the Union in 1707, Scotland also retained something of her own education system, being at that time far in advance of the English in the provision of a school in every parish for the benefit of all children, rich or poor. Scottish education has always believed itself to have a great egalitarian tradition, but in Edinburgh the reverse tends to be true. The city is richly provided with privately-endowed schools, and out of 145,000 schoolchildren in Edinburgh and surrounding districts, no less than 13,000 are receiving some form of private or semi-private education.

Until recent years many of these schools, although privately governed, received substantial Government grants, and provided a good education at reasonable cost. Now the grants have been withdrawn, and schools must choose to become wholly independent or enter the state education system. Many an Edinburgh parent, who still places a very high value on education, has found that the cost of keeping a child at one of these schools has gone up from £40 per term to £200. But it is significant that the numbers attending private schools have hardly dropped at all.

After all this intensive schooling, followed by long hours in a Government office thinking of new laws for the lawyers to amuse themselves with and for the Kirk to condemn, what do the citizens do for recreation? Even the supposedly dour, patrician, withdrawn, haughty Edinburghers have been known to take an hour off for play.

Christianity is the second religion of Scotland. The first does not have quite the fanatical following here that it does in Glasgow, but there are still two professional football teams in Edinburgh, Heart of Midlothian and Hibernian, to amuse, excite, and enrage their supporters on a Saturday afternoon. Any comment on one is certain to invoke fearful retribution from the supporters of the other, so we had best leave it at that.

Rugby union – the amateur game – has a religious following in only two parts of the United Kingdom, the Scottish Borders and South Wales; in those areas it is a people's game, played and watched by ordinary men to the exclusion of football. In Edinburgh rugby union is the game of the classier schools and of the universities and colleges, although any rugby international at Murrayfield will attract an enormous, enthusiastic, and generally well-behaved crowd.

Edinburgh is a fine place from which to go walking in the hills, sailing on the Forth, or fishing on the Tay or the Tweed. But the principal participant sport of the people is, naturally, golf. It is not, as in England, the game of the moderately rich or the faintly snobbish; the city invented the game, offers facilities for it in profusion, and plays it without taking any notice of wealth or social class.

The other major participant sport is played, also by every social class, in public houses. I used to think that the Scots were the most enthusiastic consumers of alcohol in the world, but that was before I visited Iceland, Russia and Finland, and I conclude that the nearer the North Pole and the more repressive the liquor laws, the more spectacular the indulgence. Compared with the dwellers of the sub-Arctic regions, the Scots are effete amateurs in the sport of drink; but among contenders in the more civilized temperate zone, they are undoubtedly in the premier league.

That two-sided Scots personality comes forcefully into play where drink is involved. An Edinburgh man is rarely drunk, although he may be *legless, stottin', trousered, steamboats,* or *as fu' as a puggy.* Upright citizens of the suburbs, who are probably elders of the Kirk as well, might choose to perish in the Calvinist hellfire before being seen in a pub, but they know that they can always rely on that useful Scottish institution, the licensed grocer. As the canny shopkeeper makes up the weekly order in a cardboard box for some stout city matron, he will quietly and solicitously inquire: 'Will madam be requiring a little something under the potatoes?'

Our behaviour under the influence has greatly improved, at least on the city streets, since the repressive licensing laws were eased in 1977. But we still retain one of the vilest drinking habits I know. We produce the finest whisky in the world, made with patience, skill, care and a great deal of time; we profess to know it, appreciate it, love it, and tell one blend from another. And yet we put *lemonade* in it.

So here we are adulterating our whisky, wondering where our promised fortunes from Scottish oil have gone, breeding and educating men who can run both black African marxist people's democracies and embattled white settlers' enclaves, trying to clean up our city after accusations that she is an old lady who has powdered her nose but forgotten to wipe her behind, speaking our bastard lowland dialect of English vocabulary and Doric idiom, readily accepting £50 million in tourist revenue each year, yet squabbling over money to such a degree that we have a hole in the ground where we should have had an opera house.

It is as well that we can still laugh at ourselves. A man from the city, a man of unimpeachable character, went to heaven and was interrogated by St Peter at the gates to establish the stainless nature of his earthly life. 'I see,' said St Peter, consulting his ledger, 'that you were a shopkeeper, a magistrate in the burgh court, and an elder of the Kirk. How very commendable.' The man agreed, and pointed out that he had never cheated a customer, had always shown mercy to offenders, and had served God dutifully through the Presbyterian faith. 'You have certainly led an upstanding and unblemished life,' said the keeper of the gates. 'Did you say you were from Edinburgh?'

The man agreed he was. 'Well,' said St Peter, 'you can come in, but you won't like it here.'

# CHAPTER 2

# The First City

♣ ♣ ♣

The earliest origins of Edinburgh are obscured in a thick Scotch mist, and even the derivation of the name is fogged by uncertainty. More might have been known had not Edward I, the 13th century Hammer of the Scots, carried off the nation's records from Edinburgh Castle, consigning them to London or to flames. Still, a little romantic mystery is no bad thing.

When the army of Julius Agricola reached Lothian in AD 80, the area from the Tyne to the Forth was settled along the coast by the Ottadeni, and inland by the Gadeni, two of the twenty-one Caledonian tribes then occupying north Britain, and both of sufficiently threatening demeanour to require the building of Hadrian's Wall. But Agricola did not stay to conquer. Lollius Urbicus ventured north of Hadrian's Wall in AD 139 to establish control over the turbulent Lowland tribes which constantly threatened the northern frontier of the Roman empire; he turned Lothian and Strathclyde into the sixth British province of Valenta, and established a more lasting Roman presence. Forts were established in the Scottish Borders, at Fisherrow to the east of Edinburgh, and at Cramond to the west, the latter being a supply station for the building of the Antonine Wall, a fortified earthwork from the Forth to the Clyde. Traces of a causeway from Fisherrow to Cramond have been found, possibly part of the Roman Dere Street from York to the Tay, but the imperial military engineers appear to have ignored the natural defensive properties of the Castle Rock. It is however probable that the Ottadeni occupied it with a rough hill fort of earth and wooden palisades, and as the Roman occupation developed in time into an amicable partnership of co-existence and trade, there they doubtless remained. Ptolemy, mapping the Roman empire in the 2nd century AD, referred to it as *Castrum Alatum*, from a fancied resemblance to a spread eagle.

After the Romans finally left Britain in AD 443 the northern tribes, by now collectively known as the Picts and with a reputation for warring amongst themselves which has clung to the nation ever since, probably continued to occupy the rock until ousted by the Saxons of Northumbria in 452. Thus began 600 years of largely uncharted struggle for the rock between Pict and Saxon. By now it may even have acquired a name, *Dun Edin* ( the fort on the hillside), or *Obsessio Etin*, mentioned in the *Annals of Tigernach* of 638, or perhaps it was *Eden Oppidum*, a place known to have been abandoned by the Angles in 954, although anyone who has savoured the occasional purgatory of its climate must wonder what misguided motives the ancients had for giving it the name of Paradise.

King Edwin of Northumbria now enters the lists to advance his claim to the naming of the city. Edwin came to the northern end of his kingdom in AD 682 and rebuilt the fort on the hill for the first time in stone, probably quarried at Craigmillar in the south-eastern quarter of the present city. His successor Egfrid promptly lost the northern half of his kingdom to the Picts under King Brude in 685, and the Pictish border was established for the first time on the river Tweed, where it has remained – more or less – ever since.

With a frontier established fifty miles to the south a measure of security came to the Castle Rock, and gradually a huddle of huts grew up around it. By 854 the huddle had grown to a sufficiently sized township for the bishopric of Lindisfarne in Northumberland to establish a small wooden chapel dedicated to St Giles, a saint then popular in France. But the kings of the newly united nation of Picts and Scots preferred to keep court well up country, at Scone in Perthshire or Dunfermline, safely across the Forth. The boundary of Scotland was more clearly defined in 1018 when Northumbria formally and finally ceded Lothian to the Scots; but for all that, it was Saxon rather than Pictish influence that subsequently shaped Edinburgh, and it has always remained the most anglicized of Scottish cities.

Fifty years later King Malcolm III, son of Shakespeare's murdered Duncan and successor to Macbeth, took the throne and married Margaret, the grand-niece of Edward the Confessor who had fled from England at the Norman Conquest and was shipwrecked in the Forth. Their capital was at Dunfermline, but they chose to build another, more fortified, royal residence on the Castle Rock. From this point the known history of Edinburgh begins, and the marker is the tiny chapel the saintly Margaret had built for herself on the very summit of the rock. It still stands, 900 years on, the oldest building in Edinburgh.

Her youngest son David I succeeded to the throne in 1107, and it was he who first properly established Edinburgh, moving the garrison out from its protective huddle on the Castle Rock to form a little medieval walled town on the eastern slopes of the hill, reaching from the Castle to the present-day intersection of the High Street and South Bridge. This 12th-century wall, not a trace of which remains, was of turf and earth, with wooden gates surmounted by iron spikes. Inside, the new burghers were allotted plots of land on either side of a single main street, on the line of the present Lawnmarket and High Street, but fourteen feet wider. Each citizen had his 'enclosure', a croft or smallholding of not less than a rood (¼ acre), upon which he kept cattle, pigs, sheep and poultry, and upon which he built his house, wooden-framed with clay or plaster infill, and a roof of turf or thatch. As often as not, the houses had their gables to the street and their entrances at the side, reached by an alley running down the side of the enclosure to a lane at the rear. The alleys were the foundation of the dark, narrow closes (from *enclosures*) which became a feature of the old town when building extended behind the single rows of houses, and which still remain in abundance. One of the back lanes, that on the southern side, remains as the Cowgate, along which cattle were taken to their daily grazing on the common land of the Burgh Muir.

Even in the 12th century, the rudiments of town planning regulation existed. Under the 'Law of the Four Burghs' the houses had to be at least three feet apart, and officials known as 'liners' ensured that the law was observed. It must have been an attractive little town, the lime-washed walls of its houses framed by carved and painted beams of oak, hewn from the forest of Drumsheugh to the north. In the centre of the wide street, the monks of Lindisfarne were rebuilding the 9th-century wooden chapel of St Giles as a substantial structure in stone with timber roof, fragments of which survive in the massive pillars under the crown spire.

In 1128 King David further embellished his metropolis by granting to a convent of Augustinian canons residing within the Castle the new abbey of Holyrood, and with it a substantial parcel of land upon which they established their own burgh of Canongate, to the east of Edinburgh. According to tradition, on 14 September 1128, when he should have been at prayer, it being a holy day, King David chose to go hunting in the forest of Drumsheugh. A stag, maddened by the 'noys and dyn of bugillis', leapt at him, knocking him from his horse, and he was only saved from further injury by the sudden and miraculous appearance of a cross between its antlers. In gratitude for this divine intervention, he founded the abbey, and the crest of the Burgh of Canongate ever afterwards bore the representation of a cross and a stag's head.

Edinburgh now had all the attributes of an important medieval town: the King in his Castle, the citizens in their walled burg with their church, and the canons in their abbey at the foot of the hill. It prospered and expanded; King David had brought with him Norman barons from his long residence at the court of Henry I of England, and to them he gave lands around the town. Many of their names – de Brade, de Doding, de Lestalric, Napier – survive in the names of modern city districts. They in their turn attracted other immigrants, and by the close of the 12th century the little town was home to considerable numbers of French, Flemish and English.

Alexander II convened the first Scots parliament in Edinburgh in 1215, and his son, Alexander III, repaired and strengthened the Castle, making it the repository of the regalia and records of Scotland. His wife Margaret, daughter of Henry III of England, was not so enamoured of it. She complained to her father that it was 'a sad and solitary place, without verdure, and by reason of its vicinity to the sea, unwholesome'.

The death of Alexander III signalled the end of Edinburgh's first golden age, with a disputed succession to the throne and the arrival of Edward I of England, called in as an umpire, but seizing the chance to subjugate once and for all the northern kingdom. Edward took Edinburgh Castle in 1291 and burned the town which, being chiefly of timber and thatch, burned well. It was the first of many attacks and counter-attacks during the ensuing thirty-year war of independence, in which the Castle changed hands several times.

Robert Bruce's victory at Bannockburn in 1314 established Scotland's nationhood and rid her of the English oppressor, but only for the time being; the fire and sword of invasion was to be visited upon Edinburgh many more times throughout the 14th century. That the Scottish nation was still far from secure is shown by the Declaration of Arbroath, a stirring document of national purpose drawn up by the Scots barons in 1320 appealing to the Pope to recognize Bruce as King, which states in part: 'So long as an hundred of us remain alive we are minded never a whit to bow beneath the yoke of the English. It is not for glory, riches or honours that we fight; it is for liberty alone, the liberty which no good man loses but with his life.'

Despite the march and counter-march of armies, the pillage and the sheer uncertainty of life, Edinburgh retained and consolidated its position as the principal burgh of the kingdom. In 1296 it had its first chief magistrate, William de Dederyk, the start of an unbroken line of succession to the present-day Lord Provost. And in 1329 it became a Royal Burgh with the granting of its first charter by King Robert Bruce, ten days before his death; the charter makes mention of Edinburgh's mills, and grants to the Burgh the port of Leith, an indication that it was already an established centre of industry and commerce.

With the English repulsed, at least for the present, Edinburgh had an opportunity to recover and rebuild. David II enlarged and strengthened the Castle, adding a 60-foot Great Tower which was rediscovered beneath subsequent building in the early years of this century. Under the Castle Rock, to the south-west, he built a great stables and jousting ground – the 'Barras' – and a new suburb grew up at the West Port to house the workmen employed in its building, while the old turf wall was rebuilt in stone. At the same time the original burg was indulging in some modest expansion to the south of the

Castlehill ridge, known as the Newbiggin (New building), in the areas of the present-day Grassmarket and Cowgate. This was partly to accommodate the continuing flow of immigrants attracted to Edinburgh from England and the Continent, many of them merchants and a large number from Berkick, which, being a frontier town in the thick of the Anglo-Scottish hostilities, was no place for the orderly conduct of business. Merchants came to Edinburgh in such numbers that the town's newly-acquired port of Leith had to be enlarged to accommodate them, and duties imposed on their vessels provided a substantial revenue to the town. From Leith went Scots exports of hides, sheepskins, rough woollen cloth, salmon and herring, and in return came timber from the Baltic, wines from Gascony, linen, dried fruits, rice, sugar, ginger, honey, almonds, olive oil and vinegar. Leith which at the beginning of the 13th century was the fifth port in Scotland, was easily the largest by its end.

In 1385 an English force under Richard II laid waste the town and burned the Norman church of St Giles to the ground, leaving only a few fragments. But within two years the masons had started to rebuild it on a much more magnificent scale and their work, which took a century to complete, is the fine Gothic cathedral which, with a few additions and alterations, stands today. Not that all attacks upon the town and its fortress were successful; in 1400 Henry IV laid siege to the Castle, but it had been so well repaired by David II that its defenders needed only patience, until the wind, rain and bitter cold of the Edinburgh ridge drove the English home again before they could do any significant damage.

King James I did not much care for Edinburgh, preferring to hold court at Perth. Sitting there with his parliament in 1425, he at least took note of the dangers facing his chief burgh from within, and passed a series of laws requiring Edinburgh's magistrates to be equipped with basic firefighting equipment, including eight ladders of 20-feet length, several large saws for common use, and six or more 'cleikes [hooks] of iron to draw down timber and roofs that are fired'. Another of his laws forbade any fire to be carried from one house to another, except in a lantern or covered vessel, and yet another forbade people on social visits to live with their friends, but to put up in lodging houses. The little town was already crowded, with a population of about 2,000, and the houses were still mainly of timber or thatch, although most were of no more than two storeys, 20 feet in height.

The assassination of James I at Perth in 1437 finally confirmed Edinburgh as the capital of Scotland, its castle being the safest place in the kingdom. His successor, the boy king James II, was crowned at Holyrood on 25 March the same year, and proceeded to take a greater interest in his capital. England was preoccupied with her internal troubles in the Wars of the Roses, but James nonetheless thought it prudent to improve the defences of Edinburgh. By a charter of 1450 he empowered the magistrates to build a new town wall for, as he recognized in the charter's preamble, 'We are informed by our well-beloved Provost and Community of Edinburgh that they dread the evil and scathe of our enemies of England.'

It took twenty-two years for the Provost and Community to get the wall built. It encompassed a smaller area than previous defensive works, running along the southern edge of the ridge between the High Street and Cowgate, crossing the High Street at the Netherbow (the present-day junction with Jeffrey Street), and terminating at the eastern end of the Nor' Loch, a stretch of swamp in what is now Princes Street Gardens which was dammed and extended to complete the defences. The delay was caused by the citizens of the Cowgate and Grassmarket who, being outside the perimeter of the wall and therefore denied its protection, understandably refused to contribute to its construction. Only three fragments of the wall remain, at Tweeddale Court in the High Street, at Castle Wynd between Johnston Terrace and the Grassmarket, and in the Wellhouse Tower in the gardens below the Castle, which, although of earlier construction, was incorporated into the 1450 defences.

But the fears of attack were for once ill-founded, and it was not until nearly a century later that raiders again seriously attempted to intrude upon the city, although in the meantime there was no shortage of internecine strife between Stuart kings and jealous and rebellious nobles. The citizens of Edinburgh, however, enjoyed a long period of relative peace in which to go about their business, and in the latter half of the

15th century the town grew and prospered. By 1451 it was already the most populous in Scotland, and in succeeding years, encouraged by the security of the wall and the pre-occupation of the English with their own affairs, numerous churches, chapels, and hospitals were founded and endowed, Scottish abbeys opened hospices in the High Street, and even an occasional bishop's palace began to appear in the Cowgate. One of the churches founded at this time was that of Trinity College (1462) by Mary of Gueldres, a rebuilt fragment of which remains in Chalmers Close, off the High Street. Richer residents took to building bigger and better houses of stone although, not wishing entirely to abandon the old pattern of smallholdings, they reserved the ground floors for pigs and cattle, building outside staircases to take them to their own living quarters on the first floor.

James III entertained a morbid fear that his closest rela-tives were about to deprive him of the throne, and he impris-oned his brothers, the Duke of Albany and the Earl of Mar, in Edinburgh and Craigmillar Castles. But at least he was positive, practical and generous towards his capital; in 1481, in gratitude for Edinburgh finding the money to pay the dowry of his daughter, he granted the town its so-called 'Golden Charter', giving its provost and bailies the power of sheriffs, and confirming its exclusive right to all customs dues from trade through the port of Leith. But the charter is best remembered for its recognition of the town's several craft guilds, and its granting to the tradesmen a banner which still exists. The Blue Blanket is a silk swallow-tailed flag 10 feet long and 6 feet broad, embroidered with the legend: 'Fear God and honour the King with a long lyffe and a prosperous reigne. We that is Trades shall ever pray to be faithfull for the defence of his sacred Maiesties royal person till Death.' It is said to have been embroidered by the Queen and the ladies of her court, and became the rallying point of the tradesmen, and later of the Town Guard, in every war or civic broil. That, at least, was its proper purpose, but a later Stuart king, James VI, complained: 'The craftsmen think we should be content with their work how bad soever it be; and if in anything they be controlled, up goes the Blue Blanket.' It was the first known trade union banner, and it may be inspected at the Trades Maiden Hospital in Melville Street.

As the 15th century drew to a close Edinburgh was entering her second golden age, encouraged by one of the abler of the variable Stuart line, James IV, crowned at Kelso in 1489. Edinburgh became famous throughout Europe for its jousting and other knightly feats, held in pageantry and splendour in the Barras under the Castle Rock. Knights came from all over the Continent to compete for golden-headed lances; Scottish knights held their own, the champion being Sir Patrick Hamilton, who reputedly could sustain close combat with a heavy two-handed sword for a full hour against the cream of European opposition. The pageantry reached its zenith in 1503, when James married Margaret Tudor, daughter of Henry VII, at Holyrood Abbey, probably the greatest spectacle seen in the city up to that time. James, dressed in a jacket of crimson velvet trimmed with cloth of gold, met his new bride at Dalkeith, and escorted her in great procession to Edinburgh, where the houses were covered with tapestry and a fountain ran with wine.

It was also a time of learning and of building. King James founded the Royal College of Surgeons, Gavin Douglas, Provost of St Giles, translated Virgil's *Aeneid* into Scots verse, and in 1507 Walter Chepman, an Edinburgh merchant, introduced the printing press to Scotland in a shop in the Cowgate. At the same time James superintended the completion of the great Gothic cathedral of St Giles, by now raised to the status of a collegiate church, adding its majestic crown spire; and in honour of his new Queen he took over the guest house of the abbey of Holyrood and commenced its conversion and enlargement to a royal palace. He decided to equip himself with a respectable navy, and founded the little port of Newhaven for the construction of the biggest ship then built, the *Great Michael*. The city was prospering, too, from trade with her English and European neighbours; in 1501–2 customs dues levied at Leith totalled £1,758, a handsome sum at the time. But this golden age came to a tragic and abrupt end in 1513 when King James, answering a call for assistance from Scotland's old ally, France, which was facing invasion from King Henry VIII, assembled the largest army Scotland had ever seen, upwards of 100,000 men, and marched it to annihilation at Flodden Field.

The greatest military disaster in Scottish history set Edinburgh and the whole nation in a panic, and rekindled fears of an imminent English invasion. Edinburgh immediately organized a standing watch, the forerunner of the Town Guard, and set about building a new defensive wall, the citizens being heavily taxed to pay for it. When an English force eventually arrived to lay waste the city, thirty-one years later, the wall had still not been completed. So much for the apparent urgency. The Flodden wall was 18 feet high and 5 feet thick, with six gates or 'ports', battlemented and turreted, and enclosed an area of about 140 acres, considerably more than the wall of 1450, with the Nor' Loch continuing to form the defence on the northern side. In sixty-three years the town had grown, with new suburbs spreading down the southern slope of the ridge to the Cowgate and Grassmarket to house an expanding population which, by the time of Flodden, stood at about 10,000. So great was the shock of defeat that the town did not venture outside the confines of its wall for any major development for another 250 years.

When finally completed in 1560, the town wall ran due south from the Castle across the western end of the Grassmarket, where was situated the West Port; it continued south up the alley now known as the Vennel, where the best preserved portion of it remains, and turned east, along the back of the Grassmarket houses to Greyfriars Kirk and the Bristo Port, at the modern junction of Bristo Place and Forrest Road. It continued east along the line of the present-day Royal Scottish Museum, University Old College and Drummond Street to the Pleasance, where another fragment remains, and turned up St Mary's Street to cross the High Street at the Netherbow Port, the principal gateway to the town. From here it continued northwards for a short distance to include Trinity College Church, on the site of Waverley station, and finally turned west to the end of the Nor' Loch, somewhere under the modern North Bridge. Other gateways were the Potterrow Port, where the short street between the museum and the Old College now stands, and the Cowgate Port, at the southern end of St Mary's Street. A final gateway, the New Port, was installed at its end by the loch, on the site of the present station.

Throughout the first half of the 16th century, expansion of the town was slow, but there were some notable improvements. In 1532 King James V founded the College of Justice, the supreme court of Scotland, an act commemorated in a fine stained-glass window in the Parliament Hall. The harbours of Leith and Newhaven, by now both gifted by the King to Edinburgh, showed steady growth, and by 1550–51 the customs dues collected at Leith had risen to £2,012. To the east of the walled town, the little unprotected burgh of Canongate grew little in size but much in status, as James V continued the work begun by his father and completed the royal palace of Holyrood. With the construction of the palace, Scottish monarchs ceased to drag their court and parliament around the country, and Edinburgh was finally and firmly established as the Scottish capital.

Enclosed by its wall, Edinburgh itself began to feel some sense of security again, and grand houses of stone replaced the humbler 2-storey timber dwellings; in the centre of the High Street, crowded around by market stalls and booths, stood the fine church of St Giles. The town was no longer a single street of crofts; the smallholdings were becoming built over, the wealthy were taking the houses fronting the main street, which was paved for the first time, and the commoners were covering the slopes of the ridge and the former smallholdings with new housing. Several of the grand houses of the period remain, including Bishop Bothwell's House in Advocates Close, and Moubray House and John Knox's House standing together in the High Street, although the two latter have been extensively rebuilt and restored. The forestairs which they still exhibit were not always to avoid the pigs in the cellar; in the houses of the merchants the ground floor formed the shop, with the living quarters above.

But behind the grand façade of the High Street, the old timber and thatch houses persisted, as the Earl of Hertford discovered when he came to set fire to the place in 1544. On the death of James V in 1542, King Henry VIII of England became anxious that his son Edward should be engaged to James's daughter Mary, a wish with which the Scots were singularly unwilling to comply; Henry sent Hertford with an army of 10,000 men, supported by 200 ships, on an expedition which came to be known as the 'rough wooing'. Hertford landed at Granton, seized Leith and Newhaven, and advanced up the High Street, slaughtering citizens on every side, and firing the town in eight places; but the smoke from the thatch and the oak-framed houses was so intense that the invaders were driven out to ravage the surrounding countryside.

Mary may have been as romantic a figure as ever trod the European stage, but during both her minority and her tragic reign she contributed little to her capital city. Scotland was again in turmoil, with pro-English and pro-French factions struggling for the succession, culminating in the siege of Leith, to which the French circle had been banished by the citizens of Edinburgh on account of their arrogance and swagger. John Knox preached for the first time in St Giles' on 1 July 1559, and the cleansing fire of the Reformation was well and truly lit in Scotland. The following year, the dissolution of the monasteries brought many hundreds of displaced craftsmen and tradesmen to swell the population of Edinburgh. On 6 July 1560 the Treaty of Edinburgh brought the Siege of Leith, and warring between Scotland, England and France, to an end; four days later, the Scottish Parliament met in Edinburgh Castle to cast off the authority of the Pope, establish a Protestant nation, and pave the way for eventual union with England. The supporters of Queen Mary fought a strong rearguard action on her behalf even after her exile, and none more valiantly than Sir William Kirkcaldy of Grange, who held Edinburgh Castle against all odds for three years.

With the final defeat of Mary's supporters, and the firm establishment of King James VI on the throne of Scotland, a period of peace returned, and the serious business of trade resumed in earnest, to such an extent that by 1597–8 the customs dues from the port of Leith had shot up to £8,833. But there was no better indication of the times than the founding, by King James in 1582, of the University of Edinburgh, the first democratically-constructed, civic university in Great Britain and one of the first in Europe. The three universities already existing in Scotland, at St Andrews, Aberdeen and Glasgow, were all ecclesiastical Catholic foundations; the Toun's College of Edinburgh owed nothing to any church, and was in the control of the town council. All that King James omitted to do was to endow it with any money, and for more than 200 years it was accommodated in a mean cluster of buildings unworthy of such a great and pioneering institution.

On the Saturday night of 26 March 1603 Sir Robert Carey, who had ridden from London in less than three days, arrived hotfoot at the gates of Holyrood Palace to announce that Queen Elizabeth was dead, and that henceforth King James VI of Scotland was also King James I of England. It was a milestone in the city's history; the King and Court moved to London, never to return, taking with them much pageantry and colour. But at the same time, with Scotland and England united, it was no longer necessary to build behind fortifications; the unwalled burgh of Canongate came into its own: it being a roomier and airier place than the tightly packed town of Edinburgh, it was favoured by the nobility for the building of fine mansions, and several of the period still exist.

Throughout the 17th century, Edinburgh itself remained cramped within its wall, and to cope with an ever-increasing population it had to build upwards. The 2- and 3-storey houses of earlier years had additional floors added and five- and six-storey tenements became common. The city was the birthplace of high-density urban living, and of the high-rise apartment block. For all its crowding, it had what modern sociologists would call 'a good social mix', the highest and lowest in the land living cheek by jowl in the same close or even the same stair. Friendly it may have been, but it was also exceedingly dirty and unhealthy.

The plague first appeared in Edinburgh in 1349, brought by troops from a raid into England, to destroy one-third of the Scottish population, and thereafter it reappeared at frequent intervals. Attempts were made by the town council to control its spread; the master of a household had to report immediately any case of sickness and the death penalty was frequently employed upon those who failed to do so. The last appearance of the plague in Edinburgh was in 1648; its eventual disappearance had nothing to do with administrative measures or advances in medicine, but to the gradual replacement throughout Europe of its carrier, the black or house rat, by the brown or sewer rat. Malaria and leprosy were common, too, and often reached epidemic proportions. In 1530 the Edinburgh magistrates decreed that no leper might enter the city, its churches or its market places, on pain of branding and banishment; elsewhere they were at least permitted, hooded and gowned and with a warning clapper or bell, to solicit alms in the streets.

It was small wonder that disease was so rife, and continued to be so for another two centuries, in the old town. There was neither running water nor sanitation of any kind; water was drawn from wells in the street, carried laboriously in buckets and casks up the steep turnpike stairs of the tenements. All manner of filth and excrement was piled at the close entrances by tidy citizens, and thrown from upstairs windows into the street by the rest. Brave was the man who walked the High Street at night; the ten o'clock bell from St Giles' was the nightly signal for the throwing open of windows, the perfunctory cry of 'Gardyloo' (*Gardez l'eau*), and the tipping of nameless unpleasantness down to the main street of the capital city of a supposedly civilized kingdom. It is no surprise that, with so much raw material to work on, Edinburgh was in later years to produce so many outstanding pioneers of public health and social medicine.

Meanwhile history was on the march through the High Street mire. In 1633 Charles I came to be crowned at Holyrood, for which event the ancient abbey was restored. He created a bishopric in St Giles', the old kirk became a cathedral, and Edinburgh a city. In 1637, when Archbishop Laud's new English liturgy was read for the first time, Jenny Geddes, an Edinburgh market stallholder, threw her stool at the preacher; her accompanying utterance of rage is variously reported as 'Daur ye say mass in ma lug?' and a curious old Scots oath, 'Deil colic the wame o' ye.' Within a year all Scotland was under arms, the National Covenant declaring support for the Presbyterian faith had been signed at Greyfriars Kirk, and the Covenanting forces were attacking every major fortress in Scotland. The assault on Edinburgh Castle was led by General Sir David Leslie, Marshal of Sweden under Gustavus Adolphus and one of the most brilliant soldiers in Europe. By 1640 there was a truce between Covenanters and the King, and the Castle was handed back to a Royalist garrison under Sir Patrick Ruthven. Within months the truce had collapsed, and Leslie attacked again; this time, of his force of 185 men, only 33 survived the murderous cannon fire.

Leslie was called into action again in 1650, when the victorious forces of Cromwell advanced upon Edinburgh. His troops, ranged behind an earthwork on the line of the modern Leith Walk, supported by cannon on Calton Hill, easily repulsed the invader, watched from the Castle ramparts by the future King Charles II. But after Cromwell's subsequent victory at Dunbar, he marched unchallenged into Edinburgh on 7 September 1650, placed the city under martial law, took up residence in Moray House, and blockaded the Castle with batteries sited in the grounds of the still uncompleted Heriot's Hospital; the hospital itself he used to accommodate his wounded.

Cromwell left Edinburgh in the charge of his second-in-command, General Monck, who built a barracks at Leith and maintained law and order in the city with an iron grip. By 1652 Monck was being fêted by the magistrates, and for ten years there was perfect peace in the city; Cromwellian officers preached in St Giles, others taught in the newly-built Parliament House, a regular stage coach was started to London, leaving every three weeks at £4 10s a head, and there was even a proposal by the magistrates to erect a large statue of Cromwell. But the Restoration intervened.

Edinburgh went wild with joy at the news that a Stuart was back on the British throne in 1660; the Mercat Cross was garlanded with flowers, fountains ran with wine, and 300 dozen glasses were broken in drinking the King's health. Scottish affairs were put in the hands of the Duke of York, later to become King James II, and he held splendid court at Holyrood, introducing tea to Scotland for the first time. But the Covenanting wars were not yet over; James, by his strong adherence to the Roman faith, was not universally popular with the citizens, and there were further scenes of joy in 1688 when the Protestant William of Orange landed in England to assume the throne. Edinburgh Castle was, however, governed by the Duke of Gordon, a Catholic and supporter of James, who by now had fled the country. As revolutionary mobs rampaged around the city, causing Cavalier families to flee, a Protestant force under Viscount Dundee besieged Edinburgh Castle for the last time. It took 500 lives, and a celebrated secret meeting on the ramparts between Gordon and Dundee, before the fortress finally surrendered.

In spite of the religious strife which disrupted life for fifty years or more, the 17th century brought extensive improvements to Edinburgh, which had a population of well over 20,000 by its close. Three great architectural ornaments had been added, Parliament House, Heriot's Hospital, and Sir William Bruce's new Palace of Holyroodhouse for Charles II. New industries were established, including a powder factory at Powderhall, glassworks and sawmills at Leith, a foundry, factories making linen, wool cloth, silk, stockings, sailcloth and ropes. Mills for paper-making, which became a major industry of the city, were established on the Water of Leith in 1675. There was some timid expansion outside the Flodden Wall, at Portsburgh and Mureburgh, and Edinburgh had bought the superiority of Canongate, though it retained its status as a separate burgh. In 1667, the city's chief magistrate assumed the title of Lord Provost, and in the same year public transport was first introduced, in the shape of the sedan chair, a form of travel which persisted, surprisingly, until the mid 19th century.

There were even some attempts to improve the living conditions of the ordinary citizens, still crammed into their dark and stinking tenements inside the Flodden Wall. The first of these was revolutionary – piped water.

Not, it must be said, water piped into every home, which was a Victorian innovation; it was water piped to a reservoir on the Castle Hill, which fed a string of wells down the High Street. In 1681 Peter Brusche, a German engineer, laid a lead pipe of 3-inch bore from the springs at Comiston, three miles to the south, later augmented by further supplies from Swanston in the Pentland foothills. The water was borne up the turnpike stairs in a small casks by 'cadies', a band of highly regarded all-purpose messengers who not only carried water, but who could be trusted to convey the most confidential of messages. The arrival of piped water also meant that the revolting pavement of the High Street could be hosed down occasionally, which went some way towards alleviating the stench.

The second improvement was an attempt by Robert Mylne to break away from the dark and airless closes by designing open squares of tenements; his earliest surviving example is at Milne's Court in the Lawnmarket.

Things had not improved much by 1724, when Daniel Defoe visited the city during his *Tour of Great Britain*: 'Although many cities have more people in them, yet I believe there is none in the world where so many people live in so little room. After ten at night you run a great risk, if you walk the streets, of having chamber-pots of ordure thrown upon your head: and it sounds very oddly in the ears of a stranger, to hear all passers-by cry out, as loud as to be heard to the uppermost stories of the houses, which are generally six or seven high in the front of the High Street, "Hoad yare hoand": that is, hold your hand, and throw not, till I am passed.'

As early as 1681 the magistrates, and even the Duke of York in idle moments in Holyrood Palace, had been thinking that it really was high time the old city burst its bonds from the old Flodden Wall. But it was another century before anything was done about it; Edinburgh has never taken its big decisions in a hurry.

There was the matter of the Union. Merging of the Scottish and English Parliaments at Westminster was not a proposal which attracted great popular acclaim, removing as it did one more prop to Scotland's sense of nationhood. But there were those who feared that, without complete unification, hostilities would once more break out between the two old enemies. Scotland was barred from reaping the advantages of England's growing empire overseas, and the general standard of living north of the border was undoubtedly lower. Scotland decided that what she needed was an overseas colony of her own, and in 1698 a fleet set sail from Leith to found the colony of Darien on the Isthmus of Panama, from which untold riches were confidently expected to flow in raw materials and trade with the American natives and their Spanish conquerors.

The Darien Expedition was a spectacular disaster. The majority of the fleet was shipwrecked, and those colonists who made it to Darien found only disease, starvation and hostile natives. It was an investment collapse comparable with the South Sea Bubble, and the resulting economic debilitation of the kingdom did much to hasten union with England. The only permanent survival of the Darien Scheme is the Bank of Scotland, founded in 1695 to help finance it.

Union was achieved on 1 May 1707 and the Scots Parliament, aided by bribes of up to £12,000 per head, dissolved itself; the Commissioners signing the Treaty were pursued by an angry mob and had to take refuge in a High Street cellar.

Edinburgh at first did not take kindly to direct rule from London. Resentment against the distant Hanoverian throne boiled over in the celebrated Porteous riot of 1736 when the mob hanged John Porteous, Captain of the Town Guard, from a dyer's pole in the Grassmarket after Queen Caroline had granted him a pardon for ordering his men to shoot and kill a number of bystanders at an execution. The incident is graphically described by Sir Walter Scott in *Heart of Midlothian*.

Edinburgh after the Union has often been presented as a dejected and demoralized provincial town; certainly many of the outward trappings of a capital city had been removed, but in the coming years much was achieved, largely through the vision of George Drummond, whose six terms as Lord Provost spanned a large portion of the 18th century. In 1738 Drummond founded the city's first proper hospital, the Royal Infirmary. In 1727 the Royal Bank of Scotland was founded, an indication that business confidence, shattered by the Darien fiasco, had returned. But before the major 18th century expansion and improvement really got under way, Edinburgh was to have one final act of stormy Scottish history played out in its streets.

On 15 September 1745 Prince Charles Edward Stuart, at the head of a Highland army of 2,000 men, entered Edinburgh unopposed and remained for six weeks before undertaking his ill-fated invasion of England. The Highlanders entered the city without trouble, and generally behaved themselves well; most injuries were to citizens caught in the occasional crossfire between Highlanders and the garrison in the Castle, held by a loyal 87-year-old Whig, General Preston. The last shot to be fired in anger from its walls was loosed off on 31 October 1745; that night Prince Charles left for England and for the final decimation of the Stuart cause at Culloden the following year.

The clearances of the Highland peasants from their crofts by the southern landowners which followed Culloden brought many thousands to the lowland towns, and by 1755 Edinburgh's already crowded population had swelled to 31,000. In September 1751 a 6-storey tenement in the High Street collapsed, and several others which were overcrowded and unsafe had to be pulled down. It was a golden opportunity.

The following year Sir Gilbert Elliot, backed by the town council, published a pamphlet of *Proposals for carrying on certain Public Works in the City of Edinburgh*, in which he described his native city thus: 'Placed upon a ridge of a hill, it admits but of one good street, running from east to west; and even this is tolerably accessible only from one quarter. The narrow lanes leading to the north and south, by reason of their steepness, narrowness and dirtiness, can only be considered as so many unavoidable nuisances. Confined by the small compass of the walls, and the narrow limits of the royalty, which scarcely extends beyond the walls, the houses stand more crowded than in any other town in Europe, and are built to a height that is almost incredible.'

The *Proposals* also bemoaned the lack of decent public buildings in the city, particularly the absence of a merchants' exchange and a public record office; but their most important clause was that the city should extend its royalty (the area of jurisdiction of the royal burgh) and commence building extensively to the north and south.

Such grandiose plans are generally consigned to a bottom drawer to gather dust, but in this case, over the next eighty years, they were carried out almost to the letter. There were delays and desperate shortages of money; and there was war with France. Great buildings stood without roofs for years. But the guiding vision of George Drummond and his successors saw it through; how odd that they never put up a statue to him.

The foundation stone of the Royal Exchange was laid in

1753, and it was completed in 1761; but the merchants made little use of it, preferring to continue their habit of doing business in the middle of the street. In 1769 the first North Bridge was opened from the Old Town across the valley of the Nor' Loch, and promptly fell down. But once repaired, it gave the vital access to the city's newly acquired land to the north, and construction of the first New Town could begin, based on a gridiron street plan submitted in a competition by a young architect, James Craig. The plan was hardly revolutionary – three parallel streets with a square at each end – but it was ideally suited to the site. Its virtues were not immediately apparent to the citizens, and a Mr John Young had to be offered a consideration of £20 by the Town Council before he took the plunge and built the first house on the new site in October 1767. It still stands in Thistle Court, a modest dwelling which gives no hint of the architectural splendour to follow.

One of the major improvements was the draining of the Nor' Loch, which had become a fetid dump for all manner of rubbish; the gardens which replaced it, laid out by James Skene of Rubislaw, were originally for the private use of Princes Street residents, and it was only much later in the 19th century that public agitation made them open to all.

Construction of the first New Town occupied the next thirty years, although the last house in Princes Street was not built until 1805. Houses were erected by a variety of architects and builders, but the town council exercised rigid planning control throughout. The grandest residences, in Charlotte and St Andrew Squares, were sold for a hefty £2,000, or rented at £100 a year. But even in the grandest New Town house, there was still no mains sewer, and it was the nightly task of the servants to collect the soil and refuse in time for the cart which bore it, at four in the morning, to the market gardens of the Lothian countryside.

While the Town Council was executing its grand plan to the north, private builders were beginning to extend the Old Town to the south. Credit for the first major development outside the Flodden Wall of 1513 must go to James Brown, a speculative builder, who erected George Square outside the southern limits of the old burgh in 1766. Expansion of the southern suburbs was greatly encouraged by the building of the South Bridge in 1786.

The first New Town revolutionized the city and its social habits. Leading citizens abandoned their mansions in the Old Town for the spacious dwellings of Princes Street and George Street, leaving the tenements of the High Street to be divided and subdivided to house the poor who flocked in from the countryside. It was the beginning of a degeneration of the noble, warm old town into a slum, from which it did not recover until preservation became a fashionable occupation of architects and town councils in the 20th century. The populace lost something of the raw pleasure of communal living, with the highest and lowest in the land sharing the same stinking turnpike stair, but in moving to the windy open streets of the New Town they lost neither their dirty habits nor their three principal social occasions, the dancing assembly, the theatre and the drinking club.

Several dancing assembly halls had existed in the Old Town throughout the 18th century, and new ones were built as the New Town took shape, one in George Street and one near George Square. The assemblies were hugely popular, but were hardly occasions of unconfined joy and abandon. Clearly, in a community so tightly-packed that each knew the other's business, no whiff of scandal could be allowed to circulate.

Theatres were gayer, their atmosphere charged with the added excitement of official censure. The Town Council disapproved of theatres, the Kirk even more so, and it was a great shock to both bodies when a man of the cloth, the Rev. John Home, had his verse tragedy, *Douglas*, performed in a High Street theatre in 1756, the more so because a large part of the first-night audience was composed of the very ministers who were supposed to condemn such licentiousness.

In the closing decades before its glory began to fade, the High Street had nurtured the first of the great men whose genius provided Edinburgh with its third and greatest golden age – men like David Hume, Adam Smith, Adam Ferguson and Dugald Stewart. Later, Robert Burns was to visit the city to seek, and win, recognition, at a time when Edinburgh's greatest son, and undoubtedly her greatest publicist, was growing to manhood – Sir Walter Scott. The city had long since lost two of the principal trappings of a capital city, the royal court and the parliament, but she still retained the headquarters of Scotland's own church and legal system, and her university had grown to become one of the most eminent in Europe, particularly in the fields of philosophy and medicine. From such rich veins of education, erudition and dry Scottish wit there came a succession of great scientists and men of letters, who lifted Edinburgh to a position of pre-eminence amongst European cities, with the possible exception of Paris, until well into the 19th century.

Immediately Edinburgh had completed its first New Town it embarked upon another, on ground to the north of Queen Street, based upon a similar but less rigid gridiron plan centred on Great King Street. This second New Town, which is preserved largely intact, was planned by Robert Reid and built mainly between 1804 and 1820, the elegant Georgian architecture of the first New Town giving way to a more severe neo-Greek fashion. On the fringes of this second New Town grew subsidiary developments promoted by private builders and landowners, including the Earl of Moray, who developed his lands behind Charlotte Square into the grandest New Town scheme of all, from Moray Place to Randolph Crescent. In 1814 the city laid plans for an enormous development stretching from the east end of Princes Street all the way to Leith, for which W.H. Playfair produced a design. But by this time the city was virtually bankrupt, having emptied its coffers, not only on erecting new residential streets, but on building the first proper docks at Leith in 1801, and the scheme never got beyond Calton Hill. And as the east end of Princes Street became cluttered with commercial development, the fashionable nucleus was tending to move westwards, to where another major extension was being privately developed on the Coates estate in the area of Melville Street. That was virtually the end of Edinburgh's publicly-sponsored extension; most of what followed was the result of private enterprise. The last major public work undertaken in the city for many years was the building of a new western approach road round the Castle Rock to give access to the Old Town in 1827.

New Town building was in full swing when King George IV

paid a state visit to the city in 1822 in an atmosphere of pomp and splendour largely stage-managed by Sir Walter Scott. The king, clad in pink silk tights beneath his kilt, was rapturously received; it was the first state visit since Culloden, and Scotland saw it as the final act of forgiveness by the British throne for the Jacobite uprising, and the recognition by London of Scotland as a nation, rather than as an adjunct of England which for some years it had been fashionable to call simply 'North Britain'.

The early Victorian era witnessed major expansion of high-class residential suburbs on the south side of the city, their development hastened by a decision in 1846 to allow commercial premises in the New Town. It also saw the coming of the railways; the first main line in the city was the Edinburgh and Glasgow Railway, opened from Haymarket in 1842, followed by the North British Railway to Berwick in 1846, and the first through trains to London in 1850 bringing Edinburgh within twelve hours of London instead of three days.

By 1856 the city's population had grown to 160,302, and an Act of Parliament of that year extended the boundary to include all the new suburbs springing up to the north and south of the Old and New Towns, and a further Act of 1882 pushed the limits farther out to include Roseburn, Myreside, Morningside, Craigmillar and Prestonfield; for a time the city lost sight of its regard for amenity and good planning, and later 19th-century working-class districts like Dalry and Gorgie mushroomed in the hothouse of Victorian industrialization. Edinburgh by now had more than twenty breweries, several large engineering works, and the biggest rubber factory in the Empire.

While the affluent built their spacious villas at Grange or Murrayfield, the poor dwelt largely unnoticed in an increasingly squalid Old Town, its numbers swelled by Irish potato famines and continuing decimation of the Highlands. It was not until tragedy struck in 1861 that the extent of their deprivation became generally realized.

In that year the public conscience was rudely awakened when a High Street tenement collapsed, killing 35 inhabitants and burying many more, and revealing that it had housed more than 100 persons in unimaginably cramped conditions. As a direct result, Dr Henry Littlejohn was appointed the city's first medical officer of health in the following year, and in a career spanning over forty years his was possibly the greatest single influence in the improvement of living conditions. The overcrowding was unsurpassed by any other town in Britain, and vice and disease – especially typhus and cholera – were rampant; in 1849 a cholera epidemic had claimed 478 lives in the city, and pulmonary tuberculosis was an ever-present killer. It was an Edinburgh man, William Budd, who first differentiated between typhus and typhoid, and another, Robert Philip, who opened the world's first tuberculosis clinic in his native city. Dr Littlejohn took office at a time when public health was for the first time becoming a subject for serious study and legislation, and his appointment coincided with an Act of Parliament which finally made running water and drainage compulsory in all houses. Littlejohn made sure the Act was carried out in Edinburgh, as well as having the closes and stairs regularly washed out, and the dunghills in the street finally removed. Between 1863 and 1913 the city's death rate was almost halved, the infant mortality rate cut by a third, the death rate of children under five by two-thirds, and the death rate from tuberculosis by well over half.

Dr Littlejohn found an ally in Sir William Chambers, the Lord Provost; together they promoted a City Improvement Act which swept away much of the worst housing in the High Street and elsewhere; Old Town closes were opened up into wider, airier and more sanitary streets, and whole rows of rotten dwellings were torn down in the area of the University to make way for Chambers Street.

A major event in the city streets in 1871 was the arrival of the first horse-drawn tramcar; within twenty years the system had grown to 300 cars and 1,000 horses. But the steep streets of the New Town proved unsuitable for animal power and in 1888 the first of the tramway routes from Hanover Street to Canonmills was converted to an underground cable operation, with a gripper on the bottom of the car lowered through the slotted centre rail to grab a continuous cable driven from a central power station at Henderson Row. By 1898 the entire system, covering

48

26 miles and operated by 52 miles of underground cable, had been converted, making it the fourth largest of its kind in the world. In 1905 the then-separate burgh of Leith introduced the electric tramcar, and Edinburgh followed suit in 1922; the tramcar lasted until 1955, when it was finally ousted by the bus.

Still the city was growing beyond its boundaries, and in 1920 an Extension Act added another 21,000 acres to the Royal Burgh, taking in outlying villages like Colinton, Corstorphine, Cramond and Liberton, some of them as old as the city itself. The 1920 Act also returned to Edinburgh its port of Leith, which had made a long-awaited bid for freedom as a separate burgh under the great Reform Acts of 1832–3. In 1896 the seaside village of Portobello had been added to the city, and in 1901 the lands of Duddingston House. By now the burgh had expanded from its tiny huddle on the ridge to an area of 53 square miles, at that time the largest area of any municipality in Britain, although with a population sparse enough to permit an abundance of open spaces. In 1975, by a stroke of the administrative pen, Edinburgh was virtually doubled in size and now covers 105 square miles.

Edinburgh in the first half of the 20th century settled down to being an industrious, prosperous, worthy if slightly dull provincial capital, remaining largely unscathed by two wars, and its great university remaining the principal magnet for the outsider. The establishment of an international festival of music and drama in 1947 put it firmly back in touch with the outside world.

The first Festival was a modest affair, dreamed up by Harvey Wood, senior official of the British Council, John Christie, founder of the Glyndebourne Opera, Rudolf Bing, then an influential impresario, and Sir John Falconer, the Lord Provost. Glyndebourne presented *The Marriage of Figaro* and *Macbeth*, Bruno Walter and the Vienna State Orchestra played Beethoven, Louis Jouvet brought Molière and Giraudoux from Paris, the Hallé and Scottish orchestras were joined from France by L'Orchestre des Concerts Colonne, Sadler's Wells Ballet danced, and Kathleen Ferrier sang. It was a huge act of faith in the austerity of post-war Britain, but it has never looked back; its only major failure was a lengthy drama of bumbledom and official meanness which deprived the city of an opera house it so badly needed, a setback made the more galling when Glasgow converted an old theatre into one with the minimum of fuss and bother.

It took a long time for the Festival gaiety to penetrate very far into the dour Scots consciousness, but in recent years even grey old Edinburgh has allowed the ghost of a smile to play upon its lips and the hint of a spring to creep into its step. Many of its finest buildings have been cleaned to reveal the delicious creaminess of their Craigleith stone; boutiques, clubs and exotic restaurants have flowered in profusion where once there was only the demure tearoom and the fish and chip shop. But best of all, in the eyes of the permanent residents, the Calvinistic rigour of ten o'clock closing has, after 60 years, been eased to allow the drinker to remain in his public house until a civilized hour of night, and he need not crawl unwillingly home while it is still daylight.

I bring this brief history up to date with mention of a public improvement for which Edinburgh has been waiting since the Pictish tribes watched the Roman advance from their wooden palisade on the Castle Rock, and which has been sorely needed in all the centuries since. In the Old Town they threw it out of the topmost windows; in the New Town they carted it away to the fields at dead of night. For the past 100 years Edinburgh has pumped it, raw and untreated, into the Forth, creating one of the most polluted stretches of seashore on the entire British coast. In 1977, at Powderhall, at a cost of more than £30 million, one of the most decorous and civilized cities in Europe finally opened a plant to treat its sewage.

# CHAPTER 3

# Visitors' Edinburgh

♣♣♣

Within its boundaries Edinburgh harbours a rich store of history, atmosphere, architecture, curiosity, open space and scenic delight. By any yardstick the Old and New Towns are outstanding attractions, but there is much more, hidden in unexpected corners, to surprise and please. This brief guide to the principal places of interest will serve as an introduction to the succeeding chapters, which explore the city in some depth. Figures in parentheses refer to the appropriate chapter.

All parts of the city are within easy reach of a bus route; detailed information and maps may be obtained from the city information office on Waverley Bridge by the main railway station and airport coach terminal, or from the Lothian Regional Transport office at 14 Queen Street. Buses to outlying areas operate from the bus station at St Andrew Square. Waverley Bridge is also the starting point for a comprehensive programme of city coach tours.

Nine hundred years of Scottish history are told in the stones of the Old Town (4), and no visitor should miss the one-mile downhill walk from the Castle to the Palace of Holyroodhouse, following the main street of the medieval burgh. Every dark, narrow close has a story to tell; every passageway reveals an ancient house or an unexpected vista. History is written too in the ruins of Craigmillar Castle (15) and the port of Leith (18), where kings and queens have come and gone, and much survives from an earlier age of commerce.

Across the valley of the Nor' Loch, the New Town (5 and 6) is one of the finest neo-classical survivals in Europe, and remains very much as it was built, aided by a major effort of conservation in recent years. It contains a wealth of excellent architecture, from the Georgian elegance of Robert Adam to the

Greek revival of Thomas Hamilton and William Playfair. The New Town grew both north and south of the Old, and many major works lie in the University area (7), with the University itself arguably Adam's finest work in the city.

Edinburgh was well served by her architects during the 19th century, and throughout the city there is a profusion of both public and domestic works by the leading practitioners of their time, David Bryce and Sir Rowand Anderson. The domestic tradition was carried into the 20th century by Sir Robert Lorimer, many of whose private houses stand in the southern suburbs. Domestic architecture of an earlier age is particularly well displayed in the ancient burgh of South Queensferry (8), but in almost every quarter of Edinburgh itself there is a 17th- or 18th-century mansion, the most notable being Lauriston Castle (8).

As the city expanded it swallowed up villages as old as the Old Town itself, and it is one of Edinburgh's most pleasing features that so many survive with their village atmosphere largely intact, some with a fine old church as their centrepiece. The Dean Village (8) is a picturesque haven only minutes from the city centre, while farther out Corstorphine (9), Cramond (8), Duddingston (16), Colinton (11) and Swanston (12) retain much charm and some notable antiquities.

It is another endearing quality of the city that, being built on a rising succession of hills, it offers so many views of itself. From near sea level, the Royal Botanic Garden (5), one of the finest in Europe, provides a wide vista inland to the Old Town ridge and the Pentlands beyond. In the city centre, the Castle Rock and Calton Hill show the urban scene spread out below at close quarters with the river and hills beyond. To the west, Corstorphine Hill (8) offers Stevenson's viewpoint at Rest and Be Thankful, and good woodland walking from the Queensferry to the Glasgow road. From the 822-foot summit of Arthur's Seat (16) the horizon recedes much further, to include the Pentlands to the south and the nearer Highland peaks to the north, with the whole Lothian plain below, and a living geological museum directly beneath the feet. In the southern suburbs, the hills of Blackford (13) and Braid (12) combine city panoramas with good walking, and are a prelude to the

Pentland Hills proper, which tower behind the city and form its boundary 1,600 feet up on the summit of Allermuir. The less energetic may let a city bus take them through the first 600 feet to its terminus at Torphin (11), the start of some fine hill walking, or drive to Stevenson's village at Swanston, from where the whole of Edinburgh is laid out for inspection.

Gentler walking is to be found along the seashore and the courses of the city's rivers. There are marine promenades at Portobello (17) and from Granton to Cramond (18), as well as a pleasant wooded seaside walk through the Dalmeny estate from Cramond to the Forth Bridges (8). From its mouth at Cramond, the River Almond is followed by a path along its wooded valley with the added attractions of a waterfall and a trail of industrial archaeology (8). It is not yet possible to walk the entire course of the Water of Leith, but a woodland path follows a substantial section from Slateford (10) through the dell of Colinton (11) out to the Pentland foothills at Balerno. Within the city there are stretches of riverside path at Roseburn (9), Dean (8) and Rocheid, behind Glenogle Road (8).

As befits a city which has some claim to being the birthplace of the game, Edinburgh is richly endowed with golf courses; there are no less than 22 within its boundaries, mostly owned by private clubs to which an introduction is normally required, but also including excellent public courses at Braid Hills (12). Other championship courses are within striking distance at Muirfield, East Lothian, St Andrews in Fife, and Carnoustie beyond Dundee.

Whole volumes have been written on Edinburgh's literary landmarks. No writer left a greater impression on his native city, nor strove so much to publicize it, than Sir Walter Scott, and the Old and New Towns are full of houses associated with him; those following his trail will also find his mark at Guthrie Street (7), Portobello (17) and Duddingston (16). Robert Louis Stevenson was second only to Scott in introducing his home town to a wider world and, as well as his several New Town houses, his holiday retreats are to be found at Swanston (12) and Colinton (11). Scott and Stevenson are two amongst dozens of literary figures who have added to the city's cultural store, and whose names will be found in the pages covering the Old and New Towns.

There will be more than sufficient occasions when Edinburgh's weather drives the visitor to shelter, but even then he need not want for things to see. The Royal Scottish Museum (7) is the largest general museum in the British Isles, and is of particular fascination to children, as are the museums of transport (18) and childhood (4). The National Museum of Antiquities (5) houses Scotland's national historical collection, and Huntly House (4) is an outstanding museum of city history. Lady Stair's House (4) contains literary relics of Burns, Scott and Stevenson, and the Wax Museum (4) portrays the good, the bad and the ugly of Scottish history.

The city is rich in art collections. The National Gallery of Scotland (5) is one of the finest small galleries of Europe, and modern Scottish painters are represented at the adjoining Royal Scottish Academy, the Scottish National Gallery of Modern Art (5), and the Scottish Arts Council Gallery (5), while figures from the nation's history are displayed in the Scottish National Portrait Gallery (5). The Georgian House in Charlotte Square (5) is a faithful record of domestic life at the period of the building of the New Town.

At Corstorphine (9) is the Scottish National Zoological Park, which apart from its merits as a first-class zoo has the added attraction of being set among 80 acres of hillside parkland. On the western edge of the city is one of the most unique and compelling sights of all; the Forth Bridge (8) is one of Europe's biggest and most spectacular monuments to Victorian engineering, now contrasted by the graceful road suspension bridge alongside.

There are many seasonal events to add to Edinburgh's permanent attractions. In May each year the General Assembly of the Church of Scotland provides pageantry and a host of ministers; in June the traditional royal visit to the northern capital offers a view of the Queen, at least one procession a day, garden parties and a great deal of colour. The Royal Highland Show, also in June, brings farmers from all over Scotland to the premier agricultural show at Ingliston (9). And in late August and early September the International Festival brings visitors in their tens of thousands.

This book must necessarily confine itself to the City of Edinburgh District, but places of interest do not end at local authority boundaries. To the east of the city is the rich rolling farmland of East Lothian, its seashore skirted by a succession of excellent springy-turfed golf links. To the south, seven miles from the city centre, the village of Roslin contains one of the best medieval churches in Scotland, with notable sculpture and its famous 'Prentice Pillar. It was intricately carved by an apprentice mason in the absence of his master. According to legend, the master on his return was so jealous that he killed the boy. To the west, a short distance beyond South Queensferry, is the huge mansion of Hopetoun House, begun by Sir William Bruce and finished by William Adam, one of the largest and most impressive country houses in Scotland, with magnificent interiors and a collection of art treasures.

# CHAPTER 4

# The Old Town

♣ ♣ ♣

*Castle – Lawnmarket – St Giles' – Parliament Square –*
*City Chambers – John Knox's House – High Street –*
*Netherbow – Canongate – Moray House – Tolbooth –*
*Huntly House – White Horse Close – Palace of Holyrood-*
*house – Holyrood Road – St Cecilia's Hall – Scott's*
*Birthplace – Magdalene Chapel – Grassmarket –*
*Covenanter's Memorial – Burke and Hare*

The Old Town of Edinburgh stretches from the Castle to the
Palace of Holyroodhouse down the main street of the ancient
medieval burgh now known as the Royal Mile, with its warren
of alleys and lanes. It is an easy downhill walk from the Castle,
where this chapter begins. Access to the Old Town is by bus or
on foot to the top of the Mound, from where a right turn into
the Lawnmarket leads on to the Castle Esplanade.

THE CASTLE is approached by a modern replacement of the
drawbridge which once spanned the dry ditch (dug 1742–52),
and of which only parts of the stone piers remain. The modern
entrance gateway carries sculptures of Robert Bruce (by
Thomas Clapperton) and William Wallace (by Alexander Car-
rick), erected in 1929 to mark the 600th anniversary of the
granting of the first known charter to the city by Robert Bruce.
Also built into the gateway walls are two late 16th-century
stone panels depicting ordnance.

Directly inside the gate is the massive retaining wall of the
Half-Moon Battery, built by Morton in 1574. It hides the
remains of David's Tower, an L-shaped fortification 60-feet
high, built in 1367, destroyed in 1573 and rediscovered in 1913.
Discovery of the tower also unearthed a gun loop, now visible
in the battery wall, which covered the approach to the Castle

from the street. Near the entrance are the remains of the inner barrier, and the curtain wall of the Forewall Battery, on which is a memorial plaque to William Kirkcaldy of Grange, who held the Castle for Mary, Queen of Scots between 1568 and 1573.

The steep roadway passes under the Portcullis Gate, erected by the Regent Morton in 1574 and extensively restored in 1886. The eastern wall depicts the arms of the King of Scots, which is modern, surrounded by the original arms of Morton. The upper part of the gateway, by Hippolyte J. Blanc, is an 1886 restoration of Argyle's Tower, the old state prison.

Beyond the gateway on the left are the 15th-century Lang Stairs, leading to the Upper Defence. At the bottom is a tablet to Thomas Randolph, Earl of Moray, who scaled the rock to recapture the Castle from the English. On the right is the Argyle Battery, built c. 1750 on top of earlier fortifications, and displaying a range of muzzle-loading eighteen pounders of the same period. Below is the Low Defence, on the wall of which is an old iron basket for the lighting of beacons. Immediately beyond is the small building of Mills Mount Barracks, erected in 1746 on the site of a 17th-century storekeeper's house. The large block adjoining is the hospital; the north wing was rebuilt in Scottish Baronial style in 1897, while the south wing remains largely unaltered from its construction in 1753 by William Skinner as an armoury. On this site was formerly the 17th-century powder magazine.

Behind the hospital, on the western edge of the fortress, is a fragment of the Sallyport, a postern doorway, where in 1093 the body of Queen Margaret was smuggled out to its burial place at Dunfermline. Here too took place the last meeting between Viscount Dundee and the Duke of Gordon, Governor of the Castle, in 1689, when the former scaled the steep western face of the rock in the vain hope of persuading the latter to join with him in raising the Highlands against William of Orange.

In front of the hospital is the Governor's House, erected in 1742 with a symmetrical, rubble-built front, followed by the 6-storey New Barracks, (Thomas Rudyard, 1796). Nearby is the entrance to the Casemates, a series of vaulted chambers beneath the Great Hall used as dungeons, and occupied by French prisoners, some of whom carved their names in the woodwork, during the Napoleonic Wars. Here the roadway swings round sharply through Foog's Gate, a 17th-century arch, to reach the Upper Defence, the site of the earliest known Castle.

St Margaret's Chapel, on the very summit of the rock, is the oldest surviving part of the Castle, the oldest building in the city, and probably the oldest and smallest chapel of Roman Christianity surviving in Scotland, built *c.*1080 by Queen Margaret, wife of Malcolm Canmore, who was chiefly responsible for introducing Roman Catholicism to Scotland. Excavation suggests that it stands on the site of a still-earlier chapel. The interior of the simple Norman structure is only $17 \times 11$ feet; it consists of a nave, originally timber-roofed, and a semi-circular stone-vaulted apse. The two are separated by an archway, ornamented on its west side, probably added in the mid 12th century; the shafts of each jamb are restorations, but the bases and caps are original. The westernmost of the three windows on the south side is original, with the outside check for holding the window frame. The chapel suffered severe alterations in the 17th century, but was restored as near as possible to its former state by order of Queen Victoria in 1853. The modern stained-glass windows by Douglas Strachan depict Saints Andrew, Ninian, Columba and Margaret, and William Wallace. The chapel was further restored by H.J. Blanc in 1886.

By the chapel is the celebrated 5-ton 15th-century cannon, Mons Meg. Opinions differ about its origin, although it is agreed that it was forged about 1486. One theory states that it was made in Flanders, hence its name; it is similar to the great cannon of Ghent, known as 'Mad Marjorie', and to other Continental cannon. Another theory has it made within the Castle itself by Robert Borthwick, the King's master gunner, and first fired on the day that King James V was born; still another states that it was made in Galloway and first used at the siege of Threave Castle by King James II. It burst during the firing of a salute in 1682 to the Duke of York, lay derelict in the Castle for some time, and was removed to the Tower of London in 1754, where it remained until returned to Edinburgh in 1829 at the instigation of Sir Walter Scott. The carriage is a modern replica, copied from that depicted on the stone tablet by the Castle gateway. The iron barrel, of flat bars girded by iron hoops, is 13 feet 4 inches long, with a bore of 1 foot 8 inches. An old legend states that Mons Meg could fire a stone cannonball for about 1½ miles.

On a ledge below Mons Meg is a small garden used as a burial place for soldiers' dogs. To the east is the top of the Lang Stairs, situated beside the Forewall Battery, equipped with 18th-century muzzle-loading eighteen pounders. At the far end is the Fore Well, the Castle's ancient water supply, 110-feet deep, mostly hewn from the solid rock.

Beyond is the Half-Moon Battery, built partly on the ruin of David's Tower, and partly on the ancient water tanks served by the Fore Well. The Tower and the tanks can be inspected from an entrance on the battery. Nearby is the Lyon's Den, a reminder that in the time of King James VI a lion was kept in the vaults.

To the rear of the Half-Moon Battery is the entrance to the Palace Yard around which are ranged most of the royal apartments. On the east side of the square is the Palace, or King's Lodging, originally 15th century but restored and extended in 1617 by William Wallace, master mason, for the ceremonial return of King James VI to his birthplace. This was the Royal Palace of Scotland from the 15th century until the later 16th century, when Holyrood came to be preferred. The north stair tower, with its ogee roof, its original, with the date 1615, but the west tower, from which the flag now flies, is an early 19th-century addition. The exterior has much fine stone carving by Wallace.

One of the most interesting apartments remaining is Queen Mary's Room, in the original part of the palace, where she bore the future King James VI in 1566; over the courtyard entrance is the cypher of Mary and Darnley, and the date 1566. The Palace also contains the Crown Room, where the Honours of Scotland are displayed.

The crown, of Scottish gold and pearls, of uncertain origin, was remade for the coronation of King James VI and used again for the coronation of Charles II at Scone in 1651; the bonnet and ermine were renewed for the State visit of Queen Elizabeth II after her coronation in 1953. The sword and sceptre were presented to James IV by Pope Alexander VI and Pope Julius II. The case also displays the Order of the Garter presented to James VI by Elizabeth I, and the Garter badge presented by Cardinal York, brother of Prince Charles Edward, to George IV.

On the south side of the square is the Great Hall, built by James IV in the early 16th century as a banqueting hall, and where the Scottish Parliament met from 1537 until 1632. Its main feature is the magnificent and original hammerbeam roof, the corbels ornately carved with royal motifs, including the cypher of James IV; the windows and other interior fittings date from a restoration by H.J. Blanc in 1888. The hall now houses a collection of arms and armour.

The west side of the square is occupied by the Scottish United Services Museum, housed in a former barrack block built in 1707. There is a large collection of war relics, established in 1933, representing all the Scottish fighting units, and unique in housing such a comprehensive collection under one roof.

On the north side is the Scottish National War Memorial (Sir Robert Lorimer, 1927), in Scots Gothic and displaying the stonemason's art to great advantage. The plain severity of the building gives little hint of its awesome interior, a sumptuously decorated mausoleum resplendent with stained glass and bronze. The Hall of Honour is filled with regimental memorials; every Scottish regiment, whether raised at home or overseas, has its own display of battle colours and its Roll of Honour. The shrine, behind its ornate gates, is entirely the work of Scottish craftsmen. The bronze frieze depicts Scots in all manner of wartime occupations, and the Casket in the centre, given by King George V, contains the names of a hundred thousand Scots who fell in the First World War. The stained-glass windows are by Douglas Strachan. Through the floor of the Shrine projects the living rock on which it is built.

In front of the Castle is its Esplanade, an open area 140 yards long by 100 yards broad, laid out in the early 19th century as a parade ground. Along its northern edge is an array of memorials to Scottish soldiers and regiments, including an equestrian statue by G.E. Wade of Earl Haig, presented by a Bombay parsee in 1923. Nearby, under a huge granite block, are the remains of Ensign Ewart, a sergeant in the Greys, who at Waterloo captured single-handed the standard of the French 45th Infantry Regiment; the standard is in the United Services Museum in the Castle.

Here too is a statue of the Duke of York, later James II (Thomas Campbell, 1839), High Commissioner for Scotland before his brief career on the British throne.

At the top end of the Esplanade is a plaque on the wall of the moat where the Earl of Stirling received lawful possession of the province of Nova Scotia in 1625, and where subsequent Scottish baronets of Nova Scotia received sasine (tenure) of their baronies. A token handful of Nova Scotian earth was sprinkled here by the Prime Minister of the province in 1953.

For centuries the Esplanade was a favoured spot for executions. At the north-east corner is a small plaque and fountain (1894) recalling that between 1479 and 1722 more than 300 women were burned here as witches. The plaque is on the wall of the Ramsay Garden reservoir, a long single-storey ashlar structure holding 2 million gallons, built in 1849 on the site of the tank holding the Old Town's first piped water supply, brought from Comiston in 1681.

Opposite, the first building is Cannonball House, built in 1630 for Alex Mure, whose monogram can be seen, largely reconstructed in the 17th and 18th century, but retaining some original gables, dormers and window features. The cannonball embedded in the western wall marks the gravitation height of the original piped water supply from Comiston.

Ramsay Lane falls steeply away on the north side. On its right is the old Edinburgh Original Ragged Industrial School, founded in 1847 for the benefit of the city's poorest children by Dr Thomas Guthrie, one of the founding ministers of the Free Church. The building was originally the Tolbooth Parish School, opened in 1837, and carries an inscription. On the left is Ramsay Garden, a picturesque block of late 19th-century flats built by Sir Patrick Geddes around the poet Allan Ramsay's home. Ramsay built for himself, in 1746, an eccentric octagonal villa nicknamed 'Goosepie House'; its effect is now largely obscured by the surrounding houses, and the building itself has become a training college for bank staff. On the roofline is a carving of the Devil, now so eroded it looks like a cat.

At the corner of Castlehill and Ramsay Lane is the Outlook Tower, with a viewing platform and camera obscura which projects panoramic views of the city on to a large screen, provided the weather is fine. The lower part of the building is 17th century and was the house of Ramsay of Cockpen, immortalized in the song *The Laird of Cockpen*. Three further storeys were added in 1853, and in 1892 it was acquired by Sir Patrick Geddes, a native of Edinburgh regarded as the father of modern town planning. There is a permanent exhibition of his work inside. The doorway on the Ramsay Lane side was rescued from the demolition of Woolmet House near Dalkeith, the home of the Edmondstones, and placed there in 1955.

East of the Tower is Semple's Close, containing Sempill House, a 3-storey rubble-built mansion of 1638, with a semi-octagonal stair tower, and two door lintels, inscribed with the date and biblical inscriptions. The house is named after Hugh, Eleventh Lord Sempill, who bought it in 1743.

Across the street, no. 352 is Boswell's Court, a 17th-century 5-storey tenement with a moulded and inscribed doorway in the courtyard, named after the uncle of James Boswell, who lived here.

On the corner of Johnston Terrace is the Highland Church of Tolbooth St John's, built in 1844 by Gillespie Graham and E.W. Pugin in English mid-pointed style, with a 241-foot octagonal Gothic spire. It was built as Victoria Hall, to house the General Assembly of the Church of Scotland after the Disruption of 1843, and its unusual 2-storey interior, with imperial staircase at the west end and carved royal coat of arms, are reminders of its original purpose.

Playfair's New College, the rear of which faces the Lawnmarket, is built on the site of the 16th-century Palace of Guise, home of Mary of Guise, mother of Mary, Queen of Scots, and where the Queen of Scots herself probably resided for a short time after the murder of Rizzio. Directly opposite at the top of Johnston Terrace, is St Columba's Free Church (Thomas Hamilton, 1845) once the church of Dr Guthrie, the Free Kirk pioneer, where the present-day Free Kirk holds its annual assembly. Johnston Terrace itself was built in 1833 to give access to the Old Town from the west. The traffic island at the junction marks the site of the old Butter Tron, or Weigh House, built 1352 and rebuilt 1660, but long since demolished.

Here too is the Upper Bow, a remnant of the old West Bow, a steep, curving street which ran from here to the Grassmarket beneath. The present alley terminates high above the pavement of Victoria Street, a 19th-century 2-tier development.

Here Castle Hill becomes the Lawnmarket where cloth traders once set up their stalls on market days. The public house on the left contains mementoes of Ensign Ewart. Adjoining it is Milne's Court, built by Robert Mylne, the King's master mason, 1690; it is an early attempt to break away from the narrow, dark and stinking closes and create a housing development with some light and fresh air. The tenements are of impressive height, reaching 8 storeys in places, topped by picturesque gables, and the east block has an attractive turnpike stair. The court was extensively restored 1967–70 by the University, and is now used as student accommodation for the Faculty of Divinity which resides in the adjoining New College.

Next, on the same side, is James Court, another open square built by James Brownhill, 1723–7, with some later 19th-century alterations by Sir Patrick Geddes. Like Milne's Court, it was a fashionable quarter of the town in its time; in a house here, now demolished, David Hume lived, 1762–72. It was then rented by James Boswell, who entertained Johnson here in 1773; the house, along with a large part of the original court, was destroyed by fire in 1857. The north block has a huge 8-storey rear façade looking down the Mound.

Adjoining the court entrance on the Lawnmarket is Gladstone's Land, one of the most interesting restorations in the Royal Mile. The building is partly 16th century, but most of what is now visible, including the frontage, is 17th century, the result of renovations carried out by Thomas Gledstanes (a remote ancestor of Prime Minister W.E. Gladstone) when he bought the property in 1617. Most of the best features of the house were hidden until 1934, when restoration by the

National Trust for Scotland brought it to its present fine condition. Ground floor arcades were once common in old Edinburgh, but this is the only genuine one surviving. Its outside stair, also a typical Old Town feature, gave direct access to the first floor house over the ground floor shops. Restoration uncovered some fine 17th-century painted ceilings.

Behind is Lady Stair's Close. Most of the original buildings have gone, including a house on the east side in which Robert Burns stayed during his first visit to Edinburgh in 1786, and a tavern in which the essayist Sir Richard Steele gave a dinner to a company of eccentric beggars in 1717. The building on the Lawnmarket side is a 19th-century reconstruction by Sir Patrick Geddes, retaining some original features, including a moulded doorway and 3 projecting gables. Blackie House, at the rear of the court, is of the 17th century reconstructed in 1894 and again in 1950 by the University, its best side again being the north wall that faces the Mound. In the north-west corner of the close is Lady Stair's House, built in 1622 and much remodelled, but retaining a door lintel bearing the date and the initials of William Gray and his wife, for whom it was built. Lady Stair, a noted beauty and leader of fashion, bought the house in 1719. It has a corner stair tower with ogee roof, and now houses a small literary museum with relics of Burns, Scott and Stevenson. When the Mound was first opened in the late 18th century, this close became the main access between the Old Town and the New.

On the south side of the Lawnmarket is Riddle's Court. The first part, nearest the street, was built by Captain George Riddell in 1726, and the stair tower has a doorway with this date over it; the door leads to another of the houses occupied by David Hume in 1751, although the houses themselves have been rebuilt, largely at the instigation of Sir Patrick Geddes, who made them one of the first student residences in the city. The romantic-looking outside wooden stair is a 19th-century addition. The archway at the far end of the close is part of the 16th-century house of Bailie McMorran, built in 1591, and a grand mansion in its time. John McMorran was one of the wealthiest citizens of his day; he was shot dead in 1595 when pupils at the High School rioted and barricaded themselves in the school in protest at a refusal of extra holidays. The house was inherited by his brother, and in 1598 it was used by the Town Council to give a sumptuous banquet to King James VI and his Queen, Anne of Denmark. The interior has unique 16th- and 17th-century painted beams, and 17th-century plaster ceilings, one of which has the royal cypher of Charles II and the date 1684, suggesting that he too was a visitor. A later ceiling painting of 1890 depicts the famous banquet. The house is now an adult education centre.

Adjoining the entrance to Riddle's Court is the Scottish Central Library, an 18th-century façade with a 20th-century steel-framed building behind. The semi-octagonal stair tower in Fisher's Close, dating from 1699, is the oldest part, the rest being by Thomas Fisher, 1752. The library was opened in 1953 after restoration by the Carnegie Trust. Fisher's Close also contains Baden-Powell House, now the Edinburgh Scout headquarters, formerly a Methodist church, in Italian Gothic by Paterson and Shiells, 1865. The Close gives access to the upper level of Victoria Street. The block between Fisher's Close and Brodie's Court has a fine 17th-century front, behind which is the Roman Eagle Hall, a masonic building of 1646 (the Celtic Lodge) with an ornate plaster ceiling, where Robert Burns was entertained by the Freemasons.

Brodie's Court was the home of a most colourful citizen, Deacon Brodie, a respected cabinetmaker and town councillor by day and burglar by night. Brodie, while working in the houses of his customers, would take wax impressions of their keys, and return later for less honourable purposes. One night, while burgling the Excise Office at Chessel's Court in the Canongate, he was disturbed, but escaped and fled to Holland, where he was arrested and brought back to the gallows in 1788. He bribed the hangman to let him wear a steel collar in order that he might survive the rope, but his device failed. The gallows were of his own design, and clearly efficient. R.L. Stevenson used Brodie as the model for *Dr Jekyll and Mr Hyde*.

Brodie's name is also preserved in a public house opposite, remodelled from the lower 2 floors of a late 17th-century block, one of the few remaining examples of the domestic architecture of the period. The 6-storey block adjoining (nos. 443–9) is 18th century.

Here the Royal Mile crosses Bank Street, and becomes High Street. At no. 12 Bank Street Sir Robert Philip, public health pioneer, opened the world's first tuberculosis clinic in 1887.

On the north-east corner is the city's Sheriff Court House (1937), and opposite are Midlothian County (now Lothian Region) Buildings, in an Edwardian Palladian style (J. McIntyre Henry, 1905). On this corner are 3 brass studs in the street which mark the site of the last public execution in the city, in 1864. William Burke, the notorious murderer, was hanged here on 27 January 1829. Nearby is one of the Old Town's 18th-century wellheads.

The High Street now widens into Parliament Square, dominated by the west front of St Giles' Cathedral. Before it is the Queensberry Memorial to Walter Francis Scott (1806–84), 5th Duke of Buccleuch and 7th Duke of Queensberry, who built Granton Harbour out of his own fortune at a cost of £500,000, was Lord Lieutenant of Midlothian, a Knight of the Garter, and a patron of agriculture, science and the arts. The statue is by Sir Joseph Boehm, 1887, on a plinth by Rowand Anderson decorated with panels of allegorical figures. In the street alongside is the Heart of Midlothian, immortalized by Sir Walter Scott. The heart-shaped pattern of cobblestones marks the position of the doorway of the Tolbooth, the town prison demolished in 1817. The prison's heavy wooden door was presented to Scott, and it can still be seen at his house at Abbotsford. The outline of the Tolbooth is marked by studs, some of which carry the dates of successive reconstructions.

St Giles' has not really been a cathedral at all since 1688, when the Church of Scotland finally did away with bishops. But although it is more properly known as the High Kirk of Edinburgh, no one ever calls it anything but a cathedral.

A church has stood on this site at least since AD 854, when the monks of Lindisfarne Priory in Northumberland had an outpost here. A larger Norman church was erected in mid 12th century but was largely destroyed by Richard II of England in 1385; all that remains of this ancient structure are the 4 massive pillars in the nave beneath the spire. Rebuilding began almost at once, although the bulk of the church existing today is 15th century. Its external appearance was substantially altered in 1829 when William Burn performed an unfortunate facelift by cloaking the ancient rubble-built walls in a coat of smooth ashlar masonry, leaving only the spire in its original state. Burn also removed many original Norman features, including a fine doorway.

In 1454 the church acquired a religious relic, the reputed arm bone of St Giles, mounted in gold with a diamond ring on its finger, brought from France by Preston of Gordon, but lost during the upheavals of the Reformation. In 1467 St Giles' had grown sufficiently in importance for the Pope to declare it a collegiate church. It was about this time that the crown spire was added.

By mid 16th century idolatry was taking over from true worship, and at one time there were more than 50 altars inside St Giles', the grandest being that of St Giles himself. Only with the advent of the reformers led by Knox, who first preached in St Giles' on 1 July 1559 were they all swept away. In the 130 years of religious strife which followed, first against Papacy, and then against the episcopacy forced upon Scotland by English kings, St Giles' was divided up into as many as 4 separate churches, and parts of it were in use for secular purposes, including a police station in the nave, up to the mid 19th century. In 1871 major renovations began to restore it to its former glory and to a single church, and in 1883 it was reopened in the state in which we find it today. Since then the major addition has been the Thistle Chapel, erected in 1910.

St Giles' is basically cruciform in plan, with numerous additions, particularly on the south side, making its overall shape irregular. In spite of the 1829 'improvements' it remains a spectacular Gothic building inside, 206 feet long and 129 feet wide across the transepts, its crown spire rising to 161 feet.

We enter St Giles' opposite the Queensberry statue, by the west door, built as part of the 1871 restorations and incorporating statuettes of monarchs and ministers associated with the church. To the left of the nave, with its fine medieval vaulting (the sections of plaster vaulting are a 19th-century recon-

struction) is first the Albany Aisle, in the north-west corner of
the church, built 1401–10, by Robert, Duke of Albany, after his
nephew had been murdered by the Duke of Rothesay. It now
contains a war memorial, dedicated in 1951, with a perpetually
burning lamp of remembrance and a simple cross surrounded
by panels depicting the 4 elements of earth, air, fire and water.
In the west wall, beside the door just entered, is a fine stained-
glass window by William Morris, commemorating Lord Currie-
hill.

Proceeding along the north aisle we come to the north bay,
which contains the memorial to Archibald Campbell, first
Marquis of Argyll and one of the outstanding leaders of the
Covenanters, who was beheaded in 1661. The marble monument is by Sydney Mitchell, and is enhanced by a floor of Irish
marble, and a window, showing the coats of arms of the principal Covenanter leaders, by the Glass Stainers' Company of
Glasgow.

This bay was originally the Hammermen's Chapel, where
the city's tradesmen dedicated their celebrated Blue Blanket.
Adjoining, in the north transept, is the entrance from the High
Street, and immediately beyond, in the north aisle of the chancel, a small chapel of youth, where the colours of youth organizations in the city are laid.

We cross from the north transept to the south, beneath the
spire and between the original Norman pillars. In the chancel is
the oak communion table, enlarged in 1953 to take the
Honours of Scotland which were placed on it during the
National Service for Queen Elizabeth II after her Coronation.
The table is flanked by the ceremonial stalls of the Moderator
of the General Assembly of the Church of Scotland on the left,
and the Dean of the Thistle and Chapel Royal on the right. At
the near end of the chancel is an ornate pulpit in Caen stone by
John Rhind, with panels depicting the 6 Acts of Mercy. In the
south transept are the organ and university stalls.

We cross to the railings flanking the south aisle; here is a
display of old service books, including Laud's Liturgy, the use
of which episcopal book in St Giles' sparked off the Covenanting wars. Also in the south aisle is a pre-Reformation
relic, the Vesper Bell of 1452. Behind the railings lies the Moray

Aisle, built 1387–91. James Stewart, Earl of Moray, was married here by Knox in 1562; eight years later, as Regent of Scotland, he was murdered and his body was brought back here to be buried, with Knox again officiating. He is buried beneath the aisle, and there is a memorial incorporating the bronze plaque from the original tomb, with a Latin inscription by George Buchanan.

The aisle also has a fine canopied pulpit by Rowand Anderson, erected in 1884 to mark the resumption of a daily service in the Cathedral after a break of 200 years.

Here too, beneath the oriel window in the west wall, is a large memorial bronze to R.L. Stevenson by Auguste St Gaudens.

Moving east past the organ we come first to the Chepman Aisle, built in 1513 by Walter Chepman, who introduced printing to Scotland. It contains an ornate memorial to James Graham, Marquis of Montrose, who was hanged in Edinburgh in 1650, and his body reinterred here in 1661. The memorial, by Rowand Anderson, was erected in 1888 by the clan Graeme. Exhibited nearby is a copy of the National Covenant of 1638.

Beyond is the Preston Aisle built in 1455 in gratitude to William Preston who donated St Giles' arm bone. Here is the Royal Pew, occupied during the General Assembly by the Queen's representative, the Lord High Commissioner. At the east end, set into the wall, is the oldest known representation of the coat of arms of Edinburgh.

The gates at the east end of the Preston Aisle lead to the antechapel of the Thistle Chapel. Consecrated in 1911, it is the work of Sir Robert Lorimer, and is the most ornate building of its kind erected in Scotland since the Middle Ages.

The Order of the Thistle is the oldest and most senior of Scotland's orders of chivalry, founded in the 15th century by James III, and this chapel is its shrine. It was the gift of the earls of Leven, who wished to restore the ruined Chapel Royal at Holyroodhouse, but on finding the scheme impractical donated this building instead. Under a remarkably ornate vaulted ceiling are the 14 exquisitely carved stalls of the Knights of the Thistle, decorated with the arms of famous Scotsmen, past and present members of the Order. The Queen's stall displays an elaborate carving of the Royal Arms of Scotland, and the windows are decorated with some fine stained glass by Douglas Strachan and Louis Davis. From the Thistle Chapel the exit to the street is by the south-east door, a survival from the 1387 rebuilding, originally sited in the Moray Aisle, and replaced here in 1910.

Behind St Giles' lies PARLIAMENT SQUARE, once the home of the Scottish Parliament but now housing the high courts of Scotland. Where the square narrows at the south-west corner of the cathedral is the Parliament House, built 1631-40 by Sir James Murray; the Scots Parliament moved here from the Castle in 1639, and remained until the Treaty of Union in 1707. It is a fine old Scots Gothic building, with interesting rubble stonework, turrets and window tracery, but is completely hidden by a Greek frontage added by Robert Reid in 1807 to complete a unified façade round the square. The only sight of the original is to be had from George IV Bridge, alongside the National Library. Parliament Hall has an imposing interior, with a splendid hammerbeam roof, erected in 1639 by John Scott. The hall is 122 feet long and 49 feet broad, and is decorated with statues of eminent legal figures. The stained-glass window, added in 1868, depicts the founding of the College of Justice by James V in 1532.

Parliament Hall once housed some of the high courts, but is now used only as a promenade by advocates waiting to be called for their cases. Beneath it is the Laigh (Low) Parliament House, with rows of massive stone pillars supporting its roof.

Adjoining Parliament Hall on the east, behind the central Ionic portico, are the High Court of Justiciary and the Court of Session, the principal criminal and civil courts of Scotland. This, like the rest of Parliament Square, is 19th century; the unified Ionic frontage, built by Robert Reid in stages between 1807 and 1834, borrows much of its detail from Robert Adam's University Old College. After a great fire in 1824 which destroyed many of the older buildings, Reid's scheme was continued along the east side of the square.

In the centre of Parliament Square is a statue of Charles II, erected in 1685 and the oldest lead equestrian statue in Britain. Said to be of Dutch origin, it has had to be repaired many times, most recently in 1972, because of weakness at the knees under the weight of the lead. The plinth (1835) carries a panel from the original 17th-century base.

Against the wall of St Giles' is a statue, by Pittendrigh Mac-Gillivray, of Knox, which marks the approximate site of his grave, somewhere under Parliament Square, formerly St Giles' churchyard.

The narrow gap leads to the western half of the square, occupied by the Signet Library, by Robert Reid (1810), continuing Reid's design for the rest of the square. The interior is one of the finest anywhere in Edinburgh, and is the work of William Stark, 1812–13, with a staircase by W.H. Playfair (1819). Both the lower and upper libraries are very fine, lined with Corinthian columns and containing between them some 150,000 books. The upper room is 136 feet long, and is lit by a central saucer dome, with ornate paintings of Apollo and the Muses by Thomas Stothard, RA. The lower hall was built with an ingenious central heating system, which circulated hot air through the legs of small cast-iron tables, which can still be seen.

To the rear of the Parliament Square complex is the Advocates' Library, not normally open to the public, founded in 1682 by Sir George Mackenzie of Rosehaugh; David Hume was a former keeper. In 1925 this massive and ancient collection, with the exception of its law books, was handed over to the nation to form the nucleus of the National Library of Scotland, whose present premises adjoin at the rear.

At the east side of Parliament Square, by the south-east door of St Giles', is the Mercat Cross, erected in 1888 at the instigation of Prime Minister Gladstone who, according to a Latin inscription on the cross, claimed purely Scottish descent through both parents (although himself born in Liverpool). The shaft is from the original burgh cross which stood a few yards to the east from 1617 until 1756, and whose site is marked by stones in the street at the entrance to Old Fishmarket Close.

We return to the High Street, and pick up the north side again at the corner of St Giles' Street; the frontage here, down to no. 367, dates from *c.* 1800. The adjoining block, nos. 343–63, is mid 18th century but incorporating older work, some of which can be seen in Advocates Close, built mainly about 1610, but with some earlier remnants.

The close is named after James Stewart, Lord Advocate (1692–1713), who lived here, and its narrow gulley opens out to a fine view of the New Town rooftops. Here too lived Sir John Scougal (1645–1730), one of the early Scottish portraitists, who painted William of Orange. On the left of the close stands the late 16th-century mansion of Adam Bothwell, Bishop of Orkney, who married Mary, Queen of Scots to Bothwell. The rubble-built house is of 3 storeys with attic, and with a 3-sided apse facing north. At the top of the close is an 18th-century projecting stair tower. Both the Bothwell mansion and the block on the right-hand side of the close have inscribed door lintels, some dated 1590.

In the centre of the street opposite here, hard by the north wall of St Giles', there stood, until their demolition in 1817, a rambling block of tenements with ground floor shops known as the Luckenbooths (locked booths). Among the shops was that of William Creech, bookseller, who published an edition of Burns' poetry following the latter's visit to Edinburgh in 1786, and the shop of Allan Ramsay, wigmaker, who opened Scotland's first circulating library there in 1725.

The north side is next occupied by the CITY CHAMBERS, home of the City of Edinburgh District Council. The original building is in the centre courtyard, and modern extensions flank the street on either side. This is where classical Edinburgh was born.

The buildings round the courtyard (John and Robert Adam, 1753–61) were the first of a succession of major improvements to the Old Town, carried out at the instigation of Lord Provost George Drummond, and which culminated in the building of the New Town. This was the Royal Exchange, a meeting-place for Edinburgh merchants, but they never used it much, preferring to do business in the street. It has been a council chamber since the early 19th century.

The main façade has a Corinthian centrepiece and a piazza where the merchants were supposed to stroll. The building is deceptive from this side; it has 12 storeys altogether, and its massive rear wall, seen from Cockburn Street, makes it one of the highest remaining buildings in the Old Town. In the entrance hall are panels listing the names of all the city's chief magistrates from William de Dederyk in 1296. The later extensions enclose the remains of Mary King's Close, an ancient alley abandoned during the plague of 1645, and rediscovered largely intact. In the quadrangle is Sir John Steell's statue of The Taming of Bucephalus by Alexander the Great (cast 1883). The arcaded screen to the street, a modern addition, contains a simple war memorial. The building has a committee room panelled in timber from New Zealand, a reminder of the link between Edinburgh and Dunedin.

The eastern extension incorporates Anchor Close, site of Dawney Douglas' Anchor Tavern, a favourite haunt of Burns and the home of the Crochallan Fencibles, a celebrated drinking club of which Burns was a member and upon which he based *Rattlin' Roarin' Willie*. 'Willie' was William Dunbar, a noted lawyer and the club's 'colonel'. Here too were the printing works of William Smellie, who produced the Edinburgh edition of Burns in 1787, and the first edition of the *Encyclopaedia Britannica* in 1768. In a house in the close Sir Walter Scott's parents lived until 1771.

Writers' Court, leading to Warriston's Close, incorporated in the west wing of the City Chambers, contained Cleriheugh's Tavern, another celebrated 18th-century inn frequented by Burns. Warriston's Close contained the mansion of Sir Archibald Johnston, Lord Warriston, a champion of the Covenanters, and also a manse occupied by Knox during his early years at St Giles', 1560–66.

The eastern wing also incorporates Craig's Close, now remembered only by a plaque, where Archibald Constable, Scott's publisher, had his first premises, and Old Post Office Close, where the first proper Post Office in Scotland was set up in 1713.

By Geddes' Entry, on the shop front of a mainly 18th-century block is a plaque marking the site of a snuff shop owned by James Gillespie, who endowed a famous Edinburgh school. Old Stamp Office Close was the home of the Scottish Inland Revenue until 1821, and of Fortune's Tavern, one of the most elegant in the city in the 18th century, where the Lord High Commissioner of the General Assembly held his receptions. Here too was the home of the Countess of Eglinton, who had 7 beautiful daughters, all over 6 feet tall; the family progress, in 8 gilded sedan chairs to a ball in the Assembly Rooms directly across the street, was one of the sights of the 18th-century town. Flora Macdonald, saviour of Prince Charles Edward, attended a school in the close. From here to the Cockburn Street corner the frontages are mainly *c.*1700 with a fine tenement above the Black Swan public house.

The south side of the High Street between St Giles' and the Tron Kirk was largely destroyed in a great fire in 1824, and little remains except the old closes running down to the Cowgate. Parts of the block are reconstructions of ruins which did not collapse in the fire, and most of the present frontages date from about 1825. The first, by the entrance to Old Fishmarket Close, was built *c.* 1846 in a Scots Jacobean style to house the new office of the *Edinburgh Courant* newspaper, founded by Daniel Defoe.

Old Fishmarket Close and Borthwick's Close afford fine views to the Italianate roofs of the Royal Scottish Museum. Old Assembly Close was the site of the second of the Old Town's halls, where the formal dancing assemblies took place having moved from old premises in the West Bow; this hall was in use between 1720 and 1766, and the assemblies here were described by Oliver Goldsmith, a medical student in the city, after his one and only visit. The close was also the home of Clement Little, an advocate who, in 1580, bequeathed his library of 300 books for the founding of the University library. The house of an engraver at the head of the close is said to have been the origin of the 1824 fire. Further down the Close is an old preparatory school built for George Heriot's school in 1839.

In New Assembly Close is the only surviving building of the 1824 fire, now occupied by the Edinburgh Wax Museum. Built in 1813 by Gillespie Graham as St David's Masonic Chapel, it is decorated with Roman Doric columns, fanlight and arched wrought iron lampholder. This was also the site of the third dancing assembly hall, opened in 1758, but enjoying only a brief life until the present-day Assembly Hall was opened in George Street in 1787. The street frontage here houses the Royal Mile Centre and headquarters of the Festival Fringe Society.

At the eastern corner of High Street and Cockburn Street, now occupied by a bank, stood the Union Cellar where, according to tradition, the Treaty of Union was signed in 1707. A plaque on the Cockburn Street frontage of the Black Swan recalls the site of the house of Lord Provost Sir Simon Preston where Mary, Queen of Scots spent her last night in Edinburgh on 15 June 1567 on her way from defeat at Carberry Hill to imprisonment in Loch Leven Castle.

Cockburn Street is named after Lord Cockburn, the distinguished judge and man of letters. It was built mainly in 1860, 6 years after his death, by Peddie and Kinnear, and exhibits some good snecked rubble frontages in Scottish baronial style. No. 30 was the office of *The Scotsman* newspaper, and its masthead is carved in the stonework of the façade. This was one of the most advanced newspaper offices of its time, with private telegraph wires to London and a printing plant capable of producing 60,000 copies an hour.

Hunter Square was built *c.* 1790 as part of the improvements connected with the opening of South Bridge. The south-west corner was the site of a house where George Buchanan, historian and poet, died in 1582. No. 4, now a bank, was built in 1788 by John Baxter as the Merchants' Hall for the Edinburgh Merchant Company, with Doric pilasters and balustraded parapet.

Hunter Square is dominated by the Tron Church, built 1637–47 by John Mylne for Charles I, but much altered and shortened at the building of the surrounding square. There is some fine window tracery, and a hammerbeam roof by John Scott, dating from the church's original construction. The Tron originally had an unusual wooden spire, burnt in the fire of 1824, and replaced by an octagonal tower and spire (R. & R. Dickson, 1828). Above the main doorway is a representation of the city coat of arms and a Latin inscription, but the rest of the church is in a rather nondescript style. It was closed for worship in 1952, and has recently been restored by the city. During reconstruction in 1974, excavations under the floor revealed the cobbles of Marlin's Wynd, an ancient roadway covered over to build the church foundations in 1637, along with the massively thick foundation walls of the adjoining tenements.

The church takes its name from the Tron, or public weigh-beam, which stood nearby. Merchants whose goods were found to be underweight were occasionally nailed to the beam by the ears.

Beyond the junction of North and South Bridge, on the south-east corner, is an imposing Bank of Scotland branch (formerly British Linen Bank), by Dick, Peddie and Walker Todd, 1923, in Renaissance style with a large fluted portico on the High Street side. Opposite, on the north-east corner, is a Royal Bank branch (Mitchell and Wilson, 1898) in Scots Renaissance style with corbelled parapet and angle turrets with ogee roofs.

Adjoining is Carubber's Close, named after William de Carriberis, a merchant who had a mansion here c. 1450. At the foot of the close is Old St Paul's Episcopal Church (Hay and Henderson, 1883), built to replace an earlier one to which Bishop Rose took a congregation from St Giles' when episcopacy was abolished from the Church of Scotland in 1688. (The episcopal – Anglican – church was disestablished for its Jacobite allegiance and its refusal to accept William of Orange as rightful king in place of the Stuart line.) The Seabury Chapel (1904) commemorates Samuel Seabury, first bishop of the American church, who worshipped here while a student in Edinburgh. The Warriors' Chapel (1926) commemorates 140 of the congregation killed in the First World War. There is a fine iron choir screen on a rich marble base. Because of the church, Carruber's Close became a Jacobite stronghold. Here too, in 1736, Allan Ramsay opened the first regular theatre in Edinburgh, only to have it rapidly closed by the magistrates.

In the nearby Bishop's Close, now closed, Archbishop Spottiswoode, historian of the Scottish church, was born in 1565, and in the same house Henry Dundas, Viscount Melville, was born in 1742.

Bailie Fyfe's Close and the adjacent Paisley Close were the site of a major disaster in 1861 when one of the ancient towering tenement blocks collapsed, killing 35 of the inhabitants. At the time of the crash the 7-storey block was said to have nearly 100 people living in it; the tragedy focused public attention on the gross overcrowding and insanitary conditions in the Old

Town and led to the appointment of Edinburgh's first medical officer of health. Above the entrance to Paisley Close is a memorial window and inscription: 'Heave awa' chaps, I'm no deid yet', recalling one lucky youth who narrowly escaped with his life.

Chalmers Close gives access to Trinity Church Apse, an ancient structure. The original church, which was founded by Mary of Gueldres in 1462 on a site where Waverley Station now stands, was demolished in 1848 and rebuilt here in 1872 using the original stones. In 1964 it was partly demolished, leaving only the apse as a scheduled monument.

South Gray's Close, opposite, was the birthplace of Thomas Erskine, Lord Chancellor of England (1750), and of his brother Harry Erskine, Lord Advocate of Scotland (1746). Adjoining it, in Hyndford's Close, is the Museum of Childhood, displaying toys from earliest times to the present day.

The block containing the museum is late 17th and early 18th century, originally 6-storey, now demolished to 2. The museum entrance is a fragment of an arcade, a once-common feature of the Royal Mile; the rear wing has a slightly projecting stair tower and moulded doorway.

On the north side of the street, adjoining Trunk's Close, is one of the oldest remaining buildings in the High Street, Moubray House, originally built by Robert Moubray in 1477, but with 16th and 17th-century alterations and additions, and a recent restoration. The house retains its outside stair, a reminder that the ground floors were once used for separate shops or the keeping of pigs, and its projecting wooden gable at attic level. The portraitist George Jameson (1586–1644), who studied under Rubens and who was known as the Scottish Van Dyck in his day, lived here while executing portraits of past Scottish monarchs for Charles I at Holyrood. Daniel Defoe edited the *Edinburgh Courant* briefly from here in 1710. Trunk's Close exhibits the side wall of the house, with corbelled features, and on the front is an old Sun Insurance plate. In the street outside is an 18th-century well.

Next door is JOHN KNOX'S HOUSE, which displays relics of the great reformer inside although it is not certain that he ever stayed here. The house is of great age and architectural interest;

it is originally 16th century, and is first mentioned in 1525 as the property of Walter Reidpath, being later inherited by his descendant James Mossman, goldsmith to Mary Queen of Scots, who extended the house and added his initials and those of his wife, below the first-floor window of the west wall. The legend above the ground-floor windows, 'Lufe God Abufe Al and yi nyghbour as yi self', was added during a much more recent restoration. Although extensively rebuilt, the house exhibits several notable Old Town features, including the projecting timber galleries facing the street, two projecting wooden dormers in the roof, and an outside stair.

Adjoining is the Church of Scotland's Netherbow Arts Centre (1972), retaining a tablet from an earlier building, dated 1606, in the courtyard at the rear. The bronze sign depicting the old city gate at the Netherbow is fanciful, and a better picture is given by a carving above the door of no. 9 High Street, a few yards to the east.

On the south side of the street is Tweeddale Court, entered through a 6-storey block of early 18th-century date. The court contains a few vestiges of the first city wall of 1450, but its main feature is the small mansion built in 1576 by John Layng, Keeper of the Signet. The court takes its name from the first Marquis of Tweeddale who inherited the house in 1645 from his grandmother, Lady Margaret Kerr. From 1791 to 1807 it was the first headquarters of the British Linen Bank, who added the Doric porch, and in 1806 it was the scene of one of the city's great unsolved murders when William Begbie, a bank messenger, was found stabbed to death in the court, with £4,392 of the bank's money missing.

A few yards to the east, in an early 19th-century block, is World's End Close, the last in the street before the old city wall and the world outside. At the junction of Jeffrey Street and St Mary's Street, brass studs in the roadway mark the site of the Netherbow Port, one of the main gateways to the old town, built as part of the Flodden Wall of 1513 and finally demolished in 1764. The Port marked the end of the old burgh of Edinburgh, and the beginning of the separate burgh of CANONGATE. No. 2 St Mary's Street was the first building to be erected under Sir William Chambers' city improvement scheme,

1867, and no. 26 is on the site of Boyd's Inn, where Dr Johnson stayed in 1773.

Many of the Canongate buildings are 20th-century reconstructions of 17th- and 18th-century tenement blocks, built to harmonize with the street as a whole rather than copy exactly those they replace. Such a block is Morocco Land (nos. 265–7 Canongate), rebuilt 1957 but retaining some of the original stones, including the effigy of a Moor which gives the block its name. A curious legend is attached to the Moor. A young Edinburgh man, Andrew Gray, condemned to death for leading a riot, escaped from prison to Morocco; in 1645 he returned to demand a pardon for his unjust treatment but, on learning that the provost's daughter was dying of the plague, offered to cure her. She was cured, he won his pardon, they married, and lived in a house on this site.

Across the street, nos. 250–54 were built in 1700, and the green stuccoed block, nos. 246–8, is mid 18th century; both blocks have been completely rebuilt behind their frontages. Next door is Chessel's Court, an outstanding reconstruction which retains a large part of the original. The court was built in 1748 by Archibald Chessel as high-class apartments, with a large garden and fine views to Arthur's Seat. The south block, with notable interior work, is original, the west blocks mainly so, and the front block is a reconstruction of 1963, when the entire scheme was restored. The south block became the Excise Office for a time and it was here, in 1788, that Deacon Brodie performed his last ill-fated burglary. All the remaining buildings on the north side of the street, as far as the New Street corner, are modern reconstructions.

On the south side, next to Chessel's Court, a modern public house recalls the tradesmen's Blue Blanket. The house next door (no. 206) has a plaque to George Chalmers (1773–1836), a wealthy Canongate plumber who bequeathed his fortune to found Chalmers Hospital at Lauriston.

On the eastern corner of New Street no. 231 was restored and opened as the Old Sailors' Ark, dispensing shelter and hot food to the poor and old of the city. Opposite is Old Playhouse Close, entered through a restored 17th-century block, largely rebuilt in 1969, but retaining a turreted stair tower at the rear.

The close was the site, 1747–69, of the Playhouse Theatre, one of the earliest in Edinburgh and one of the most successful at avoiding closure by the magistrates. John Home's *Douglas*, a now forgotten work, was first performed here in 1756, and caused a scandal because it was written by a minister of the Kirk and its first night was attended by many of his fellow preachers, at a time when the church was strong in its condemnation of the stage.

In the street by the close entrance is a ring of stones marking the site of St John's Cross, the old burgh cross of the Canongate, to which the Town Council of Edinburgh would repair to greet important visitors arriving from the east.

At the entrance to St John's Street is a house where the novelist Tobias Smollett stayed with his sister in 1766 while writing *Humphrey Clinker*, and the Edinburgh scenes in this early novel reflect his visit. The entrance block is of 1755, restored in 1955 and now part of Moray House. St John's Street was a fashionable address; the only remaining house of the 18th-century row, on the west side of the street, has been restored as the headquarters of the Priory of Scotland of the Most Venerated Order of St John, a 13th-century order of chivalry revived in 1947. But the oldest building is that immediately beyond the archway, the Canongate Kilwinning Lodge of Freemasons, of which Burns was a member and which claims the oldest masonic chapel still in use in the world. The northern part is 17th century, although the crowstepped dormer heads and re-entrant turret at the south-east are modern. The southern section, containing the chapel, was built in 1735, and contains an organ of 1757 and a Master's chair of 1800.

Next to St John's Street is one of the grandest of the Canongate mansions, MORAY HOUSE, with first floor balcony and entrance gatepiers with pyramid finials. It was built in 1628 for Mary, Dowager Countess of Home, was visited by Charles I, and on two occasions, in 1648 and 1650, was occupied by Cromwell. From its balcony the Marquis of Argyll, champion of the Covenanters, watched on his wedding day as James Graham, Marquis of Montrose, Captain-General of the armies of King Charles of Scotland, was wheeled to his execution in 1650. The original 2-storey house, much extended, has a semi-octagonal stair tower on the west side, and some fine plasterwork within. In its garden is a summerhouse where, tradition affirms, the Treaty of Union was being signed in 1707 until an angry mob drove the signatories to seek shelter in the Union Cellar in the High Street.

Opposite, at nos. 195–7, is Shoemakers' Land, a 1956 reconstruction of a 1725 tenement, using some of the original stones. It was built by the Canongate Incorporation of Cordiners (shoemakers), and their crest, a shoemaker's rounding knife, appears on a stone tablet, with Biblical text: 'Blessed is he that wisely doth the poor man's case consider.' A few doors farther down, beyond further 1958 reconstructions, is Bible Land (nos. 183–7) built in 1677, also by the cordiners, whose badge can also be seen here, as well as an open Bible with a text from Psalm 133: 'Behold how good a thing it is and how becoming well, together such as brethren are, in unity to dwell,' and another Biblical epithet: 'It is an honour for men to cease from strife.'

Nos. 167–9 is a 4-storey house of 1624, with a turnpike stair and pedimented dormers, partially reconstructed. It adjoins the CANONGATE TOLBOOTH, built 1591 in French style and one of the oldest survivals in the Canongate. The 5-storey turreted steeple and the bulk of the building are original, but the stone dormers and outsize clock were added during Victorian renovations. It is now a branch of the City Museum, housing a collection of Highland dress. Beside its forestair, which led over the jail to the council chamber and court house, is the Canongate's war memorial.

Across the street is HUNTLY HOUSE, one of the finest of the preserved houses and the home of the city's principal museum of local history. Originally 3 adjoining timber tenements, built *c*. 1517, it was rebuilt in stone in 1570; it takes its name from the first Marquis of Huntly, who is supposed to have lived here in the late 16th century but his connection is doubtful. In 1647 it was bought by the Incorporation of Hammermen (smiths) of the Canongate, who used it as their headquarters. It was bought by the city in 1924 and extensively rebuilt, although retaining the unusual cantilevering of its upper 2 floors, and its 3 wooden harled gables to the street. The Latin inscriptions on the front are modern; the originals are inside. The interior is well preserved and should be seen for its own sake as well as for the exhibits which show the growth of Edinburgh. On the east side of Bakehouse Close entrance is another 16th-century house, with wallhead gable and balcony, and square crowstepped stair tower to the rear, which forms an annexe to the Museum. Bakehouse Close also gives access to Acheson House, another of the Canongate's great mansions. Built in 1633 for Sir Archibald Acheson, a judge in Ireland under Charles I, his monogram and that of his wife, Dame Margaret Hamilton, appear on the dormer heads. The house was restored for the Marquis of Bute in 1937, and is now the Scottish Craft Centre.

In the street here was the site of the old Canongate Burgh Cross, removed as an obstruction in 1888 and re-erected a few yards away in front of the CANONGATE KIRK. The Kirk was built by James Smith in 1688 to house the congregation ousted from the church of Holyroodhouse by James II, who wished to convert the latter building into a Chapel Royal. The church is cruciform, and rubble-built except for the ashlar gable frontage of curvilinear outline, and with Doric portico and central circular window with the royal arms above. The fine interior was restored in 1950.

It was in this church that Prince Charles Edward held prisoner the captured English officers from the Battle of Prestonpans, 1745. In more recent times, the church's wartime minister, Dr Ronald Selby Wright, achieved national fame as a radio padre. The churchyard contains the graves of many eminent Scotsmen, listed on a board at the gate, including the poet Robert Fergusson, with a headstone erected by Burns, the economist Adam Smith, Burns' 'Clarinda' (Mrs Agnes McLehose) and George Drummond, 6 times Lord Provost and father of the New Town.

On the north side further down is Panmure Close (entry by Little Lochend Close) which leads to Panmure House, a late 17th-century L-plan mansion, rubble-built with crowstepped gables, first occupied in 1696 by the fourth Earl of Panmure, a leading Jacobite. From 1778 until his death in 1790 it was the home of Adam Smith. After lying empty for many years it was restored by Roy Thomson (later Lord Thomson of Fleet) who gave it to the Canongate Boys' Club. Since 1973 it has been a young people's training centre. Also in Panmure Close (at no. 129) is Cadell House, an 18th-century 3-storey edifice restored as flats in 1954.

Reid's Court on the north side contains Canongate Manse, an early 18th-century 2-storey house with advanced wings added later (restored 1958). At the court entrance is Russell House, another late 18th-century 3-storey rubble-built house; the modern houses adjoining are by Sir Basil Spence.

Across the street, no. 82 is a 1954 replica of Nisbet of Dirleton's house (1619) incorporating some of the original stones, including fine carved lintels. The house has crowstepped gables, and a crowstepped stair tower on the west. Among the mottoes carved on the lintels is that of the city, *Nisi Dominus Frustra*.

On the north side beyond Reid's Court, the adjoining modern housing block carries a plaque recalling the site of Golfer's Land, and a celebrated golf match between James II (then Duke of York) and John Paterson. Paterson's motto, 'I hate no person' is an anagram of his name, and his other motto, 'Far and sure' has been adopted by golfers everywhere.

Next on the north side is Whitefoord House, (Robert Mylne, 1769) the town house of Sir John Whitefoord, who died here in 1803; he was one of the early patrons of Robert Burns. Much extended and altered, this and the adjoining Callander House, built c. 1770 for John Callander of Craigforth, a noted antiquary, now serve as a war veterans' home. They were built on the site of the town mansion of the Earl of Winton, better known as Seton's Lodging in the Canongate, from Scott's *The Abbot*; a plaque at Forsyth's Close records this fact.

Directly opposite is Queensberry House, now an old people's hospital. Built 1681 by Charles Maitland of Hatton, it has 18th-century additions, and was extensively rebuilt as a barracks in 1808, when an extra storey was added. It was sold in 1686 to the first Duke of Queensberry, and remained in the Queensberry family until 1801. The second Duke of Queensberry was a commissioner for the Treaty of Union in 1707, accepting a bribe of over £12,000 to see the Act passed. His son was a grotesque insane monster; while the Duke was out signing the

Treaty, his son, left in the house, roasted a young kitchen boy alive on a spit and was eating him when discovered.

On the north side, through a restored arcade at no. 27, is WHITE HORSE CLOSE, a picturesque renovation of a 17th-century inn and courtyard, restored in 1889 and again in 1964. The inn stood at least as early as 1623, which date it carries. It was the starting point of one of the first regular stage coaches to London, a fact commemorated on the label of a well-known whisky. The yard was probably the site of the stables for Holyrood, and is thought to be named after Mary Queen of Scots' favourite white palfrey. It was the Jacobite headquarters during Prince Charles Edward's brief occupation of the city in 1745. The close contained the forge of William Dick (1793–1866), a farrier, who founded the city's Royal Dick Veterinary College.

At the corner of Abbeyhill is a recently restored (1975) late 17th-century 4-storey house with crowstepped gables. In the centre of the street is a circle of stones marking the site of the Girth Cross, the extremity of the Holyrood Abbey sanctuary, within which debtors were safe from their pursuers.

The limits of the Abbey sanctuary are also marked by brass studs in the roadway denoting the letter S. The earliest record of a debtor seeking relief from his pursuers here is in 1531, and the practice continued until the abolition of imprisonment for debt in 1880. All that was necessary for the escapee was to find himself lodgings within the Abbey precincts and sign a book kept on the premises by the Bailie of Holyrood. The author Thomas de Quincey made much use of this privilege between 1833 and 1840.

Here, in the last few yards of the Royal Mile, Canongate becomes the Abbey Strand. The house on the Abbeyhill corner is early 16th century, with 17th-century additions and a 19th-century upper floor, presenting 6 dormer gablets to the street. Adjoining it, hard by the palace gates, is a 2-storey 17th-century house with 3 crowstepped gables, and outside stairs typical of the period. Opposite, in the wall of the old Abbey Court House, is a restored heraldic panel taken from the ancient Abbey gatehouse which stood near this site, bearing the monogram of King James V and the royal arms of Scotland.

We now enter the palace yard of HOLYROODHOUSE through

one of three sets of magnificent wrought-iron gateways. Designed by Sir George Washington Browne, they were erected in
1920 as part of the national memorial to King Edward VII,
which is completed by a statue of 'Edward the Peacemaker'
(H.S. Gamley, RSA), on the west side of the courtyard. Above
the Abbey Strand gateway is a representation of a stag's head
surmounted by a crucifix, a reference to the generally accepted
legend of the founding of Holyrood Abbey.

The ruined abbey stands to the north-east of the Palace. The
earliest buildings are now little more than patterns in the
ground; the roofless nave was built between 1190 and 1275,
incorporating parts of the earlier work in the south aisle wall.
The abbey church was originally cruciform, but the choir and
transepts, whose outline can still be traced to the east, were
demolished in 1569 by order of John Knox's reformed Kirk,
although before that the abbey had been desecrated by the Earl
of Hertford during the 'rough wooing' of 1544, and again in
1547. When the choir and transepts were demolished the nave,
no longer a monastery, was repaired to become the parish
church of the Canongate. Enough remains to indicate the size
and ornament of the old Abbey, which was richly decorated
and furnished.

Externally the ruin is chiefly in First Pointed Gothic style
and is mainly early 13th century, with some later additions. The
finest part is undoubtedly the west wall, with a 13th-century
deeply-recessed Norman doorway surmounted by two remarkable windows, which date from a restoration of the Abbey by
Charles I in 1633; two inscriptions from Charles' restoration,
one in Latin and one in English, adorn the doorway. This west
façade was originally flanked by two square Norman towers,
one of which was demolished to make way for the adjoining
palace, the other still there but shortened and without its spire.
This tower contains a memorial to Robert Douglas, Viscount
Belhaven (died 1639), a Scottish patriot at the time of the Covenant. The north wall, one of the oldest existing parts, is late
12th century, but its 7 flying buttresses were added in the 15th
century. The east wall was built after the choir and transepts of
the original church had been demolished, and its huge window
also dates from the Charles I restoration. The south wall is

early 13th century and contains, in the blocked-up doorway at the south-east corner, the only remaining vestige of the original kirk of 1128. Here too is the royal burial vault, restored by Queen Victoria in 1898, containing the remains of several Scottish kings and their queens: David II, James II and Mary of Gueldres, James V and Magdalene of France, and Darnley, consort of Mary, Queen of Scots. The remains here were collected from the individual tombs desecrated at the time of the Reformation and again in 1688.

In the rest of the ruined nave are many gravestones and monuments, including those of Bishop Bothwell of Orkney, who married Bothwell to Mary in this church, and Bishop Wishart of St Andrews, chaplain to the Marquis of Montrose.

King James II, the last of the Catholic kings of Great Britain, refurbished the Abbey – then serving as a parish church – established a college of Jesuits, and turned it into an ornate Chapel Royal for the Order of the Thistle. Before it could be used for its new purpose, news came that William of Orange had landed at Torbay, and the Edinburgh mob burst into the abbey, burning and destroying most of the Catholic artefacts, and even bursting open the royal vault to scatter the bones of ancient kings. The Abbey was never used again, and in 1768 the low-pitched stone roof added by Charles I in 1633 collapsed in a storm leaving the building in the ruinous state in which it remains today.

The adjoining Palace of Holyroodhouse originated as the guest house of the Abbey, used as occasional lodgings by the Scots kings. The present palace was begun in 1498 by King James IV, who established Edinburgh firmly as the Scottish capital. James' palace, a 4-storey rectangular structure, now forms the north-west tower; James died at Flodden in 1513, and the palace was completed by his son James V, mainly 1528–32. The old palace was severely damaged during the English invasion of 1543, and again by a fire during Cromwell's occupation of it in 1650. In 1658 Cromwell ordered its restoration, but all his work was pulled down in 1671 when the construction of the major part of the palace as it stands today was begun under the direction of Charles II, who finally carried out the intention of James IV to have a façade of 2 matching towers.

The 17th-century palace is to the design of Sir William Bruce, erected by Robert Mylne, the King's master mason. At the south-west corner, Bruce built a replica of the old King James' Tower, its architecture heavily influenced by the French style of Louis XIV, and he linked the two with a 2-storey Doric façade and gateway, surmounted by the arms of the King of Scots and a cupola clock dated 1680.

The gateway leads to the courtyard, where the style changes to Palladian classic, displaying the 3 orders of architecture, Doric, Ionic and Corinthian, one above the other, and the royal arms of Great Britain in the centre pediment, flanked by the crowned initials of Charles II.

Visitors to the interior come first to the royal apartments, of which the largest is the Picture Gallery, 124 feet long and 24 feet wide. Here Prince Charles Edward held a series of great balls during his brief occupation of Edinburgh in 1745. The tradition is continued today by the High Commissioner of the Church of Scotland during the General Assembly. There are 111 portraits of Scottish monarchs on the walls, all painted between 1684 and 1686 by Jakob de Wet of Haarlem, and mostly bearing only a notional resemblance to their subjects. Next, the Duchess of Hamilton's drawing room has a fine plaster ceiling, with rich detail including the cypher of Charles II.

The visitor then enters King James' Tower by Lord Darnley's apartments, consisting of an audience chamber, a dressing room and bedroom, containing interesting tapestry and furniture, mainly 17th century. From the audience chamber, a turnpike stair leads to Queen Mary's Apartments on the first floor. The stair itself is of curious design, being an early example of a double staircase. These apartments were extensively restored during the Charles II rebuilding, but the oak ceilings, with their emblems and initials of Scottish sovereigns, and the portion of frieze above the fireplace in the audience chamber, date from Mary's time. The bedroom contains relics of the Queen, including examples of her needlework above the fireplace; the dressing room has ancient and decayed tapestries of the period, and the supper room has a brass plaque marking the spot where Mary's secretary, Rizzio, was stabbed to death with 56 wounds on the night of 9 March 1566.

The remainder of the palace is occupied by the state rooms and throne room built for Charles II, and still used by the reigning monarch. After Prince Charles Edward's departure from Edinburgh in 1745 they lay unused for 50 years until the Count d'Artois, later Charles X of France, sheltered here during the French Revolution. George IV paid a state visit to Edinburgh in 1822, but did not reside at the Palace, although he held a grand ball here. Queen Victoria, King George V and King George VI all used the Palace regularly, and Queen Elizabeth II is in brief residence each summer, although it is said to be one of her least favourite Royal residences.

There are several antiquities of interest in the Palace grounds. In the forecourt is an ornate fountain, a copy of a 16th-century original at Linlithgow Palace. This one, designed by Robert Matheson and executed by John Thomas, was erected at Queen Victoria's request in 1859. In the north garden of the Palace is a sundial of 1633, made by John Mylne, the King's master mason, and known as Queen Mary's Dial. The reference is to Henrietta Maria, Queen of Charles I. In the north-west corner of the grounds is a curious late 16th century pavilion known as Queen Mary's Bath, rubble-built with a pyramid roof, probably a pavilion serving an adjoining tennis court. In 1789, during repairs, a richly chased dagger was found stuck in the roof. At the extreme north of the Palace grounds by Abbeyhill is a curious L-plan building of late 16th century date known as Croft-an-Righ (The King's Farm). The 3- and 4-storey rubble-built house originally belonged to Lord Elphinstone, but was subdivided for use as cottages for the gardeners of Holyrood.

The visitor may return to the Canongate, or turn into Horse Wynd by the Palace Gate and proceed back by Holyrood Road, now mainly occupied by the large Holyrood Brewery and modern housing development, to the Cowgate. This dark and gloomy chasm was the back lane of the old walled town used chiefly, as its name implies, for the driving of cattle to and from the common grazing land on the Burgh Muir.

Holyrood Road becomes Cowgate at the junction of St Mary's Street, an old High Street close widened during the 19th century as a sanitary improvement. On the north side of the

Cowgate is St Patrick's Church (1774) originally the Cowgate
Episcopal Chapel, of rectangular plan, with a Renaissance
façade added in 1928. The interior has painted murals and
semi-dome by Runciman. A few yards along is Blackfriars
Street where, at no. 8, is the remains of the much altered late
16th-century house of the Earls of Morton, 5-storey, rubble-
built, with a stair tower projecting into the street, and doorway with an ogee head. By no. 31 is an early 18th-century L-
plan house with a large octagonal stair tower and moulded
doorway, once the Skinners' Hall, used for a time as a theatre,
and latterly the home of one of Dr Guthrie's first Ragged
Schools in 1847. At the south-east corner of Blackfriars Street a
stone tablet marks the site of a house built in 1512 by James
Beaton, Archbishop of Glasgow, and afterwards the palace of
Cardinal Beaton, who crowned Mary Queen of Scots at Stirling
in 1543.

On the south side of the Cowgate here was the Blackfriars
Monastery, a Dominican friary founded in 1230, and beside it
was the residence of Gavin Douglas, Bishop of Dunkeld, who
translated Virgil into Scots in 1513. All trace of these buildings
has long been swept away.

At the corner of Niddry Street is St Cecilia's Hall, a fine
18th-century small concert hall carefully restored by the University in 1966 and now housing the unique Russell Collection
of early keyboard instruments. It is the work of Robert Mylne,
1763, with a classical exterior and notable oval concert hall
inside. The hall served for a period as the venue for the town
dancing assemblies in the 1760s, but fell into disuse in the early
19th century.

The Cowgate passes under the one exposed arch of the 19
that form South Bridge, and enters a deep valley between the
Heriot-Watt University on the south and the National Library
on the north.

On the south side is Guthrie Street, leading to Chambers
Street. In the long-demolished house, marked now by a stone
tablet at the top of the street, Sir Walter Scott was born on 15
August 1771. At the foot of Guthrie Street is the disused Argyle
Brewery, containing the ancient Tailors' Hall, built 1621 for the
Incorporation of Tailors but now sadly neglected, having been

used for years as a granary. The 4-storey L-plan hall has a projecting stair tower and moulded doorway. It was in this building, in 1638, that 300 ministers of the Church of Scotland drew up the National Covenant.

Cowgate then passes under the exposed arch of George IV Bridge. Immediately beyond, on the south side, is the tiny MAGDALENE CHAPEL, founded *c.*1547, and containing the only examples of pre-Reformation stained glass surviving in Scotland. The windows show the royal arms of Scotland, the emblems of the Queen Regent, Mary of Guise, and of the founder, Michael Macquan and his widow Janet Rhynd.

The chapel was taken over in 1614 by the Incorporation of Hammermen of the Canongate, who added the little spire in 1622 with their coat of arms above the rich Renaissance doorway. The spire contains a bell of 1632. Nearby, nos. 30–36 Cowgate is a late 17th-century rubble-built block of 5 storeys with 2 wallhead gables to the street, scroll skews and a stair tower at the rear. At the corner of Cowgate and Grassmarket, the Greyfriars Hotel is a 1930 copy by E.J. MacRae of early 18th-century Scottish vernacular style.

Cowgate opens into the Grassmarket, which had a regular weekly market continuously from 1477 to 1911, when it was moved to Saughton in the west of the city. There are some fine early 18th-century survivals at the corner of the West Bow, which formerly led to the Castle but which in the 19th century was remodelled as Victoria Street to join the new George IV Bridge. No. 91–3 West Bow (Crocket's Land) is a 4-storey stuccoed building *c.* 1705, with curvilinear gable and *oeil-de-boeuf* garret window; the interior is well preserved, with extensive original panelling. No. 89, adjoining, is late 17th century, also with fine interior, and a crowstepped wallhead gable with an entrance for pigeons. Nos. 95–9 and 101–7 are *c.* 1729, with later restoration, showing a picturesque assortment of gables to the street. Nos. 94–6 and 98–102 are extensively restored early 18th-century tenements also with a fine array of gables, and a pigeon entrance at garret level. Nos. 98–102 is a modern replica.

Nos. 110–18 are later 18th century, ashlar built, with arched ground floor. The upper part of Victoria Street altered the line of the old West Bow. It was planned by Thomas Hamilton in 1827, and carried out (1840–46) by George Smith, as an unusual 2-tier street, with shops at pavement level, and the reconstructed backs of the Lawnmarket closes above. India Buildings (nos. 1–6) at the top, is in a Scots Jacobean style by David Cousin, 1864. Victoria Terrace, the upper level, contains the back of Baden-Powell House. Nos. 5–6 Victoria Terrace was built as the Mechanics' Library (George Smith, 1840) in Scots Jacobean, with crowstepped dormer heads.

Back in the Grassmarket, the Bowfoot well stands at the West Bow junction, with the original well of 1671 encased in a stone top of 1861. In the centre of the street nearby a small enclosed garden marks the site on which the city's public gallows stood until 1784. Inside the garden the old paving stones in the pattern of a St Andrew's Cross are preserved as a memorial to the Covenanter martyrs, more than 100 of whom were hanged here in the years preceding 1688. The inscription reads: 'For the Protestant faith on this spot many martyrs and Covenanters died.' Which is a little ironic, as it was Protestants who were doing the hanging.

This too was the scene of the famous Porteous riot on 7 September 1736 when John Porteous, captain of the town guard, was hanged from a dyer's pole by an angry mob of citizens.

On the north side of the Grassmarket is the White Hart Inn, an early 18th-century inn with wallhead gables to the front and 2 semi-octagonal stair towers at the rear. Both Robert Burns and William Wordsworth lodged here at various times on visits to the city. Nos. 66–8 is *c.* 1800, and 70–72 is late 18th century. Nos. 74–84 is dated 1634, with the initials IL and GK (James Lightbody and Geillis Kniblo, the builders), but was extensively rebuilt in 1930.

From the east end of the Grassmarket, Candlemaker Row leads to George IV Bridge; at the west end King's Stables Road leads to Lothian Road, along the site of the Barras, the 16th-century jousting ground. The road leads under the King's Bridge, a semi-elliptical tunnel arch of unusual profile built by Thomas Hamilton, 1832, to carry the new western approach road. Also at the west end, West Port leads to the junction of

Lady Lawson Street, where stood the long-demolished Tanner's Close, home of Edinburgh's most notorious murderers, Burke and Hare, who killed between 16 and 30 persons during 1827, and sold the bodies to Dr Knox at the Surgeon's Hall for medical study.

On the north side of the Grassmarket is Castle Wynd, leading back to the Castle Esplanade; on this steep path clear traces of the Flodden Wall of 1513 can still be seen.

# CHAPTER 5

# The New Town

♣♣♣

GPO – Register House – Princes Street – The Mound –
Charlotte Square – George Street – St Andrew Square –
Queen Street – Moray Place – Heriot Row – Drummond
Place – Great King Street – Stockbridge – Silvermills –
Canonmills – Stevenson's Birthplace – Royal Botanic Garden
– Broughton Street – Melville Street – St Mary's Cathedral

The New Town of Edinburgh is one of the finest and best-preserved examples of neo-classical town planning in Europe. Since 1970 the area has been the subject of an intensive programme of conservation to preserve the fabric of its rich store of domestic architecture. The New Town area, as defined by the conservation programme, covers 310 hectares, from Princes Street in the south, to Stockbridge and East Claremont Street in the north, from Haymarket in the west to London Road in the east.

The first New Town, from Princes Street to Queen Street has undergone considerable change, and many of its original houses have been replaced by Victorian commercial architecture, some of it excellent. The later New Town extensions remain three-quarters residential, containing 14,000 of Edinburgh's population of 470,000. It is best seen on foot, starting from Princes Street and heading north. This chapter begins from the General Post Office and covers the whole New Town area with the exception of its eastern extremity, which is covered in the following chapter on the Calton Hill.

The GENERAL POST OFFICE, on the corner of North Bridge, is by Robert Matheson, architect of the Board of Works for Scotland, in a moderately rich Italian style with a 140-foot frontage to Princes Street and a 180-foot façade to North Bridge. The foundation stone was laid by Prince Albert on 23 October 1861, one of his last public acts before his death 2 months later. The building, finished in 1866 at a cost of £120,000 stands on the site of the old Theatre Royal, where Mrs Siddons performed. Edinburgh is the home of the British Post Office Philatelic Bureau (housed in a Government office in Lothian Road) and the GPO has a philatelic counter and gallery, with regular stamp exhibitions. The present building replaced an earlier post office which still stands in Waterloo Place, a few yards to the east.

On the opposite corner of North Bridge is the North British Hotel (Sir William Hamilton Beattie, 1902) which clearly belongs to the Victorian railway age, but with its huge bulk enlivened by Scottish Baronial detail. The clock tower is just short of 200-feet high.

On the north side of the street is REGISTER HOUSE, the Public Record Office for Scotland. Designed by Robert Adam and his brother James, the clean lines and perfect proportions of its 200-foot Palladian façade put it in the first rank of British public buildings. In the centre is a tetrastyle Corinthian portico surmounted by the royal arms of Great Britain; at each of the four corners is a square turret crowned with a cupola and vane. Register House was the first major work to be started in the New Town, in 1774, with a £12,000 grant taken from the profits of forfeited Jacobite estates. By the time it was opened, still uncompleted, in 1789, it had cost £80,000, and it was not finally finished until 1827, when Robert Reid added the little-seen north wing. It was one of the first buildings anywhere to be designed for the specific purpose of storing archives, with more than 100 vaulted rooms, each separated by thick stone walls to inhibit fire, and even in its early days it had a primitive form of ducted central heating to keep the documents free from damp. Beneath its central dome is a fine circular room, 50 feet in diameter. Register House contains many of the major documents of Scottish history, including the charter of King David I to Melrose Abbey (1140), the Declaration of Arbroath (1320), and the Scottish copy of the Treaty of Union (1707). It also contains the court of the Lord Lyon King of Arms, the final authority and arbiter on all matters of heraldry and genealogy in Scotland.

Directly behind is New Register House (Robert Matheson, 1860) in a Palladian style with Greek details and a galleried dome, the headquarters of the Registrar-General for Scotland.

Dominating the adjoining pavement is an equestrian statue of the Duke of Wellington (Sir John Steell, 1852), containing 12 tons of bronze. Wellington was so pleased with 'the Iron Duke in Bronze by Steell' that he had a copy of the bust made for his own home at Apsley House, London.

In West Register Street is the Café Royal; built in 1862 as a plumber's showroom, it is today a celebrated bar and restaurant exhibiting a fine array of Victorian plasterwork, stained glass, and ceramic murals.

The store of F.W. Woolworth occupies the site of two notable houses. The first house to be built in Princes Street stood here; John Neale, a silk mercer who occupied it in 1769, was induced to move from the Old Town only when the town council agreed to waive his rates. Next door, no. 10 was the office and shop of Archibald Constable, Scott's publisher. Constable rose to fame by paying up to £3,000 for a single poem, but in 1826 he went spectacularly bankrupt, dragging Scott down with him. In the adjoining block, now John Menzies' bookshop, was the office of *Blackwood's Magazine*, founded in 1817, rising to become the most influential literary publication of the early 19th century with such eminent contributors as 'Christopher North' (Professor John Wilson), and still published.

On the corner of South St Andrew Street is the shop of R.W. Forsyth, a large and sumptuous Edwardian Renaissance store (Sir John James Burnet, 1907), the first steel-framed building in Scotland. Immediately behind, the YMCA (Sir G.W. Browne, 1915) completes an attractive grouping.

By the North British Hotel are the Waverley Steps leading to the station beneath. The top of the steps is one of the windiest corners in Britain, especially when the wind is from the southwest. The main access to the station is by Waverley Bridge (1873), which reaches 879 feet across the valley of the old loch from Princes Street to the lower cliffs of the Old Town. On the bridge is a city information office, and the starting point for city coach tours.

WAVERLEY STATION is the second largest in Britain, and

among the largest in the world, covering 25 acres. Designed by James Bell, chief engineer of the North British Railway, it was built between 1892 and 1902 to replace an earlier station on the same site which had become congested. When opened, its 13-acre glass roof was among the largest in the world, and its eastern signal box was one of the largest manual boxes ever constructed, with 260 signal levers in one continuous frame. The station interior retains fine Victorian ironwork, and its main booking hall has an unusual ornate roof. A railway line, now long forgotten, ran due north from the site of the present station, by way of a 1,052-yard tunnel under Princes Street, St Andrew Square and Dublin Street to Granton Harbour. The tunnel fell at a fierce 1 in 30 incline from the station, and trains went down by gravity and were hauled back up at the end of a rope. The tunnel was opened in 1847, but closed 30 years later when an alternative line was built. The line served the world's first train ferry, opened from Granton to Burnt-island in 1850.

To the west of Waverley Bridge in East Princes Street Gardens is a bronze of David Livingstone, the Lanarkshire-born missionary and explorer, by Mrs D.O. Hill. Opposite is Jenners department store, one of the last of its period surviving in the street (Sir William Hamilton Beattie, 1895), built to replace an earlier store destroyed by fire. Its stonework is a riot of late Victorian exuberance, full of detail culled from the Bodleian Library building in Oxford. The interior is an interesting period piece, with balustraded galleries and a cast-iron saloon.

Facing Jenners is the SCOTT MONUMENT, commemorating Edinburgh's greatest publicist and the largest memorial in the city. The work of George Meikle Kemp, a young self-taught architect, it is in the form of an open Gothic cross surmounted by an ornately detailed spire rising to 200 feet, completed in 1844 at a cost of £16,000. The statue in grey Carrara marble by Sir John Steell depicts the seated Scott wrapped in a shepherd's plaid with his staghound Maida at his feet. The exterior is decorated with 64 statuettes of characters from Scott novels and figures from Scottish history; the 4 most prominent, above the main arches, are of Prince Charles Edward, the Lady of the Lake, Meg Merrilees and the Last Minstrel. A staircase of 287 steps inside the spire gives access to a balcony near the top.

Next in the gardens is the statue by John Hutchinson, of Adam Black (1784–1874) founder of the publishing house of A. & C. Black, twice Lord Provost and once the city's MP. Adjoining is the statue of Professor John Wilson (1785–1854), by Steell.

The foot of the Mound is an appropriate place from which to appreciate the excellent use which James Craig made of his site when he laid out the first New Town. To the south, high on its windy crag above the valley of the drained Nor' Loch, is the skyline of the Old Town. It begins with the Castle, and gradually descends to the east by Allan Ramsay's Goosepie House, the 240-foot spire of Tolbooth St John's Church, the towering tenements of James Court and Lady Stair's Close, the Bank of Scotland, the 12-storey, 100-foot rear wall of the City Chambers, and the crown steeple of St Giles'. To the east, Princes Street stretches past the Gothic Scott Monument and the Railway Age solidity of the North British Hotel to the bizarre assembly of neo-Athenian monuments on Calton Hill. To the west, at the other end of the street, are the adjoining spires of St John's and St Cuthbert's churches, with the triple spires of St Mary's Episcopal Cathedral rising to the north-west. To the north Hanover Street rises gently for a little over 100 yards to the ridge of George Street, where the whole city falls away to give a sudden and unexpected panorama of the Firth of Forth and the hills of Fife beyond.

THE MOUND is an artificial embankment, built of rubbish dug from the foundations of the New Town. At the height of construction, 1,800 cartloads of earth and rubble were being dumped here every day; in 1781 George Boyd, a Lawnmarket tailor, was reputedly the first citizen to use the dump as a short cut between the New Town and the Old, and it became known as 'Geordie Boyd's Mud Brig'. Dumping continued until 1830, when the Mound assumed its present shape and a proper road was laid on it.

The two neo-classical galleries at the foot of the Mound are by W.H. Playfair, although more than 30 years separated their construction. At the front is the ROYAL SCOTTISH ACADEMY (1826, subsequently altered and enlarged), in purest Doric, with

fluted columns rising from a uniform base of steps, and surmounted by a pure Greek entablature. The roof is decorated
with 8 sphinxes, and above the triple octostyle portico at the
front is a massive statue of Queen Victoria by Steell.

Behind is Playfair's NATIONAL GALLERY OF SCOTLAND, in
simpler Ionic style (1859), housing the national collection of
painting and sculpture from the 15th century. Lippi, Tiepolo,
Rembrandt, Velazquez, El Greco, Van Dyck, Vermeer, Goya,
Watteau, Pissarro, Degas, Gauguin and Monet are all represented in the permanent collection. In addition the Gallery has on
loan from Bridgewater House 4 Titians, 4 Rembrandts, 2 Tin-
torettos, a group of Raphaels and several others. There is an
excellent Scottish collection, and an English representation including Constable, Gainsborough, Reynolds and Turner. It is
one of the finest of the smaller art galleries of Europe.

Above the galleries, on the east side of the Mound, is a memorial to the Black Watch (Birnie Rhind, 1908), commemorating
the regiment's part in the Boer War and consisting of a bronze
kilted figure on a red granite plinth with a bronze relief. At the
top of the Mound, its rear wall dominating the view from
below, is the Bank of Scotland, founded in 1695 to help finance
the ill-fated Darien Expedition, and now the senior of the 3 surviving Scottish banks. The original building is by Richard
Crichton and Robert Reid (1802–6), considerably extended and
remodelled by David Bryce (1870) as a picturesque Italian-
style composition with central dome and flanking turrets with
octagonal domes. The building rests on a massive sub-structure
with a huge retaining wall to Market Street.

Opposite the bank, no. 17–20 Bank Street is a 1961 restoration of a 17th-century tenement, and 15 North Bank Street,
containing the offices of the Free Church, is an 1857 reconstruction of the rear of James Court, in Scots Jacobean style
with some original interiors. On the west side of the Mound,
Mound Place contains 18th-century survivals at no. 1 and at
Lister House, but its chief building is New College, erected by
W.H. Playfair (1846–50), as the headquarters of the then-new
Free Church, but now the University's Faculty of Divinity and
the meeting place, in the adjoining Assembly Hall, of the General Assembly of the Church of Scotland. The College is aligned

with the spire of Tolbooth St John's Church behind, giving the impression from a distance that one belongs to the other.

The college, with its twin pinnacled towers at the front, is 2-storey quadrangular; the Assembly Hall was added by David Bryce (1859), and reconstructed, 1901.

At the western corner of the Mound and Princes Street is the world's oldest floral clock, 1903, a major attraction every summer, when it is laid out with 20,000 or more plants, often depicting a topical motif. When filled, the electrically-driven hands together weigh 130 lbs.

Overlooking the clock is Steell's marble statue of the poet Allan Ramsay, depicting him wearing a silk nightcap. The pedestal bears medallion portraits of his wife, his grandson General Ramsay, his two great-granddaughters, and Lord Murray, a descendant who had the statue erected in 1854.

In the gardens towards the railway and directly beneath the Mound, is the memorial to the Royal Scots, the Edinburgh-based oldest regiment of the line in the British Army (Sir Frank Mears, 1952). It lists the regiment's battle honours and bears a quotation from the Declaration of Arbroath of 1320. Directly opposite Frederick Street is an equestrian statue (Birnie Rhind, 1906) to another famous Scottish regiment, the Royal Scots Greys, commemorating officers and men who fell in the Boer War.

Behind the Ross Bandstand, built in 1935, is a footbridge across the railway which leads directly under the Castle Rock to the ruin of the Wellhouse Tower, one of the oldest relics in the city. It was built in 1362 by King David II to supply the Castle with fresh water, and in 1450 was incorporated into the city wall. On the rock above is a remnant of the crane house which hauled the water up to the Castle.

To the west of the bandstand, on the main garden walk below street level, is the Scottish-American War Memorial (Professor R. Tait Mackenzie, 1927). Entitled 'The Call', it was erected by American citizens of Scottish blood or sympathies in memory of Scottish soldiers who fell in the First World War, and shows a young kilted soldier, seated and gazing upwards, against a frieze depicting Scottish volunteers from all walks of life.

At this point, near the junction of Frederick Street and

Castle Street, a number of original Princes Street houses, built
1780–1800, are visible above modern shop fronts, notably at
nos. 94–9. No. 95 (Tartan Gift Shop) is the only one in the
street to retain its original cellar.

No. 109 is the former Liberal Club, built as the Palace Hotel
(John Lessels, 1869) in French Renaissance style. No. 110 has a
notable cast iron saloon inside, one of only two surviving in the
city. No. 112, the former Conservative Club, is by Rowand Anderson, 1884, in Renaissance style with balconies and sculptured frieze. In Rose Street behind, no. 149 was built by the
National Telephone Company in 1901 as one of the earliest
exchanges.

Opposite Castle Street is the statue (F.W. Pomeroy, 1911) to
Thomas Guthrie (1803–73), founder of the city's Ragged
Schools, and a founding minister of the Free Church, who
raised £116,000 to provide the rebel ministers with manses. To
the west is William Brodie's memorial to Sir James Young Simpson (1811–70), the pioneer of anaesthesia. In the gardens
behind is a large ornamental fountain, made for the Paris Exhibition and erected here in 1869, the gift of Daniel Ross, a local
gunmaker. The last memorial in the street is a large granite
Celtic cross by Rowand Anderson to the memory of Dean
Ramsay (1793–1872), the author of *Reminiscences Of Scottish
Life And Character*, and minister of the adjacent St John's
Church. Across the street, more original façades are visible at
nos. 137–140, where new offices have been built behind the
frontages. The Royal Bank branch nearby is also a recent reconstruction behind a delicate classical façade by John Mac-
Lachlan, 1888.

The west end of Princes Street is occupied by St John's
Episcopal Church, in later Gothic style (William Burn, 1817).
The church is 113 feet long, and has a 120-foot square tower,
originally crowned by an open lantern which blew down in
1818. It has a splendid interior, with detail modelled on St
George's Chapel, Windsor. The 30-foot high stained-glass
window at the eastern end depicting the 12 apostles is by Egg-
inton of Birmingham, and was added in 1871. The reredos,
perhaps the church's finest feature, is by Peddie and Kinnear.
Among those buried here are Sir Henry Raeburn; Sir Walter

Scott's mother; James Donaldson, founder of Donaldson's Hospital; Catherine Sinclair, the novelist; and Macvey Napier, who produced the seventh edition of the *Encyclopaedia Britannica*.

At the West End we continue through the original New Town by turning north into Hope Street and CHARLOTTE SQUARE, one of the finest examples of its kind anywhere in the world. It is partly the work of Robert Adam, and is the crowning achievement of his many works of urban domestic architecture, deriving its inspiration from his tour of Italy in the 1750s, his study of the Palace of Diocletian at Spalata, and his desire to create a new and pure classicism. Any imperfections in the square result from its being completed by lesser architects when Adam died.

Each of the 4 sides is designed as a symmetrical entity, but the finest is undoubtedly the north side, the only section begun (1791) before Adam's death a year later. It contains 11 houses behind a façade like the front of some great palace. At the centre is a large pediment supported on 4 stout columns, decorated with festoons, balustrades and circular panels. From each side spring identical, plainer wings, furnished with simple square-headed windows, and each end is terminated by another decorated block surmounted by a sphinx set before a triangular roof to suggest a pyramid. The ground floor is of rusticated ashlar masonry to give the impression of a solid base, with smooth ashlar above; the front doors are surmounted by semi-circular fanlights, and the whole is finished off by fine wrought iron railings with lamps and torch snuffers.

Most of the houses in the square were long ago turned into offices, but a few distinguished residences remain. On the north side, no. 5 is the office of the National Trust for Scotland; no. 6 is the official residence of the Secretary of State for Scotland, and the upper floors of no. 7 are the official residence of the Moderator of the General Assembly of the Church of Scotland. The remainder of no. 7 was converted by the National Trust in 1973 into a domestic museum, furnished throughout in the style of the period when the house was built. The interior is plain by Adam standards, without his more ornate plasterwork, but the restoration gives a good impression of how the house would have looked at the end of the 18th century.

The rest of the square, if less perfect, is still elegant and imposing, and it remains probably the finest neo-classical square in Britain. On the west side is the great bulk of the former St George's Church, now an annexe of the Scottish public record office and renamed West Register House. The original intention was to have a church at both ends of the New Town, the one facing the other down the length of George Street, but only one was built. Adam submitted a design for a church here, but it was rejected on the grounds of cost, and the cheaper proposals of Robert Reid were preferred. Reid's church is square in plan and heavy in appearance, with an Ionic portico and Corinthian colonnade. The enormous green dome rises to 160 feet, and is a scaled-down copy of the dome of St Paul's Cathedral. Opened in 1814, the church cost £33,000. Nearby, no. 19 houses the Scottish Arts Council gallery. Sir William Fettes, founder of the city's famous public school, lived at no. 13 in 1810. Joseph Lister, pioneer of antiseptic surgery, lived at no. 9, 1870–77. Lord Cockburn was an early resident at no. 14. Viscount Haldane, who as Secretary for War between 1905 and 1912 remodelled the British Army, was born at no. 17; and Earl Haig, who led the remodelled armies to victory in the First World War, was born at no. 24. At the south-east corner, at no. 16 South Charlotte Street, Alexander Graham Bell, inventor of the telephone, was born in 1847.

In the centre of the square is Edinburgh's own Albert Memorial, a large equestrian statue of the Prince Consort resting on a huge block of Peterhead granite 17-feet high. Albert is depicted in the uniform of a field marshal. Queen Victoria herself unveiled the work, which cost the city £16,500, in 1876.

From the east side of the square runs GEORGE STREET, perfectly straight, 115-feet wide, and intended as the centrepiece of the first New Town; many original houses survive above modern shop fronts, some of them exhibiting curious circular slated dormers in the roofs. It is now a street of banks and insurance offices, and some of the remaining Georgian houses, occupied as offices, have been restored and cleaned. There is also much noteworthy Victorian commercial architecture.

No. 133 George Street was the home of Sir John Sinclair of Ulbster, the great agrarian reformer and compiler of the *First*

*Statistical Account Of Scotland*, the forerunner of the modern census, from 1815 until his death in 1835. He was well over 6-feet tall, as were all his 15 children by 2 wives, causing the pavement outside his home to be known as the Giant's Causeway. Nos. 127–9 (First Chicago National Bank) is a recent reconstruction of the original façade, as is nos. 82–4 (Northern Lighthouse Board).

At no. 121 are the offices of the Church of Scotland in an elegant and highly original Venetian style, built originally as the headquarters of the United Free Church (Mitchell and Wilson, 1911). At no. 108 Sir Walter Scott lived briefly as a young man in 1797. On the south side is Freemasons' Hall, opened in 1859 as the Grand Lodge of Scotland, and now used as one of the principal concert halls of the Edinburgh Festival.

At the junction of Castle Street is a statue (Sir John Steell, 1878) of Thomas Chalmers, the minister who led the Disruption of the Church of Scotland and became the first moderator of the Free Church. A few yards to the north, at no. 39 North Castle Street, is a bow-fronted house, reputedly by Adam, which was Sir Walter Scott's home, 1800–26, and where he wrote the greater part of the Waverley Novels. In Castle Street to the south, a plaque at no. 32 marks the birthplace (1859) of Kenneth Grahame, author of *The Golden Age* and *The Wind In The Willows*.

No. 75 George Street was another of Scott's homes; his mother, Anne Rutherford, lived here for many years and died in the house in 1819. No. 80 is by Sir J.J. Burnet (1903) for the Civil Service Stores, now vulgarized by the National Westminster Bank.

Halfway along on the south side, are the Assembly Rooms and Music Hall. The original building, with its handsome arcaded front, is by John Henderson, 1787, and was the focus of social life in the New Town, with its regular dancing assemblies. The 92-foot main ballroom with its great crystal chandeliers is still in regular use. The building was variously extended in 1818, 1834 and 1843, to the designs of William Burn, and incorporates a fine music hall 108-feet long.

It was here, at a dinner of the Edinburgh Theatrical Fund Association on 23 February 1827, that Scott first publicly admitted authorship of the Waverley Novels. Charles Dickens and W.M. Thackeray gave readings at the Assembly Rooms, and during the First World War it became a recruiting centre. During the Edinburgh Festival the building becomes the Festival Club.

At no. 60 Percy Bysshe Shelley lodged in 1811, when he ran away from home with his 16-year-old sweetheart Harriet Westbrook, and was married to her in Edinburgh. He returned in 1813 and lodged briefly at no. 36 Frederick Street.

At the junction of Frederick Street is a statue of William Pitt by Chantrey, 1833. To the north, Howe Street falls away to give a fine view of the Forth and the hills of Fife beyond. At the foot of the hill is Playfair's St Stephen's Church which blocks what would otherwise be a fine view of the Edinburgh Academy.

No. 45 George Street, which now houses a building society, was the office of *Blackwood's Magazine* from 1830 until recently, and has a fine interior.

On the south side, now a Bank of Scotland branch, is the former head office of the defunct Union Bank of Scotland (David Bryce, 1874). Its 100-foot frontage is in a Tuscan style with porticos of Ionic columns; the interior is equally grand, with a vast telling room 80 feet by 50 feet. Adjoining is the Royal Society of Edinburgh, a scientific institution of great eminence, founded in 1783; Scott was its president from 1820 to 1832, and its distinguished Fellows have included Benjamin Franklin, Goethe, and R.L. Stevenson. The building houses an outstanding library of scientific literature and periodicals.

At the junction of Hanover Street is a statue of King George IV by Chantrey, 1831, commemorating the state visit to Edinburgh in 1822. To the south, in Hanover Street, is the head office of the Edinburgh Savings Bank (Oldrieve, Bell and Paterson, 1940), and Merchants' Hall (David Bryce, Jnr, 1866), the premises of the Company of Merchants of the City of Edinburgh, and until 1879 the office of the City of Glasgow Bank, which collapsed.

The remaining section of George Street contains two notable bank buildings. The chief Edinburgh office of the Clydesdale Bank, on the north side, is by David Bryce (1847); much grander is the old head office of the Commercial Bank of Scotland (now an office of the Royal Bank), on the south side opposite the George Hotel. By David Rhind, 1847, it is in a mixture of Greek and Roman styles with a huge hexastyle portico. In the tympanum above is an interesting sculpture group by A. Handyside Ritchie, which formerly appeared on the banknotes. The Commercial Bank, founded in 1810, has since disappeared in a merger with the Royal Bank group.

No. 25 was the home from 1784 to 1829 of James Ferrier, Principal Clerk of Session, and his daughter, the novelist Susan Ferrier. Robert Burns, a friend of the family, was a frequent visitor to the house. At no. 18 Sir Henry Raeburn set up his first studio in 1787.

On the north side is St Andrew's Church, the scene in 1843 of one of the greatest religious upheavals in Scotland. At the General Assembly of the Church of Scotland here on 18 May in that year, 470 ministers, angry at the appointment of ministers by patronage, and dismayed at the Kirk's apparent loss of its evangelical spirit, walked out and formed their own Free Church of Scotland. The event has since been known as 'the Disruption'. The church itself, which has an unusual elliptical nave, is by Major Andrew Fraser, Royal Engineers, 1785. The slim spire, 168-feet high, was added four years later by William Sibbald.

George Street is concluded on the north side by the office of the Standard Life Assurance Company; in the tympanum is a sculpture by Steell depicting the parable of the 10 virgins.

St Andrew Square, at the eastern end of George Street, was a speculative development, and does not have the harmonious unity of Charlotte Square, but one house is by Adam, and on the north side particularly, many of the pleasing original dwellings remain. They were mostly constructed between 1772 and 1775. No. 23 and no. 26 (both 1772), by Sir William Chambers, are finely detailed. No. 21 was the birthplace (1779) of Henry Brougham, a future Lord Chancellor.

On the east side, no. 35, the house immediately to the left of the Royal Bank of Scotland, is the oldest in the square, built in 1768 by Robert Adam. It was formerly Douglas's Hotel, where the dying Scott stayed on his return from Italy in 1832, and where the Empress Eugénie, wife of Napoleon III, resided while consulting Sir James Simpson, the most eminent obstetrician of his day. Queen Victoria also patronized it.

The Royal Bank was built in 1774 by Sir William Chambers as a private house for Sir Lawrence Dundas, commissary-general of the Army in Flanders. The site was intended for St Andrew's Church to balance St George's Church in Charlotte Square, but Dundas got there first. No sooner had he occupied the house than he lost it in a card game to a military crony, General John Scott. He was allowed to keep his new home only after agreeing to build the general a new house in Dublin Street. The house, modelled on a Roman villa, was taken over by the bank in 1820, and in 1857 they added a fine telling room by Peddie and Kinnear.

In front of the bank is an equestrian statue by Thomas Campbell (1834) of the Earl of Hopetoun, colonel of the 92nd Gordon Highlanders in the Peninsular campaign, who took command at Corunna on the death of Sir John Moore; the plinth incorporates an epitaph by Sir Walter Scott. Immediately to the right of the Royal Bank, no. 36, by John Young (1781), is a copy of the Adam house at no. 35.

Next door is the former head office of the old British Linen Bank (David Bryce, 1851), incorporating a splendid telling room with stained glass cupola, columns of Peterhead granite and a Roman tile floor. This famous old bank, founded in 1746 as part of the British Linen Company, disappeared in a merger some years ago, but the name has recently been revived by the Bank of Scotland for its merchant banking division. On the façade, the statues atop the 6 fluted Corinthian columns portray navigation, commerce, manufacture, art, science and agriculture. Next to the British Linen Bank, the Royal Bank head office is a tall Renaissance block by Arthur Davis, 1942. No. 8 has a plaque noting the site of David Hume's house, 1771–6.

In the centre of the square is the 150-foot Melville Monument (William Burn, 1821), copied from Trajan's Column in Rome. The 14-foot statue is by Robert Forrest, and the foundations were constructed on the advice of R.L. Stevenson's engineer father. Henry Dundas, Viscount Melville, was administrator of Scotland under William Pitt, and achieved such power over the land that he was known as King Henry the Ninth of Scotland.

Just off St Andrew Square, in Thistle Court, is the first house to be built in the New Town, in 1767. Mr John Young had to be offered a consideration of £20 by the town council before he would agree to be the first resident. There are other early survivals, *c.* 1770, at nos. 7–9 Thistle Street, and westwards at nos. 1–15, 2–24 and 21–3 Hill Street, built 1788–94. Nos. 21–3, owned, 1809–50 by Lord Jeffrey, has the coat of arms of the royal house of Orleans, commemorating the residence here of the three grandsons of Louis Phillippe, 1859–60.

North St Andrew Street leads to Queen Street, and the NATIONAL MUSEUM OF ANTIQUITIES OF SCOTLAND. The building, in a 14th-century Gothic style, is by Rowand Anderson (1890), with sculptures by Birnie Rhind. It was erected with a donation of £30,000 from J.R. Findlay, proprietor of *The Scotsman* newspaper, who bequeathed the museum to the city and the nation. Its splendid collection includes the priceless Traprain Treasure, a huge hoard of Roman silver found at Traprain Law in East Lothian, and John Knox's pulpit from St Giles' Cathedral. In the same building is the Scottish National Portrait Gallery (founded 1882) with a chronologically arranged collection starting with the early Stuart kings, and a large library of photographs and engravings.

Nos. 2–3 Queen Street are recent restorations. No. 4 is the studio of the BBC; it formerly housed the Philosophical Institution, founded in 1848, which had Thomas Carlyle as a president.

No. 8 is one of the finest buildings in the street, a town house by Robert Adam, erected in 1770 for Chief Baron Orde of the Scottish Exchequer. Now occupied by the General Medical Council, it is in a good state of preservation, with outstanding plaster ceilings.

Next door, no. 9 is the hall of the Royal College of Physicians of Edinburgh, by Thomas Hamilton (1844); its façade displays large statues of Aesculapius, Hippocrates and Hygeia. In the rest of the street, many of the original houses remain, with notable restorations at nos. 30 and 31. No. 19 was the home of

Sydney Smith, clergyman and co-founder of the *Edinburgh Review*. No. 52 was the home of Sir James Young Simpson, appointed professor of midwifery at Edinburgh University in 1840, who became one of the best known and respected medical men of his day, and an outstanding pioneer of modern medicine. He was known and honoured throughout Europe for his work in obstetrics, but is best remembered for his discovery of anaesthesia in 1847, after experimenting with chloroform on his medical colleagues at his home. He died here in 1870; 1,700 medical men and public figures joined his funeral procession to Warriston Cemetery, and 100,000 spectators lined the route. His bust was placed in Westminster Abbey in 1879.

No. 53 was the home of Professor John Wilson. No. 62 was the home of Lord Jeffrey, and later of Sir John Leslie, a pioneer of physics, who invented the differential thermometer in 1800 and wrote his *Essay on the Nature and Propagation of Heat* in 1804. There are several fine fanlights at nos. 49–59, and 64.

At the west end of Queen Street is a memorial to the novelist Catherine Sinclair, who first guessed the identity of the anonymous author of the Waverley Novels. She also performed many good works in the city, introducing workers' canteens and paying for the first street fountain, at the west end of Princes Street.

To the north of Queen Street lies the first extension of the New Town, begun in 1802 and largely completed by 1823. This northern New Town is, like its 18th-century predecessor, based upon a regular parallelogram with open squares at each end. But its architecture is much grander, its gridiron street plan is less rigid, and it is entirely surrounded by subsequent development. Great King Street is its principal thoroughfare, with the open aspect of Royal Circus at its western end and Drummond Place at the east. As in the first New Town, single-sided terraces with open views were planned for the northern and southern edges.

Heriot Row and Abercromby Place form its southern edge, facing the wooded gardens of Queen Street. Its northern boundary was Fettes Row and Royal Crescent, but the open view to the north which they once enjoyed has been blocked by later building.

From the west end of Queen Street, St Colme Street leads to Ainslie Place which, with Randolph Crescent, Moray Place and adjoining streets, forms part of a separate and slightly later development of great elegance on the Earl of Moray's estate. It was designed by Gillespie Graham with the assistance of William Burn in 1822, and mostly completed by 1826. No. 17 Randolph Crescent, the last house at the north-western end, has a fine balustraded stair on the Randolph Cliff side.

Ainslie Place is a graceful and pleasing ellipse of symmetrical blocks with Roman Doric pilastered frontages, the ground floor masonry rusticated in typical New Town fashion to give the appearance of a solid base. William Blackwood, founder of *Blackwood's Magazine*, lived at no. 3 (1830–34); Dugald Stewart, professor of moral philosophy, died at no. 5 in 1828; Sir Charles Bell, who discovered the sensory and motor nerves of the brain in 1807, lived at no. 6 (1836–42); George Cranstoun, Lord Corehouse, the eminent 19th-century judge, lived at no. 12; and Dean Edward Ramsay, whose memorial stands in Princes Street, lived at no. 23.

Great Stuart Street leads into MORAY PLACE, one of the largest circuses in the entire city and certainly the most imposing, although many have found its grandeur pompous and forbidding. It is strictly a duodecagon; each of its 12 sides has a symmetrical façade in Roman Doric, with 6- or 8-column centre blocks and pilastered end blocks. Some regard Moray Place as being built back-to-front; the front windows look inwards to a circus which can tend towards the gloomy, while the rear windows afford a splendid view, high on a sheer cliff top above the Water of Leith, across the northern city, the Forth estuary, and the hills of Fife beyond.

Moray Place has traditionally been the home of legal men; Lord Jeffrey lived at no. 24 and died there in 1850. No. 36 was presented by Scottish Lord Provosts to Queen Elizabeth II in 1954 as a 'grace and favour' residence. In the adjoining Forres Street, no. 2 was the home of the surgeon James Syme, 1835–37, and Dr Thomas Chalmers lived at no. 3, 1831–5.

From Moray Place, Darnaway Street (also by Graham) with a slight curve to its frontages, leads to Heriot Row, the first street to be built in the New Town extension, with no. 13

generally regarded as the first house. The street is the work of Robert Reid, and is generally in an excellent state of preservation, although some houses have suffered alterations or additions to their upper floors. In no. 6 the novelist Henry Mackenzie (1745–1831), author of *The Man of Feeling*, lived and died.

But the street's best-known resident was Robert Louis Stevenson, whose parents took him to live at no. 17 in 1857, at the age of 6. Here he remained until 1880, when the city's inhospitable weather forced him to the south of France, to America, and eventually to Samoa, where he died in 1894. When young, he spent much time in bed with chest trouble, and his inspiration for *Treasure Island* is said to have come from his gazing from the bedroom window at an ornamental pool in Queen Street Gardens opposite. Another fond memory of his native city was the lamplighter on his evening rounds, and a verse from his *Leerie Lamplighter* is inscribed on the railings by the front door.

No. 44 Heriot Row was the home of the Rev. Archibald Alison, who published a celebrated *Essay on Taste* in 1790, and whose sermons were so popular throughout Scotland that they were published as a collection in 1817.

Abercromby Place, the continuation of Heriot Row, was the first street in Edinburgh to be built on a curve. It is by Robert Reid and William Sibbald, built between 1806 and 1819. No. 17 was the home of one of the principal architects of classical Edinburgh, W.H. Playfair.

Parallel to Heriot Row and immediately to the north is Northumberland Street, built between 1804 and 1819, and it still exhibits fine wrought-iron balconies at first-floor level. No. 25 was the home (1821–5) of John Gibson Lockhart, biographer and friend of Sir Walter Scott, whose eldest daughter Lockhart married. Admiral Sir William George Fairfax, who distinguished himself as captain of the *Venerable* at the Battle of Camperdown in 1797, lived at no. 53. The Earl of Hopetoun, who took command after the death of Sir John Moore at Corunna, lived at no. 57.

From the east end of Abercromby Place, Dublin Street leads north into DRUMMOND PLACE. Less pompous than Moray Place,

more austere than the Adam finery of Charlotte Square, it is by
Robert Reid, with later revisions by Thomas Bonnar, built between 1806 and 1823 as a series of symmetrical blocks. Named
after George Drummond, the visionary Lord Provost who set in
motion the building of the first New Town, it forms one of the
two balancing squares of the second New Town. No. 28 was
the home, until his death in 1851, of Charles Sharpe, a noted
wit, antique collector and friend of Scott, whose visiting card
bore only the musical notation for C sharp. No. 38 was the
home of Adam Black, publisher, who produced some of the
early editions of the *Encyclopaedia Britannica*. No. 31 was the
home of the novelist Sir Compton Mackenzie, where he held
lively court until into his nineties in a house filled with 12,000
books. At the south-west corner is Nelson Street, a row of handsome flats, with fine fanlights and wrought-iron balconies. Sir
Alexander Mackenzie, the composer and for 36 years director
of the Royal College of Music in London, was born at no. 21 in
1847.

From Drummond Place westwards runs Great King Street,
the centrepiece of the second New Town, built by Robert
Reid 1817–23, mainly as a series of symmetrical blocks. That
between Drummond Place and Dundas Street features a tetrastyle Ionic portico, with a wallhead chimney above, and that
between Dundas Street and Howe Street has a giant order of
Ionic pilasters on the Howe Street corner. The playwright J.M.
Barrie had lodgings (1879–82) at no. 3 with a Mrs Edwards
who was reputedly the inspiration for *The Old Lady Shows
Her Medals*. Sir William Hamilton, philosopher and professor
of logic at Edinburgh University for 20 years, lived at no. 16
until his death in 1856. The Rev. Edward Irving (1792–1834)
lived for a time at no. 60; Irving was the founder of the Catholic Apostolic Church in 1835, after his excommunication from
the Presbyterian Church for his heretical views regarding the
humanity of Christ. The architect W.H. Playfair lived at no.
63, and no. 72 was the home until his death in 1850 of Sir
William Allan, RA, the historical painter who became president
of the Royal Scottish Academy in 1838.

From the end of Great King Street, St Vincent Street leads
down to St Stephen's Church (W.H. Playfair, 1827), built in

classical style on a giant scale; it is square in plan but its interior is octagonal, set diagonally behind the pinnacled 165-foot tower with its tunnel porch. The interior was extensively rebuilt in 1956.

Facing the end of Great King Street is Royal Circus, which, with its two tangential terraces, was built by Playfair (1821–3) as the western end of the New Town extension. No. 24 was the home of Sir Henry Littlejohn, the city's first medical officer of health.

Joining this street to Heriot Row is India Street, built 1819–24 by William Wallace, who himself lived at no. 22. The blocks on either side of the entrance to Gloucester Place form a near-symmetrical composition, and in the rest of the street there are attractive iron balconies and fanlights. No. 14 was the birthplace, in 1831, of James Clerk Maxwell, regarded as the father of modern physics. After professorships at Aberdeen and London, he became the first professor of experimental physics at Cambridge in 1871, where he did important pioneering work on gases, optics and colour. His theoretical work on electricity and magnetism, published in 1873, paved the way for the development of the telephone and radio. He died at the height of his powers in 1879.

On the west side of India Street is Gloucester Place (Thomas Bonnar, 1822), where at no. 6 Professor John Wilson lived from 1826 until his death in 1854. Here the visitor on foot may choose to return to the city centre by Gloucester Lane or Doune Terrace, or continue through Stockbridge and round the northern and eastern perimeters of the New Town.

Doune Terrace is an attractive single-sided street built on a slight curve (Gillespie Graham, 1822), its frontage decorated in places by Roman Doric pilasters and pediments. No. 1 was the home of Robert Chambers, the historical writer and one of the founders of the publishing house of W. & R. Chambers.

To continue around the New Town, we turn right at the end of Gloucester Place down the hill of Gloucester Street. A few yards down is Duncan's Land, a recent restoration of a late 18th-century rubble-built, 2-storey house, with later mansard attic, and a stair tower at the rear. The front wall contains a door lintel inscribed 'Fear God Only. 1605', rescued from an

1 The view over the city from Calton Hill

2 The Castle seen from the Grassmarket

3 John Knox's House in the High Street

4a (*Left*) The sign of the museum of the city's history, in the Canongate

4c (*Below*) This sign can be seen in the High Street

4b (*Above*) A memorial to a lucky escape from the collapse of a High Street tenement

5a (*Above*) Moray Place in the New Town

5b (*Below*) South Queensferry Harbour with the Forth Railway Bridge

6 The North Gate of the Palace of Holyroodhouse

7 The Nelson Monument and the National Monument on Calton Hill

8 A mews in the West End

earlier building in the Old Town. The house was the birthplace of David Roberts, RA (1796–1864), the landscape painter, and is one of the few remnants of the 18th-century village of Stockbridge that bordered the Water of Leith here.

By the bridge at Stockbridge, Saunders Street gives access to a pleasant riverside walk by the Water of Leith, leading to the historic Dean Village (see Chapter 8) and enabling the walker to return to the city centre by Queensferry Road. The path leads past St Bernard's Well, a large Roman Doric open rotunda covering a mineral spring discovered about 1780 and regarded at the time as having powerful curative properties. The name comes from an unlikely legend that St Bernard, on a mission to the Scottish court, received such a cold reception that he had to take refuge in a cave nearby. There is no record of any of the various St Bernards setting foot in Britain, although there is thought to be a cave behind the masonry of Randolph Cliff. The circular temple is by Alexander Nasmyth, 1789; the statue of Hygeia, by D.W. Stevenson, was erected in 1888, when the rotunda was restored at the instigation of the publisher William Nelson.

Immediately across the bridge at STOCKBRIDGE, on the left, is a handsome residential development (James Milne, 1824) on the estate of Sir Henry Raeburn, the painter, who was born in a long-since demolished cottage nearby. Dean Terrace leads up the west bank of the Water of Leith to Ann Street, the original development on this site and one of the most delightful residential streets in the entire city. Built mainly between 1815 and 1825, to Raeburn's own design and named after his wife, it is one of the earliest examples in the country, and almost the only example in the Georgian New Town, of an urban street with front gardens. The overall effect is much less austere than the rest of the New Town, chiefly because of the gardens, which in many cases retain their original wrought-iron lamp brackets at the front gates. No. 29 was another home of Professor John Wilson, where in 1829 he had as a lodger the author Thomas de Quincey, who was then at the height of his opium-eating. Robert Chambers, the publisher, lived at no. 4.

From the west end of Ann Street, the hill leads down to St

Bernard's Crescent, the inspiration of Sir David Wilkie, a fellow artist of Raeburn's. It has a frontage of giant Greek Doric columns, balustraded parapets, and fine iron balconies, and gives the impression of being designed tongue-in-cheek to contrast with the simple charm of Ann Street. In Danube Street opposite, no. 7 was the home of the distinguished landscape painter Horatio McCulloch, RSA.

Back in the main street of Stockbridge, Raeburn Place leads west to Comely Bank, where there is a pleasing ashlar terrace of 1818; no. 5 was for a time the home of the artist John Ewbank, and at no. 21 Thomas Carlye began his married life. No. 11 was the home of James Browne, publisher of some early editions of the *Encyclopaedia Britannica*, and a devoted Liberal who entertained the first Irish Catholic MP Daniel O'Connell here many times. At the corner of East Fettes Avenue, St Luke's Church is an interesting neo-Norman work by P.M. Chalmers, 1908. Back at Stockbridge, the poet James Hogg ('the Ettrick Shepherd') lodged in Deanhaugh Street in 1813, and Sir James Simpson lodged at no. 2 Deanhaugh Street and at his brother's bakery at no. 1 Raeburn Place.

Hamilton Place leads north-east from the bridge, and immediately on the left in Deanbank Lane are further vestiges of the old village. Deanbank Cottage is a late 18th-century 3-storey dwelling of rubble construction, and the nearby Deanbank Lodge (now Kartro House) is of similar age, with a Victorian porch added. Further along Hamilton Place is Saxe-Coburg Place, an elegant little U-shaped development built *c.* 1828, chiefly by Adam Turnbull. Unfortunately the street was never completed, and the symmetry is spoiled by the intrusion of a swimming bath. St Bernard's Church nearby is by James Milne, 1823.

To the rear, in Glenogle Road, is a development of 10 parallel terraces known as The Colonies. Set in semi-rural surroundings, this is the best of several attempts by the old Edinburgh Co-operative Building Company to provide artisan housing at modest cost. The scheme incorporates Glenogle House, an 18th-century 2-storey dwelling converted and enlarged, and the surrounding terraces were erected in 1861. The gables facing Glenogle Road are decorated with a variety of craft and masonic symbols. At the west end, at the corner of Arboretum Avenue are the old gatepiers of Inverleith House.

Where Hamilton Place becomes Henderson Row is the district of SILVERMILLS. In 1607 considerable quantities of silver were found at Linlithgow, 15 miles west of Edinburgh, and mills were set up on the Water of Leith to refine the ore. From the early diggings, each hundredweight of ore yielded 24 ounces of silver; King James VI bought the mine and mills for £5,000, but the yield of silver mysteriously dropped, and the project was abandoned some years later. Traces of the mills remain on both sides of West Silvermills Lane.

East Silvermills Lane leads to Fettes Row and Royal Crescent, the original northern boundary of the New Town extension, containing some fine façades by Thomas Brown built between 1821 and 1828. No. 23 Fettes Row was the first major restoration project by the New Town Conservation Committee.

On the north side of Henderson Row is William Burn's 1-storey neo-Greek Edinburgh Academy. Built between 1823 and 1826, it has a central portico of 6 unfluted Greek Doric columns, an elliptical rooflight above the pediment, and a Greek inscription which extols the benefits of learning. The building, of extreme simplicity, is one of Burn's best. The Academy was founded in 1823 by Sir Walter Scott, Lord Cockburn, James Skene of Rubislaw, and other eminent old boys of the city's High School, who jointly hated their schooldays and who, considering the educational standards of their own *alma mater* to be pitifully poor, founded their own school to provide a sound classical education. Beside the Academy, at no. 54, is the original Donaldson's School for the Deaf, a plain classic house of 1823 by Gillespie Graham.

Beyond the Academy gates, Henderson Row exhibits some fine 3- and 4-storey frontages with porches of Ionic columns and balustrated parapets (William Burn, 1825).

From Henderson Row, Brandon Terrace turns north to the district of CANONMILLS. King David I, when he granted the building of Holyrood Abbey to the Augustine canons in 1128, also granted them land in this area, and built for them a large mill on the Water of Leith. North of Canonmills bridge, on the left off Inverleith Row in Tanfield Lane, is a remnant of

Tanfield Hall, now buried in the depths of a printing works. Built in 1825 as an oil works, the hall was the scene in 1835 of a great banquet in honour of Daniel O'Connell, MP, given by his Liberal supporters in Edinburgh. In 1843 the same building witnessed the formation of the Free Church of Scotland at the time of the Disruption.

Opposite Tanfield Lane is Warriston Crescent where, at no. 10, Frédéric Chopin lodged in 1848. A short distance to the north, on the east side of Inverleith Row, is Howard Place, where, at no. 8, Robert Louis Stevenson was born on 13 November 1850. When he was 3 the family moved across the road to no. 1 Inverleith Terrace, and in 1857 to no. 17 Heriot Row.

Howard Place is by Gillespie Graham, 1809–20. The rest of Inverleith Row contains a number of fine houses, mostly by Thomas Brown. No. 8, with Greek Doric columns flanking the doorway, is by Playfair, and retains its cast-iron gatepiers and lampholder, as does no. 7.

Further up Inverleith Row is the main entrance to the ROYAL BOTANIC GARDEN, one of the finest in Europe, world-renowned for its work on taxonomy, the classification of plants, and specializing in the flora of the Himalayas and south-west China. The Garden has been at its present site in the grounds of Inverleith House since 1830 but there has been a 'physic garden' in Edinburgh since 1670, on the site of what is now Waverley Station. It therefore claims to be the second oldest botanic garden in Britain, pre-dated only by that at Oxford, founded in 1621. Among its many attractive features are a rock garden covering 4 acres, heather, woodland and peat gardens, an azalea lawn, an arboretum, and a magnificent rhododendron walk. It also boasts two splendid iron and glass palm houses; the older and smaller was built in 1834, the larger by Robert Matheson in 1858. The latter, 70 feet 6 inches high, is the tallest greenhouse in Britain, exceeding by some inches the large palm house at Kew. In contrast, more than 1½ million plant specimens are displayed in the modern exhibition plant houses (G.A. Pearce, 1967). The garden also contains a memorial by Robert Adam (1778) to Sir Carl Linnaeus, the 18th-century Swedish botanist who evolved the present-day method of plant classification.

In the centre of the Garden is INVERLEITH HOUSE, (John Henderson, 1774), now containing the Scottish National Gallery of Modern Art. Among its finest possessions are two Henry Moore sculptures on the lawn outside. The Gallery will be moving in 1982 to John Watson's School in Bedford Road.

From Canonmills bridge, Warriston Road follows the Water of Leith northwards to Warriston Cemetery, burial place of dozens of eminent Edinburgh citizens, and including a remarkable variety of gravestones and ornate memorials; sadly, many of them are untended and overgrown. At no. 1 Broughton Road, east from Canonmills, is Heriot Hill House, a plain old dwelling of 1788.

From Canonmills we return to the city centre by Rodney Street, which leads into Bellevue and the eastern extremity of the northern New Town. Bellevue Crescent forms an elegant and near-symmetrical sweep with a church at its centre. The southern section is by Thomas Bonnar, 1819–32, incorporating giant Ionic pilasters in the façade. The northern section was built by David Cousin, more or less to Bonnar's original design, in 1882. St Mary's Church in the centre (Thomas Brown, 1826) has a Corinthian hexastyle portico and a steeple of superimposed orders with pointed dome and cupola. Bellevue Terrace, opposite, is by Thomas Bonnar, 1834–56, as is Mansfield Place, built in 1820. Nos. 1–85 East Claremont Street are by Thomas Bonnar, 1824–30; nos. 2–24 are by John Chesser, 1860–69.

At the roundabout, London Street runs west into Drummond Place, and is by Robert Reid, 1807–23, mirroring the grand style of Great King Street, which continues the line to the west. East of the roundabout is East London Street, containing Gayfield House, a notable suburban mansion by Charles and William Butter, dated 1763. Built for David, Earl of Leven, and at one time occupied by a veterinary college, it is of 2 storeys, with attic and basement, and a 5-window ashlar front, incorporating a 3-window pediment with urn finials, an Ionic-columned doorway, and interesting chimney gables.

On the corner of East London Street, facing the roundabout, is the former Catholic Apostolic Church, now a Baptist church, built 1873–94 by Rowand Anderson in a neo-Norman style, with an impressive set of murals by Mrs Phoebe Traquair. Broughton Place Church, with its tetrastyle Greek Doric portico, is by Archibald Elliot (1820), while the rest of Broughton Place was built *c.* 1809.

Most of Broughton Street is by Robert Burn, *c.* 1808, but nos. 65–79 are late 18th-century artisan dwellings. No. 22, now a warehouse, was the original Apostolic Church, in neo-Greek style by John Dick Peddie, 1843. At the corner of Albany Street is the Church of the Nazarene, with Venetian detail and Ionic pilasters, by David Skae, 1816, now the office of a building society. Albany Street has pleasant rows of 2-storey houses, built *c.* 1802 by George Winton and not part of the original New Town plan, with an array of fanlights and iron balconies. No. 2 was the home of John Playfair, professor of natural philosophy.

At the corner of Broughton Street and Picardy Place, a plaque on the eastern corner recalls the now-demolished birthplace of Sir Arthur Conan Doyle, creator of Sherlock Holmes, in 1859. Doyle, son of an Irish-born clerk, studied medicine at Edinburgh University, and he based Holmes on Dr Joseph Bell, professor of anatomy, and Sir Henry Littlejohn, the city's first medical officer of health. Both men had, like Holmes, a fondness for the close observation of facts and the intelligent interpretation of them.

At the top of Broughton Street is St Mary's Roman Catholic Cathedral, a modest structure as cathedrals go, by James Graham, 1813, and substantially altered several times since. Beside is the site of the Theatre Royal, where between 1853 and 1946 no less than 5 theatres and museums were burnt to the ground.

Picardy Place leads east to the top of Leith Walk and the Playhouse Theatre, opened in 1929 within 2 months of the advent of the talkies, and an outstanding example of cinema architecture. Its 3,017-seat auditorium, the largest in the city, is built on a steeply sloping site, and the main entrance on Greenside Place gives direct access to the upper circle. The interior is a mixture of rococo and classical, and its huge proscenium arch is 48-feet wide, giving a stage 74 feet by 37 feet. Built for use both as a cinema and a large variety theatre, it contains 50 dressing rooms on 8 floors, and retains the console of its Hilsdon theatre organ.

Returning to the top of Broughton Street, York Place leads westwards back to Queen Street and the city centre. On the Broughton Street corner is St Paul's and St George's Church, in a Tudor Gothic style reminiscent of King's College Chapel, Cambridge (Archibald Elliot, 1818), crowned with 4 octagon towers. The Rev. Archibald Alison was for a long time minister here, and there is a memorial to him by Steell. On the south side of York Place is the former St George's Chapel (Robert and James Adam, 1794), now ignominiously converted to a showroom for bathroom fittings. Although greatly altered, some fine rib vaulting remains. Adjoining the old chapel is its manse at no. 7, also by the Adam brothers.

The majority of York Place, an extension of the first New Town rather than a part of the second, was built 1790–1804. It displays some of the best New Town domestic architecture, and has survived largely untouched, with its arched and columned doorways and fanlights. No. 57 was the home of the architect Thomas Hamilton. No. 47 was the home of Alexander Nasmyth (1758–1840) father of the Scottish school of landscape painting, but who is best remembered for his portrait of Robert Burns, now in the National Gallery of Scotland. His son James, born here in 1808, built a foundry in Manchester where he invented the steam hammer. No. 32 York Place was built by Sir Henry Raeburn as his studio, which he occupied from 1798 to 1809.

One major area of the New Town remains: the western extension, from Queensferry Street to Haymarket. Development of the area, which covers the former estate of the Walker family, began in 1814, but the majority is Victorian, and building was still in progress in 1907. The main thoroughfare is Melville Street, leading from Queensferry Street, and is by Robert Brown, built mainly 1820–26. Nos. 1–41 form a symmetrical block, with a tetrastyle Ionic column centrepiece at no. 25; many of the front doors in this and the block opposite retain their arched iron lampholders. No. 61 is the present home of the Trades Maiden Hospital, one of the city's oldest girls' schools, which displays the Blue Blanket, the 15th-century banner of the Edinburgh tradesmen. The banner can be viewed by prior arrangement.

Alva Street, to the south-east, is by Gillespie Graham, 1823. To the north-west, Drumsheugh Gardens is a later development, mostly by John Lessels, 1874–8. The south-west side of the Gardens triangle, by John Watherston and Sons, 1878, is a fine 4-storey Italianate block, with balustraded balconies above the doorways and Greek Corinthian detail at the first floor.

Melville Street leads to Manor Place, whose southern half consists of symmetrical blocks by Robert Brown, while the remainder is a Victorian addition by Lessels. At its north-western end, Manor Place leads into Rothesay Place (Watherston and Sons, 1878), in Italian style, with some 3-arch windows and iron balconies, and Rothesay Terrace, also by Watherston, built in stages between 1876 and 1907.

St Mary's Episcopal Cathedral is the largest ecclesiastical building erected in Scotland since the Reformation, by Sir George Gilbert Scott in Early Pointed style. It owes its existence to the beneficence of the Walker sisters, who gave their land and their fortune for its building; the 2 smaller spires are named Barbara and Mary after them: It is a huge church, cruciform in plan, 262-feet long and 98-feet wide, with a central spire of 295 feet, built at a cost of well over £100,000. The main fabric was built 1874–9, and the two western spires were added 1914–17. The Lady Chapel in the south-east choir aisle is by George Henderson (1898), and the Chapel of Resurrection in the south transept is by Sir Robert Lorimer (1922). The cathedral has a fine peal of bells, which in still weather can be heard across the Forth in Fife.

Alongside is the Song School by Rowand Anderson (1887) containing frescoes by Mrs Phoebe Traquair (1890–92), and the Walpole Hall (Lorimer and Matthew, 1933), named after G.H.S. Walpole, Bishop of Edinburgh from 1910 to 1929, and father of Hugh Walpole, the novelist. Adjoining the Song School is the mansion of Easter Coates, dated 1615, the oldest building surviving intact in the New Town area. Scoto-French in style, it was built by Sir John Byers of Coates, who had his town house at Byers' Close in the High Street, as his country mansion. In 1813, when the house was restored, two ancient door lintels from demolished buildings in the Old Town, dated 1600 and 1601, were incorporated in the stonework, together with a window and some fragments of sculpture from an ancient mansion in the Cowgate, thought to have been the residence of the French ambassador at the time of Mary, Queen of Scots.

Beyond the Cathedral in Palmerston Place, mainly by John Chesser, 1877–80; at its south-eastern end is Palmerston Place Church, an unusual design by Peddie and Kinnear (1862) in an Italianate style with a 2-storey arcaded frontage with loggia surmounted by twin towers.

Chesser's designs for Palmerston Place are continued in the twin curves of Eglinton Crescent and Glencairn Crescent (1873–80) with much use of balustraded balconies and parapets. His designs for Grosvenor and Lansdowne Crescents and Grosvenor Street tend towards the Italian, with a touch of Roman Ionic in Grosvenor Crescent. In Rosebery Crescent is Coates Hall, the Scottish Episcopal Theological College, originally by David Bryce (1850) as a mansion for Sheriff Napier. At the southern edge, facing Shandwick Place, is Coates Crescent, an earlier block by Robert Brown built 1813–23, exhibiting some fanlights but with considerable alterations to the attics. Directly opposite is Atholl Crescent, by Thomas Bonnar, 1824, with Ionic pilasters and fluted Ionic columns at some doorways. In Coates Crescent gardens is the W.E. Gladstone Memorial, by Pittendrigh MacGillivray, 1917, moved here from its original site in St Andrew Square in 1955.

# CHAPTER 6

# The Calton Hill and Eastern New Town

♣♣♣

*Waterloo Place – Calton Burying Ground – Nelson
Monument – National Monument – City Observatory – Old
Royal High School – Royal Terrace – Hillside Crescent*

From the General Post Office, WATERLOO PLACE leads eastwards, and forms the beginning of the main eastern exit from
the city. At the Princes Street end a short section of the city's
once extensive cable tramway is preserved in the centre
of the street. Waterloo Place was begun in 1815; the
original need was for an access road to a new jail being planned
on the south slopes of Calton Hill, but it developed into a plan
for a grand eastern approach to Princes Street, with Archibald
Elliot as architect and Robert Stevenson as engineer. The street
is lined with buildings in a severe classical style, with matching
screen walls at the eastern end.

The first blocks on the north and south sides present identical
end elevations to Princes Street, with tetrastyle Ionic porticos
and arched ground-floor windows. Both the Waterloo Hotel
and, opposite, the old exchequer office present similar symmetrical façades to Waterloo Place, with arched ground
floors, Ionic pilastered centre sections, and balustrading along
the rooflines.

Adjoining is the Regent Bridge, spanning Calton Road below.
Built in 1816 to the design of Elliot and Stevenson, it has a
semicircular arch; the roadway is flanked by Corinthian columned arches with Ionic colonnades to either side linking the adjoining buildings, the whole being designed as a memorial to
the dead of the Napoleonic Wars. Beyond the bridge on the
north side is another symmetrical block which matches its

neighbour, and directly opposite the theme is continued in the old General Post Office, designed by Elliot and Joseph Kay, but slightly grander with Ionic columns in the centre; it has now been gutted and rebuilt behind its original façade.

Next on the north side is a long 1-storey block designed by Elliot to be the Calton Convening Rooms, and intended to match the screen wall of the CALTON BURYING GROUND across the street. The graveyard is entered through a gate in the wall on the south side of the street, and contains numerous important memorials.

By far the most prominent is the huge obelisk known as the Martyrs' Memorial (Thomas Hamilton, 1844) to the memory of 5 early Chartists who were tried and sentenced to transportation for life in 1793 for advocating parliamentary reform. Thomas Muir, Thomas Fyche Palmer, William Skirving, Maurice Margarot and Joseph Gerald were members of 'Friends of the People', an early universal suffrage movement. They were charged with treason for attempting to correspond with the French Republic, with which Britain had recently gone to war.

Nearby is the circular Roman-style tomb and memorial, by Robert Adam (1777) to the philosopher David Hume (1711–76). On the west side of the burying ground is a statue of Abraham Lincoln, the first statue of the American president to be erected in Britain, unveiled in 1893, in memory of Scotish–American soldiers who fought in the American Civil War.

Other notable graves are those of Daniel Stewart, founder of a famous city school; William Blackwood, founder of *Blackwood's Magazine*; Sir William Allan, president of the Royal Scottish Academy; Archibald Constable, Scott's publisher; and Dr Robert Candlish, one of the leaders of the Disruption which founded the Free Church in 1843. Immediately to the east of the graveyard is a crenellated structure which looks like a toy fort and is prominently visible from North Bridge. This is the governor's house, the only remaining part of the Calton Jail, built by Archibald Elliot in 1815; the rest was demolished to make way for the adjoining St Andrew's House in 1938.

On the north side of Waterloo Place the short street of Calton Hill winds round the back of Elliot's classical blocks, and contains simpler but still elegant dwellings built mainly

1770–80. No. 22, entered by stairs at first-floor level, has a fine wrought iron lampholder at the gate. At the east corner of Calton Hill and Regent Road is Rock House, dating from the same period, which was the home and studio, 1843–69, of David Octavius Hill, pioneer of portrait and landscape photography.

By Rock House a stairway leads to Calton Hill, a short climb rewarded with excellent views of the city and surrounding countryside, and a bizarre collection of monuments. At the foot of the stairs, set into the rock face, are medallions commemorating three famous 19th-century Scottish singers, Templeton, Wilson and Kennedy.

Calton Hill, a 355-foot lump of rock associated with the Arthur's Seat volcano, probably takes its name from the Gaelic *Choille Dun* (a hill covered with bushes). The path to the summit approaches first the NELSON MONUMENT, intended to represent an upturned telescope. The 106-foot tower, with its battlemented base, is by Robert Burn and Thomas Bonnar, 1816. Above the doorway is a sculpture representing the stern of Nelson's ship, the *San Joseph*, together with an inscription recording Edinburgh's gratitude to him. On top of the monument is a time ball which drops daily at 1 p.m.

Most prominent is the uncompleted NATIONAL MONUMENT which stands on the very summit. As a memorial to all the Scottish soldiers and sailors who fell in the Napoleonic wars, Edinburgh intended to erect an exact copy of the Parthenon, to be used as a grand memorial church, with catacombs beneath – a sort of Scottish Valhalla. The original design was by C.R. Cockerell, and the executant architect was W.H. Playfair. A large amount of money was subscribed, and on 27 August 1822 the 6-ton foundation stone was laid with great ceremony. But the money soon ran out, and only part of the western peristyle, which still stands, was ever completed. The massive Doric columns of fine Craigleith stone, built of blocks weighing from 10 to 15 tons, eventually cost £1,000 each to erect. The fragment, which in fact looks more like the Parthenon than the completed building would ever have done, has since been known as 'Scotland's Pride and Poverty' or 'Edinburgh's Disgrace'.

On the western edge of the summit is the memorial to Dugald Stewart, professor of moral philosophy at Edinburgh University, 1786–1828. The monument (W.H. Playfair, 1831) is a copy of the choragic monument of Lysicrates in Athens. Stewart, born within the University in 1753, where his father was professor of mathematics, rose to become one of the foremost philosophers of his day, the author of *Philosophy of the Human Mind* and named by his contemporaries 'The Bacon of metaphysics'.

The oldest building on the hill is the former CITY OBSERVATORY, a circular rubble-built tower with a short wing and gothic windows, incorporated in the walled section on the summit. It is the work of James Craig (1776), who drew up the original plan for the New Town. It has 19th-century additions in a matching castellated style. Like so many Edinburgh projects, the observatory had its financial troubles, and by the time it was completed in 1792, there was no money left for a telescope. In 1812 another attempt was made to establish an observatory; interested parties in the city formed themselves into an Astronomical Institution, and commissioned W.H. Playfair to build a proper observatory alongside. Playfair's design, erected in 1818, is a Greek cross plan modelled on the Temple of the Winds, with a 13-foot diameter dome in the middle. The old observatory became the astronomer's house. Set into the wall of the new observatory is W.H. Playfair's monument to his uncle, Professor John Playfair (1748–1819), an eminent mathematician and natural philosopher, who was for a time president of the Astronomical Institution.

Returning to the bottom of the Calton Hill steps, we continue along Regent Road, and come first on the southern side to St Andrew's House, housing the principal Government departments in Scotland, designed on a giant scale in inter-war modern style by Thomas Tait (1939). It is built on the site of the Calton Jail, whose remains form the southern retaining wall of the modern block, best seen from North Bridge. The huge bronze entrance doors carry reliefs of the Scottish saints Andrew, Ninian, Kentigern, Columba and Magnus, and the royal coat of arms with Scottish quartering is carved in stone above the entrance. The office of the Secretary of State for

Scotland, on the fifth floor, is panelled in Scottish walnut from a tree from Balmerino, Fife, said to have been planted by Mary Queen of Scots.

A few yards to the east is the old ROYAL HIGH SCHOOL, widely regarded as the finest of all Edinburgh's neo-classical buildings, and the one which more than any other earned for her the name of the Modern Athens. This splendid classical pile is the work of Thomas Hamilton, 1829, built at a cost of only £24,000, and is his finest achievement. It is in purest Greek Doric, on an elevated site which lifts it majestically above the adjacent roadway, and is best seen from the Canongate church-yard at the bottom of the hill. The centre portion, fronted by a hexastyle Doric portico, is a copy of the Theseum, the temple that overlooks the market place beneath the Acropolis in Athens. On either side, colonnaded wings lead out to 2 sym-metrical flanking single-windowed pavilions like miniature temples, their porticos facing inwards towards each other.

Effective use is made of the mass of underbuildings which were required to lift the school on its awkward, sloping site. Banks of retaining walls at the front are decorated with railings and gateways terminated by temple blocks. There is some fine interior work, particularly the impressive hall behind the cen-tral portico, with its oval debating chamber and semi-elliptical arched ceiling.

The High School of Edinburgh was founded in 1128, and is therefore one of the oldest existing educational institutions in the British Isles. In 1969 it moved to modern buildings on the western outskirts of the city. The Calton Hill building was fine as a Greek temple, but not so good as a school; it is almost devoid of windows on its southern frontage, and is so mass-ively built that any internal alterations to keep pace with changing needs were prohibitively expensive. Hamilton's magnificent temple may now house a Scottish Assembly.

Opposite the school is Hamilton's monument to Robert Burns, erected in 1832 in the style of the Greek peripteral temple of Lysicrates in Athens, and appropriately decorated with lyre reliefs.

On the southern slopes below Regent Road is the New Calton Burying Ground, opened in 1820, with an interesting terraced layout, retaining walls, and some fine late Georgian monuments and burial enclosures, including the tomb of Robert Louis Stevenson's parents. The graveyard is equipped with a circular, battlemented watch tower, and many of the graves are protected by iron mortsafes, two reminders of the days of the resurrectionists, when fresh corpses fetched good prices on the dissecting tables of the medical schools.

On the north side of Regent Road, just beyond the High School, Regent Terrace climbs to make a grand sweep round the eastern end of Calton Hill. This street, and its continuation into Carlton Terrace and Royal Terrace, was the first stage of an ambitious plan of the town council, executed by W.H. Playfair, to construct another New Town from the Calton Hill to Leith, planned in 1819, but of which only a fragment was built.

Regent Terrace, built about 1825, is an impressive continuous block decorated with a wrought iron balcony running the entire length. Carlton Terrace rounds the corner with some interesting curved frontages, but with some later additions at top floor level. ROYAL TERRACE, which continues the development along the north side of the hill, is grander than the rest, and forms the longest continuous frontage in the city, at very nearly a quarter of a mile. The façade consists of 17 sections, 7 of them colonnaded, with a large Corinthian columned section in the centre. The façade is symmetrical, although difficult to see in its entirety. Built 1821–60, it was initially unpopular because of its north-facing aspect. But it did for a time become the fashionable abode of rich merchants who could watch for their ships coming in at Leith, and because of the residence there of a number of the city's rich distillers, it became known as 'Whisky Row'.

Behind the terraces, visible from the top of Calton Hill, is a fine private garden laid out by Sir Joseph Paxton, designer of the Crystal Palace. Playfair's Royal Terrace is completed by Greenside Parish Church, a simple T-plan Gothic structure by Gillespie Graham, 1838.

At the junction of Royal Terrace and Leith Walk is a curious block of houses in Blenheim Place, another part of Playfair's scheme. The frontage gives the appearance of 1-storey villas, but they are built on a steep slope, and there are 4 more storeys below this street level with access from Marshall's Court many feet below. On the opposite corner of London Road, Leopold Place is another part of the same scheme, designed by Playfair in 1820, with circled corners. Adjoining it is HILLSIDE CRESCENT, with 3 radiating streets, a pale shadow of the original intention to have a layout reminiscent of the Piazza del Populo in Rome. Designed in 1823, it was not completed until 1884; only the frontages of nos. 1–7 are Playfair's, the rest being inferior and later copies by John Chesser, some now demolished. Nos. 1–7 forms a heavy but imposing block with a Doric colonnade, continuous iron balcony at the first floor, and other decorative ironwork. The scheme is continued along London Road in Brunton Place, of which only nos. 4–9 are by Playfair, the rest being inferior copies by Chesser. The grandiose second New Town scheme finally peters out in Brunswick Street, which Playfair managed to complete as far as no. 17, using boldly projecting porches, before the whole scheme was abandoned. The other 3 sides of the block fronted by Leopold Place are the only other remains of Playfair's grand design; Elm Row, in Leith Walk, is an approximately symmetrical block of 1821 on a sloping site. The houses in Windsor Street have a continuous iron balcony; and no. 23 was the house of the actress Sarah Siddons, 1827–30.

# CHAPTER 7

# The University and South Side

♣♣♣

*George IV Bridge – National Library – Greyfriars Bobby –*
*Chambers Street – Royal Scottish Museum – Greyfriars Kirk*
*– George Heriot's School – University Medical School –*
*George Square – Edinburgh and Dalkeith Railway –*
*Surgeons' Hall – Pleasance – University Old College –*
*North and South Bridge*

Although the officially-sponsored New Town grew on the land
to the north of the Castle ridge, there was an equally rapid
expansion of contemporary development to the south, notably
Robert Adam's magnificent new home for the University. But
there are also survivals from earlier ages, for it was here that
the city built her first tentative suburbs outside the old town
wall.

The area is packed within relatively small confines, and all of
it is within easy walking distance of the city centre. This chapter takes the form of a circular tour from Princes Street, from
the Mound back to North Bridge, and it begins at the top of the
Mound, where George IV Bridge begins at the junction of the
Royal Mile.

On the left immediately past the junction are the Midlothian
County (now Lothian Region) Buildings, by J. McIntyre Henry,
1905, in an Edwardian Palladian style. Immediately beyond
can be seen the rear of the original 17th-century Parliament
Hall, with fine decoration and window tracery. Next on the
left is the blind frontage of the NATIONAL LIBRARY OF SCOTLAND
(Reginald Fairlie, 1956), with sculpture by Hew Lorimer representing the arts and sciences. The building has 2 storeys
showing to the street, and 9 more floors below; the blind 7-bay
pilastrade keeps out noise from the main reading hall behind.

The National Library was founded in 1925, and was initially housed in the Advocates' Library, which gave the majority of its huge and historic collection to found it. It is a copyright library, entitled to receive a copy of every work published in the United Kingdom, and houses well over 3 million books.

Directly opposite is the Central Public Library, in a François I style (Sir George Washington Browne, 1890), founded on a gift by Andrew Carnegie. It is built on the site of the 17th-century mansion of Sir Thomas Hope, King's Advocate to Charles I; 2 lintels from the old mansion are preserved above internal doorways. The library has particularly fine collections on Edinburgh and Scotland. Adjoining, at the corner of Victoria Street, is the Library's Fine Art department, formerly the Highland Institute (John Henderson, 1836), with rich neo-Jacobean detail, and sculpture by A.H. Ritchie.

George IV Bridge spans the deep depression of the Cowgate on 3 arches, only one of which is visible. Sanctioned under the City Improvement Act of 1827 to link the Old Town with the expanding area of George Square, it was built by Thomas Hamilton, 1829–34.

On the west side, at the corner of Candlemaker Row, is a small statue of GREYFRIARS BOBBY, a Skye terrier and the faithful companion of a shepherd, Jock Gray. When Gray died in 1858 the dog refused to leave his graveside in Greyfriars Kirk for 14 years, and became such a legend in its lifetime that it was granted the freedom of the city. When the dog itself died, it was buried in the churchyard at Queen Victoria's suggestion, and American lovers of the dog and the legend have since subscribed to a granite headstone for it.

Chambers Street, opposite, was built as part of a major scheme of city improvements in 1871 by William Chambers, Lord Provost, in alliance with Dr Henry Littlejohn, the city's first medical officer of health. A statue of Chambers by John Rhind stands halfway down the street.

On the north side is the headquarters of the Heriot-Watt University (David Rhind, 1872), opened in 1821 as the Edinburgh School of Arts on a site across the street, and the first true Mechanics' Institute in Great Britain. Founded in memory of James Watt, whose statue stands outside, it was endowed with funds from the George Heriot estates. It is now a university in its own right, specializing in science and technology, and has moved its main campus to Riccarton, on the south-west outskirts of the city.

Opposite is the ROYAL SCOTTISH MUSEUM, the largest general museum of the arts and sciences in the British Isles. Its symmetrical front, in early Venetian Renaissance style, is by Captain Fowke of the Royal Engineers, 1861, executed by Robert Matheson, with additions in 1874 and 1889. The foundation stone was laid on 23 October 1861 by Prince Albert, his last public act before his death. Its galleried interior is in the best tradition of Victorian cast ironwork, and is a fine museum piece in itself. It houses the Scottish national collections of the decorative arts of the world, archaeology, ethnography, natural history, geology, technology and science, with everything from working models of paddle steamers to relics of space flights.

Next to the Heriot-Watt is Minto House, once an eminent extra-mural medical school. In 1829, in the ancient mansion of the Minto family which previously stood on this site, James Syme opened his own private hospital, and treated over 8,000 patients there in his first 4 years, largely at his own expense.

The remainder of the south side of Chambers Street is occupied by the University Old College, dealt with later in this chapter. Opposite in Guthrie Street, in a house long since swept away, Sir Walter Scott was born on 17 August 1771 when the street was known as College Wynd. The Police Training College, on the eastern corner, displays a memorial tablet. The College itself, by James Lessels, 1887, has rich Renaissance detail. Next door, on the site of the old Gaiety Theatre, is Adam House (by W.H. Kininmonth, 1955), a University examination hall with a small theatre in its basement.

We return to George IV Bridge, and the top of Candlemaker Row. This steep, narrow street has a fine collection of early 18th-century tenements, saved by extensive restoration in 1930. Near the top, on the west side, is Candlemaker Hall, built c. 1722 as the meeting-place of the Incorporation of Candlemakers, one of the ancient city trades guilds; the fine panelled hall inside has been extensively restored. The adjoining block, nos. 38–42, is of similar date, and known as Henry's Land. It has a rectangular stair tower and large wallhead chimneys. Nos. 46–54, also early 18th century, restored 1930, was formerly the Harrow Inn, which had associations with Dr John Brown's book *Rab and His Friends*.

At the head of Candlemaker Row is the entrance to the historic GREYFRIARS KIRK, and its churchyard of notable historic monuments and gravestones, listed on a board by the gate. Among the graves are those of William Adam, architect; Joseph Black, physicist and chemist, discoverer of the theory of latent heat; George Buchanan, 16th-century humanist and tutor to Mary, Queen of Scots; Duncan Forbes of Culloden, Lord President of the Court of Session; James Hutton, pioneer geologist; Duncan Ban McIntyre, Gaelic poet; Henry Mackenzie, novelist; Allan Ramsay, poet; Walter Scott's father; and many more. Here too is the flat gravestone upon which was signed, according to legend, the National Covenant on 18 February 1638. There are other associations with the Covenant; in the southwest corner is an area known as the Covenanters' Prison, where 1,200 of those captured at the Battle of Bothwell Bridge in 1679 were confined for 5 months without shelter. In the north-east corner is the Martyrs' Monument, to the scores of Covenanters executed in the Grassmarket for upholding their Presbyterian faith.

Greyfriars Kirk, built on the site of a monastery of the Dutch Grey Friars which stood here from the 13th century until swept away in 1559, was opened in 1620, the first church to be built in Edinburgh after the Reformation. The eastern part, an aisled Gothic rectangle, is the older, gutted and restored, with new window tracery, by David Cousin in 1857. The western half was built as a separate church in 1721 by Alexander McGill, damaged by fire in 1845 and restored by David Bryce. The entire church was restored, and the dividing wall removed to make one kirk with one congregation, in 1938.

Opposite the entrance to the churchyard is Bristo Port, the site of a gate in the 1513 city wall. Fragments of the wall remain and part has been incorporated in the western end of the Royal Scottish Museum.

Forrest Road leads to Lauriston Place and the splendid Renaissance pile of GEORGE HERIOT'S SCHOOL, built as Heriot's Hospital between 1628 and 1660 from the vast fortune of George Heriot (1563–1624) court jeweller to King James VI. The architect is unknown, although the style is that of Inigo Jones; it was actually built by William Wallace and William Ayton, master masons, the clock tower and statue of Heriot being added by Robert Mylne in 1693. The building is of square plan, with a central quadrangle, turreted corner towers, and further octagonal towers on the centres of 3 sides and at the internal angles. On the north side there is a 5-storey entrance tower with cupola. All but the north façade was faced with ashlar in 1833. The view from Lauriston Place is of the back; the front faces north, but is difficult to see well except from the Castle Esplanade. In 1650, when still incomplete, the building was used by Cromwell as a hospital for the wounded from the Battle of Dunbar, and remained as such until 1658.

The building has some 200 windows, no two of which are precisely alike, richly decorated with curious devices. The tall window in the centre of the southern side is the window of the school chapel, rebuilt by Gillespie Graham in 1840.

To the west of Heriot's grounds, on the north side of Lauriston Place, Heriot Place leads by a high wall to the Vennel, a picturesque alley containing a substantial remnant of the Flodden Wall of 1513.

The south side of Lauriston Place is occupied by the Royal Infirmary of Edinburgh. Built 1870–79 to replace the old infirmary at South Bridge, this was one of the largest and most advanced of its time, designed by David Bryce on the then-new pavilion plan, with exterior detail, including corner turrets, modelled on the palaces of Holyroodhouse and Falkland. In the forecourt is a lead statue of George II, who granted a Royal Charter to the infirmary in 1736. By James Hill, 1759, it was brought from the old infirmary.

We return to the top of Forrest Road and turn east into Teviot Place. The north side of the street was the site of Darien House, headquarters of the Darien Scheme, one of the greatest and most disastrous expeditions ever to set out from Scotland. The house later became a lunatic asylum, and in a nearby annexe the poet Robert Fergusson died in 1774 at the age of 24.

The buildings were demolished in 1871 to make way for the present block.

The south side of Teviot Place is dominated by the EDINBURGH UNIVERSITY MEDICAL SCHOOL, a Venetian Renaissance pile by Rowand Anderson, 1878–88, with very fine detail. Anderson's original plan allowed for a 200-foot campanile, modelled on that in St Mark's Square, Venice, but it was never built. The medical school itself cost £300,000 raised from the University's 300th anniversary appeal fund. The building is in the form of 2 adjacent quadrangles, separated by a hall 100-feet long. In the first quadrangle, entered through the ornate main archway in Teviot Place, are 2 tablets set into the walls. One is a memorial to the Polish School of Medicine, established here by exiles during the Second World War and maintained for some years afterwards; the other commemorates James Lind, the conqueror of scurvy, who taught here.

Adjoining the Medical School at its eastern end is the McEwan Hall, the University's graduation hall. Also by Anderson, in a matching Venetian style, it was built 1888–97, and was one of the first buildings in Britain to employ steel trusses in its large squat-domed roof. The majority of its cost was met by Sir William McEwan, MP for Central Edinburgh and a member of the brewing family. The hall, in the form of a Greek theatre, seats 2,200. The 2 stair towers to the galleries, which project to the exterior, are of an unusual double spiral design, allowing the emerging crowd from each balcony to be kept separate until they reach the street. The interior exhibits a fine collection of Victorian mural paintings, by Palin of London, on canvas, fixed to the plaster with white lead. In the hall is a very large 4-manual organ with 3,000 speaking pipes. Outside, the ornate gates and gatepiers, and the lantern pillar in Portland stone, are also by Anderson.

Next to the McEwan Hall is a courtyard containing the Reid School of Music (David Cousin, 1858), in Italian Renaissance manner, the bequest of General John Reid, a Peninsular War veteran. The School houses the Galpin collection of old musical instruments. To the east in Park Place is the University Union (Mitchell and Wilson, 1889), on a 15th-century palace theme with towers modelled on Holyrood. This was the site of a house in which Dr Archibald Tait (1811–82), headmaster of Rugby School and Archbishop of Canterbury, was born.

Lothian Street, opposite, has been largely swept away to make way for the Edinburgh University Student Centre (Morris and Steedman, 1973); the author Thomas de Quincey lived for a time in a house on this site. In that portion of the north side which remains, nos. 29–39 is a 4-storey tenement block of *c.* 1820 which housed the early workshops of John Logie Baird, the inventor of television. No. 54 is an older 2-storey block of 1725.

From Bristo Street, Charles Street leads into GEORGE SQUARE, laid out in 1766 by a speculative builder, James Brown, who named it after his brother George and attracted the cream of Edinburgh society to its fine houses. It was the first development of any size outside the old city wall, and pre-dated the first New Town by 20 years or more. During the 1960s it was progressively demolished by the University, and now only portions of the east and west sides (nos. 16–29 and 55–60) remain. Among the early residents were Walter Scott's parents (no. 25); Henry Dundas, commissioner of Scotland under William Pitt; the judge, Lord Braxfield, model for R.L. Stevenson's *Weir of Hermiston* (no. 13); Henry Erskine, Lord Advocate (no. 27); and Admiral Duncan, hero of the Battle of Camperdown (no. 5).

The University made its first acquisition in the square in 1914; redevelopment began in 1949 with the extension of the Medical School at the north-west corner, but further work was held up for 10 years while conservationists fought in vain to save the square. On the left by Charles Street is the Appleton Tower (Alan Reiach, 1965), named after Sir Edward Appleton, physicist and principal of the University (1948–63), and housing first-year science departments. Adjoining is the William Robertson Building, named after an eminent 18th-century historian and principal, housing social sciences, history and economics.

At the south-east corner is the David Hume Tower (Sir Robert Matthew, 1963), housing departments of the Faculty of Arts. The south side has the Adam Ferguson Building (1970) named after the great professor of moral philosophy (1764–85), containing social science departments, and adjoining a 600-seat theatre (Sir Robert Matthew, 1970). This side is completed by the new University Library (Sir Basil Spence, 1967), recognized as one of the finest buildings of its kind in Europe.

Behind George Square's south side is Buccleuch Place, also by Brown. The majority of the street dates from the 1780s, and was almost as fashionable as George Square. Most of the houses are fairly plain, but the overall effect is pleasing. The backs, seen from George Square or The Meadows, have bow windows. The block, nos. 17–19, is probably the best of the street; at no. 18, on the second floor, in the rooms of the lawyer and literary critic Francis Jeffrey, the *Edinburgh Review* was founded in 1802. The building now houses the Donald Tovey Memorial Rooms, in memory of the composer and professor of music at the University between 1914 and 1940. The large and isolated tenement, nos. 14–16, was for some years the fashionable Assembly Rooms for the district.

The Meadows, the large expanse of open public parkland adjoining, was once the Borough Loch, from which the town drew some of its water supply. It was partly drained in 1722 by Thomas Hope of Rankeillor, who turned it into an ornamental park.

In Chapel Street, to the east of George Square, is Chapel House, mid 18th-century, 3-storey in squared rubble, decorated with urns; it is now commercial premises (Anderson, Gibb and Wilson). On the east side of Chapel Street, at the corner of West Nicolson Street, nos. 34–6 is an attractive 2-storey house of 1756, of squared rubble, with a centre wallhead gable of 2 windows and pediment.

Nearby is Buccleuch Parish Church, built 1753 and extensively renovated in Gothic style in 1866. It contains a fine memorial window erected by the Marquis of Bute in memory of his ancestor, Flora Macleod of Raasay, who is buried in the adjoining churchyard along with Dr Thomas Blacklock, the blind poet and friend of Burns, and Mrs Cockburn, author of the lament for the Battle of Flodden, *The Flowers of the Forest*. Nearby, at the corner of West Crosscauseway, is Buccleuch and Greyfriars Free Church, in Second Pointed style, with a fine octagonal spire, by Hay of Liverpool, 1856.

On the west side of Buccleuch Street is Archers' Hall, home of the Royal Company of Archers, who act as the Queen's Personal Bodyguard in Scotland. The hall is by Alexander Laing, 1776, altered and extended by Rowand Anderson, 1900.

Nearby, in Hope Park Square facing The Meadows, is the mid 18th-century house of Thomas Hope of Rankeillor, who drained the Borough Loch. The house is in a Scottish Baroque style of 3-storeys, with round shouldered doorpiece and cornice of late 17th-century style, second-floor windows arched with hood moulding, and a low-pitched curvilinear gable with scrolled ends.

At no. 130 Buccleuch Street is a house named Hope Park End, dating from 1780.

At the southern end of Buccleuch Street, Melville Drive strikes west through The Meadows, flanked by 2 square pillars erected in 1881 by the publishing firm of Thomas Nelson, and surmounted by a lion and unicorn, the heraldic beasts from the arms of Scotland.

Immediately beyond the crossroads, in Summerhall, is the Royal Dick Veterinary College founded in 1823 by William Dick, a farrier and blacksmith who had a forge at White Horse Close in the Canongate. The college has been on its present site since 1916, and was incorporated into the University in 1951.

Hope Park Terrace joins Clerk Street, which returns north towards the city centre. Clerk Street is composed mainly of 4- and 5-storey tenements of *c.* 1810. On the west side is the Odeon Cinema (W.E. Trent, 1930), a fine example of Odeon Gothic by the best known of British cinema architects. The north side of Rankeillor Street, built on the estate of Thomas Hope of Rankeillor, dates mainly from 1812 and it displays numerous decorated fanlights and doorways.

St Patrick Square, on the west side of Clerk Street, was one of the early developments outside the old city wall, in a late Georgian artisan style. Nos. 1–21 date from 1786, with a variety of 2- and 3-window wallhead gables. The rest of the square is *c.* 1800, and a little grander, and some of the houses have decorated fanlights. St Patrick Street, the northward continuation of Clerk Street, is of the same period and style. To the east, in East

Crosscauseway, is an old well, capped with an obelisk, dated 1797.

From Hope Park Terrace, across Clerk Street, Bernard Terrace leads to St Leonard's Street. On the east side of the latter, by Parkside Street, is a yard which was the terminus of one of the earliest railways in Britain, the Edinburgh and Dalkeith, opened in 1831 using horse-drawn transport to bring coal from the Midlothian coalfield. The original terminus was at Duddingston, but it was very soon extended through a steeply-rising 350-yard tunnel beneath Salisbury Crags to the St Leonard's station. Because of the gradient trains were hauled through the tunnel by rope wound by a stationary steam engine. Horses were still exclusively used on the line in 1845, when it was sold to the North British Railway for £113,000. The Edinburgh and Dalkeith was known as 'The Innocent Railway' because, although it carried 400,000 passengers a year at the height of its short existence, it never claimed a life.

The coal yard was finally abandoned in 1968 but there remains, in a deserted state, the old railway office, an 18th-century house known in its time as 'Hermits and Termits'. The house, no. 64 St Leonard's Street, was built in 1734 by William Clifton, solicitor. Of 2 storeys with attic, it has a shouldered doorpiece, one window wallhead gable and scroll skews. The painter David Scott, RSA, lived here as a child *c.* 1806–12, and his brother the pre-Raphaelite painter William Bell Scott, RSA, was born here in 1811.

North along St Leonard's Street is St Leonard's Lane, leading to the St Thomas of Aquin's High School, a fine example of Franco-Scottish Renaissance style by John A. Carfrae, 1919, with much elegant detail. A few yards beyond, at no. 12 St Leonard's Bank, is Gibraltar House, a simple Georgian artisan dwelling of 1782. The bay windows and porch are later additions.

We return to Clerk Street which becomes Nicolson Street, with late 18th-century tenements at its southern end. Nicolson Street Church is by Gillespie Graham, 1819, in a Tudor Gothic style with pinnacles (reconstructed 1932). One of its early ministers was Dr John Jamieson, author of a noted Scots dictionary. In Nicolson Square, on the left, nos. 12–14 is *c.* 1780, one of the earliest developments in the area. Nos. 2–10 is of similar date but greatly altered. In the centre of the square is the richly decorated Brassfounders' Pillar, designed by Sir James Gowans and made by local craftsmen for the Edinburgh Exhibition of 1886.

Nicolson Square Methodist Chapel is a classical 2-storey building of 1815, with a 3-arch recessed porch, and arched windows with Roman Doric pilaster order, inscribed parapet and balustraded parapets over the advanced end bays. It was used regularly by the United States President Ulysses S. Grant during a visit to Edinburgh.

In Nicolson Street, near the corner of Nicolson Square, is the Empire Theatre, one of the city's largest, now converted to a bingo hall. It was built in 1929 by W. and T. Milburn of London on the site of an earlier theatre of 1820 which was burned down twice. Its unimposing frontage belies a fine art deco interior.

Directly opposite is SURGEON'S HALL, one of the best works of W.H. Playfair, erected 1829–32. Built on the site of an old riding school, at a cost of £20,000, it has an Ionic hexastyle portico with the front row of columns mounted on a broad screen wall with pediment, and a podium with gateways on either side. Of massive proportions, it contains a fine circular domed entrance hall with gallery, a museum hall, pilastraded with galleries in the aisles, and a glass coffered ceiling.

Some of its committee rooms contain oak panelling from the old Surgeons' Hall of 1697, which still stands in nearby Drummond Street.

A short distance to the north, Drummond Street strikes east to join the Pleasance. On its north side St Patrick's Roman Catholic School (J.A. Carfrae, 1905), is an unusual Scandinavian-Jacobean inspiration. Opposite is Roxburgh Place, containing Lady Glenorchy's Church and Hall, both finely and elaborately detailed. The hall is by Thomas Ross, 1909, and the church by P.M. Chalmers, 1913, built on the site of an earlier chapel of 1791. The church is in late Scots Gothic, but is no longer used for worship, and most of the interior furnishings and memorials have been removed.

Further down Drummond Street on the north side is the

University's Department of Natural Philosophy (David Bryce, 1853) built as an extension to the old Royal Infirmary. The rest of the old hospital has gone, demolished when the present building at Lauriston was opened in 1879, but its original gate-piers (William Adam, 1738) remain here.

Beside is OLD SURGEONS' HALL, a 3-storey rectangular build-ing with end octagons, and a moulded doorpiece with pediment on the north front. Built by James Smith in 1697, it has been greatly altered, and many of its interior fitments were removed to the new Surgeons' Hall in Nicolson Street. It was to here that the notorious murderers Burke and Hare brought corpses for dissection by Dr Knox and his pupils for up to £16 a time.

The north side of Drummond Street here is formed by a portion of the Flodden Wall of 1513, which can be seen as the lower part of the present boundary wall, turning sharply northwards at the junction of the Pleasance, where there is a fragment of a tower. THE PLEASANCE, an ancient thoroughfare, takes its name from a convent of uncertain date which stood on the site of the present Roxburgh Street, a branch of the Franciscan house of Santa Maria di Campagni in the Italian city of Placentia. The houses of the Pleasance were largely cleared away in the 1960s, being some of the worst slums in the city, if not the country.

An interesting group of buildings remains at nos. 60–80, partly late 18th century, with a semi-elliptical arch which formed the gateway to the old Quaker Meeting House of 1791 within the courtyard. The remainder of the Pleasance Trust buildings surrounding it are a 20th-century copy (by J. Inch Morrison) of the 17th-century Scots vernacular style, incor-porating some 19th-century brewery buildings.

We return by Drummond Street to Nicolson Street, which becomes South Bridge at the junction. On the corner is the OLD COLLEGE of Edinburgh University, one of the greatest and last of the works of Robert Adam, and his largest building in the city.

The University, founded in 1582, was housed for well over 200 years in a mean collection of buildings on this site, where previously had stood Kirk o'Field, the house which was blown up, causing the death of Mary Queen of Scots's husband, Darnley, on 10 February 1567; it stood at the south-east corner of the present college.

The University continued to be poorly housed until the beginning of the 19th century, when the first sections of the Old College were completed. The foundation stone was laid on 16 November 1789, but because of a shortage of funds it was not finished until 1834. The architect was Robert Adam, but he died in 1792 with only a small part completed, and the following year war was declared with France, slowing and eventually halting building work until 1815, when it was resumed under the direction of W.H. Playfair. The frontage to South Bridge is pure Adam, as are the east and west sides of the quadrangle, but much of the rest, including almost the entire interior, is the work of Playfair.

It is nevertheless a remarkable building, constructed on a giant scale, and overcoming the drawback of a difficult sloping site. It forms a huge rectangle, 356 feet by 225 feet, with an open quadrangle in the centre. Adam's original plan was for 2 quadrangles, but this was abandoned. Among its finest features is the huge main portico, the entrance flanked by 6 great columns, each a monolith of Craigleith stone 3 feet in diameter and 22 feet high, hauled from the quarry by teams of 16 horses. Adam's original plan also included a small dome above the main entrance, but this was never built, and the present prominent and much larger dome was added by Rowand Anderson in 1887, and is surmounted by a gilded figure of 'Youth holding aloft the torch of knowledge', better known as 'the Golden Boy'. On the frontage directly beneath the dome is an inscribed panel giving the dates of the founding of the University, the building of the Old College, and the names of the Lord Provost of the time, Thomas Elder, of the principal, William Robertson, and of the architect, Robert Adam.

The façades on the quadrangle are mainly the work of Playfair, and the overall style is a mixture of Greek and Palladian, having angle quadrants at each corner with arcades at the lower level and Ionic colonnades above. The south side of the quadrangle, which stands astride the line of the Flodden Wall, is almost entirely occupied by the Upper Library, one of Playfair's finest interiors, and one of the outstanding examples of

late classical architecture in Britain. It is a hall 198-feet long
and 50-feet wide, flanked by Ionic columns and rows of statues,
with a splendid arched moulded roof. The library is approached
by an equally fine staircase.

Opposite the Old College is Infirmary Street, taking its name
from the old Royal Infirmary, established on the south side in
1738, whose site is now occupied by a swimming bath. On the
north side, near the bottom, is the old Lady Yester Church
(1803), an early example of neo-Jacobean style and of the revival
of window tracery. At the foot of the street, in High School
Yards, is the Old High School of Edinburgh (Alexander Laing,
1777), 2-storey ashlar with a tetrastyle Roman Doric portico.
This was the school attended by Walter Scott, Francis Jeffrey
and Lord Cockburn; the initials WS carved at the side of the
main doorway may or may not be those of its most illustrious
pupil. In 1832 the building became part of the Edinburgh
Royal Infirmary, and Joseph Lister and James Syme practised
here. It is now University property.

Beyond Infirmary Street and Chambers Street the main
thoroughfare becomes South Bridge proper, a viaduct of 19
arches, only one of which is visible where it crosses Cowgate.
The bridge is 1000-feet long, from Chambers Street to the High
Street, and was built by Alexander Laing, 1786–8, at a cost of
£6,400. The buildings which flank the bridge are the work of
Laing, c. 1790, and are mainly 3-storey; in the original plan
every third house had a pediment with lunette window, and a
number of these remain.

At the junction of the High Street another great bridge
springs from the northern flank of the Old Town ridge. The first
North Bridge, a stone structure of 3 arches, was opened in 1769,
to the design of William Mylne, and was an essential first step
towards the construction of the New Town. Within weeks of
its opening, part of it fell down, burying 5 people in the ruins,
and it was not finally opened to wheeled traffic until 1772. The
present bridge (architect: R.H. Morham; engineers: Blyth and
Westland) was built 1896–7, and is of 3 arched iron-girder
spans totalling 525 feet, on massive ashlar piers. The west parapet has a plaque recalling the old bridge, and on the east parapet is a memorial to the King's Own Scottish Borderers who fell

in the South African War, composed of 4 giant figures in free-stone by Birnie Rhind, 1906.

The south end of the bridge is flanked by 2 massive late 19th-century blocks in ornate Scottish Renaissance style. That on the east, occupied by the Carlton Hotel, is by Hamilton Beattie and A.R. Scott, 1898. The North Bridge frontage is of 4 storeys with attics, in a semi-symmetrical treatment, rising to 5 storeys at the northern end, and decorated with a variety of circular turrets with ogee roofs, and giant arches at first and second floor level. Across the street is another Scots Renaissance pile of greater grandeur and much more elaborate detail, chiefly occupied by *The Scotsman* newspaper (Dunn and Findlay, 1899–1902). The north façade is set back behind a balustraded terrace, with an elaborate octagon staircase to Market Street below. The North Bridge frontage has ground arches and elaborate spandrel panels. The northern façade, facing Princes Street, is a riot of sculpture, including the newspaper's masthead picked out in gold. In the centre of the block, on the North Bridge frontage, is an arcade of shops with a central dome, still with its original glasswork, and a mosaic floor.

# CHAPTER 8

# The Queensferry Route

♣ ♣ ♣

*Dean Bridge – Dean Village – Bell's Mills – Daniel Stewart's College – Fettes College – Craigleith Quarry – Ravelston House – Corstorphine Hill – Craigcrook Castle – Lauriston Castle – Cramond – River Almond – Craigiehall – Dalmeny Church – Forth Bridges – South Queensferry – Kirkliston – Niddry Castle – Hopetoun House*

From the west end of Princes Street, Queensferry Street leads to the main A90 route to Blackhall, Barnton, the Forth Bridges and the north.

At the end of Queensferry Street, by Lynedoch Place (James Brown, 1823) with its early urban front gardens, the road turns sharply right across the Dean Bridge (Thomas Telford, 1832), one of the highest in the world when built, 447-feet long and carrying the road 106 feet above the Water of Leith. It was built by Lord Provost John Learmonth, who wished to develop his land on the far side of the gorge. At the east end of the bridge is a studio house (Sir G.W. Browne, 1891) in a free Jacobean style with rich detail, and at the west end, the former Church of the Holy Trinity (John Henderson, 1838) has a new role as an electricity sub-station.

Beside the Dean Bridge, Bell's Brae descends steeply into the gorge and the picturesque DEAN VILLAGE, with a much earlier bridge. The village was a milling community as early as the 16th century, and there is much evidence of 17th- and 18th-century occupation by the 'baxters' (bakers) of Edinburgh, who by the 17th century had 11 mills on this short stretch of river. In Bell's Brae, no. 6 (1881), built as stables with a curved frontage to the river, is now an architect's office. No. 17 (Bell's Brae House) is an early 18th-century L-plan dwelling, with a stair projection in the angle, restored and partly altered in 1948. At the foot of the brae is a building of 1675, known as the Old Tolbooth, built as a 4-storey granary, now being restored; it is inscribed: 'God bless the baxters of Edinburgh who built this house' and 'God's providence is our inheritance'. There is also a carved panel showing 3 cakes and a pie. Round the corner in Hawthornbank Lane are several 18th-century millers' houses.

The Water of Leith Bridge itself is 18th-century rubble built with a single span. Across it, on the north side of the river, is West Mill, with the date 1806 in the wheatsheaf roundel, now converted to flats. Across the bridge and to the left, Well Court is a romantic creation in the Scots vernacular style, a development of flats incorporating a social hall and clock tower built (Mitchell and Wilson, 1884) by J.R. Findlay, philanthropist and proprietor of *The Scotsman* newspaper.

Dean Path, which climbs the other side of the valley following the ancient coach route, retains a number of restored late 18th-century houses at nos. 10, 27 and 39–43.

Dean Path returns to Queensferry Road at the Dean Cemetery, which contains some impressive memorials and the remains of several eminent citizens, including Alexander Russell, a distinguished editor of *The Scotsman*; W.H. Playfair, the architect; Lords Cockburn and Jeffrey; the painters Sir William Allan, William Brodie, Sam Bough and Paul Chambers; the surgeon James Syme; James Nasmyth, inventor of the steam hammer; Edward Forbes the naturalist; Professor John Wilson (Christopher North) and his son-in-law William Aytoun, the poet and scholar.

We return to the Dean Bridge and follow Belford Road westwards to another ancient crossing of the river at Bell's Mills. The modern Belford Bridge replaces one which stood even earlier than that in the Dean Village. Immediately beyond it Bell's Mills leads down to the river bank and the site of an 18th-century flour mill; only the granary of 1807 and the miller's house, late 18th century, survive.

On the north side of Belford Road is the Dean Education Centre, built (Thomas Hamilton, 1833) as the Dean Orphanage, in a neo-Baroque style with a tetrastyle Tuscan portico flanked by unusual twin open chimney towers over the internal staircases. It has an interesting entrance hall and staircases, and on its front is the clock from the old city gate of the Netherbow port, demolished in 1764. On the other side of Belford Road is John Watson's School (William Burn, 1828), a 2-storey frontage of 21 windows with a hexastyle Greek Doric portico. In 1982 the Scottish National Gallery of Modern Art will move to the school.

Belford Road rejoins Queensferry Road by DANIEL STEW-ART'S COLLEGE, an H-plan neo-Jacobean extravaganza of turrets, by David Rhind, 1855; it was submitted by Rhind in a competition to design a new Houses of Parliament in London, and came second. Inside is a fine chapel with hammerbeam roof. The school, now amalgamated with Melville College, was founded by Daniel Stewart, a macer in the Court of Exchequer, and is administered by the Edinburgh Merchant Company.

Immediately across Dean Bridge are some handsome streets laid out on the grounds of Lord Provost Learmonth. Those on the north side of Queensferry Road are in a refined Italian style by John Tait, built mainly 1850–65. No. 2 Eton Terrace was the home of Professor George Saintsbury, literary critic and professor of English literature, 1895–1915. On the south side, Buckingham Terrace (John Chesser, 1860–76) has some fine doorways and ironwork.

Beyond Learmonth Terrace, on the north side of Queensferry Road, is a splendid vista of FETTES COLLEGE. This eminent boarding school, run on English public school lines, was built from a bequest of Sir William Fettes (1750–1836), a wealthy city grocer and twice Lord Provost, who left £166,000 for the purpose. The main building is a massive and richly-detailed composition in Franco–Scottish Gothic (David Bryce, 1870). The main 3-storey block has a symmetrical front under a central lead-roofed tower, cloisters from the centre to the projecting ends, and 4-storey towers with tall roofs on the end elevations. There is an ornate and flamboyant chapel on the first floor. On the Carrington Road frontage are some fine ornate iron railings and gates, also by Bryce. Readers of Ian Fleming will know that this was the school attended by James Bond.

The nearby Royal Victoria Hospital in Craigleith Road has

an unusual cantilevered and raised gatehouse by Mitchell and Wilson, 1906.

At the junction of Craigleith Road and Queensferry Road is CRAIGLEITH QUARRY, now largely filled in, from where came most of the fine hard freestone to build the New Town. When finally abandoned, because of the increasing hardness of the stone, the quarry was 200-feet deep, and in 1830 3 large fossilized coniferous trees were found in the rock. The largest stone cut here was 136-feet long, and weighing an estimated 15,000 tons, cut in 1823. It was cut into sections, some going to form the architraves of the National Monument on Calton Hill, the rest being shipped to London for extensions to Buckingham Palace.

Half a mile to the north of the quarry, in Groathill Road North, is Drylaw House, a 2-storey rubble-built mansion of 1718, built for George Loch of Drylaw. It was partly remodelled in the late 18th century, but the west elevation is original. There is some fine interior work, including mid 18th-century painting in the parlour. At the north end of Groathill Road North, behind the 'Doocot' public house, is the house's dovecot, an 18th-century crowstepped type.

To the south of Queensferry Road, in Ravelston Dykes Road, is NEW RAVELSTON HOUSE, now forming the nucleus of the Mary Erskine School for Girls, but which once provided the inspiration, with its terraces, grass walks and statues, for Tullyveolan in Scott's *Waverley*. Nearby, well secluded by trees, is OLD RAVELSTON HOUSE, a small crowstepped rectangular tower built in 1622, with a door lintel carrying the date and the initials of George Foulis, the first occupant, and his wife Janet Bannatyne. In the garden is another lintel, originally from a richly ornate mantelpiece in the house and now incorporated into a grotto, bearing the date 1624. In the grounds there is also an early 17th-century dovecot. New Ravelston House was built *c.* 1791 for Alexander Keith of Ravelston, Knight-Marischal of Scotland; it is 2-storey with basement, and has a 3-storey octagonal entrance tower with Ionic columns at the ground floor and a blind balustrade to the north side, with a 3-storey balustraded bow to the south. Screen walls reach out to the pavilions on the east and west sides; between the main house and the east pavilion are extensive additions of 1916.

Opposite the school in Ravelston Dykes Road is the start of a public footpath which climbs the wooded slopes of COR-STORPHINE HILL, skirts the rear of the zoo (no entrance this way) and descends to Corstorphine Road on the other side. On the Ravelston side of the hill is the viewpoint of Rest and Be Thankful, where David Balfour parted from Alan Breck in Stevenson's *Kidnapped*. On the 529-foot summit of the hill is Clermiston Tower, now boarded up, built in 1872 to mark the centenary of Sir Walter Scott's birth. Below the hill, in Craigcrook Road, is Craigcrook Castle, a 17th-century keep which was the home of Archibald Constable, Scott's publisher, and from 1815–50 of Lord Jeffrey, where he entertained Tennyson, Dickens, Thackeray and other literary giants. The castle is private and secluded among trees; the original 2-storey Z-plan keep was extended by W.H. Playfair in 1835, and again in 1891. The 19th-century interior work includes murals by David Roberts, RSA.

Craigcrook Road rejoins Queensferry Road at Quality Street, leading to the village of Davidson's Mains, once known as Muttonhole. East of the junction, on the north side of Hillhouse Road, Marchfield is a 2-storey house of 1810, in 18th-century style with small Doric porch and bow at the rear. Quality Street has some houses of 1827 by Gillespie Graham (nos. 7, 9 and 13–31). The simply styled Holy Cross Church, with unfinished central tower, is by J.M. Dick Peddie, 1912.

Cramond Road South continues from the village towards the shore, passing the gateway to LAURISTON CASTLE, set on a picturesque terrace above the Forth. The Castle is a city museum, with a fine collection of furniture and Flemish tapestries; it is best known as the birthplace (1671) of John Law, founder of the Bank of France and promoter of the ill-fated Mississippi Scheme to colonize Louisiana. It collapsed along with the Bank and Law died in poverty and disgrace in Venice in 1729.

It consists of a late 16th-century rubble-built rectangular turreted and corbelled tower, remodelled in 1827 with the addition of a large Scots Tudor style wing by William Burn, and further alterations and internal improvements by W.H. Playfair in 1845. The castle, originally built by Sir Archibald Napier of Merchiston, father of the inventor of logarithms, was the home of the Law family for 140 years, and was finally bequeathed to the city by its last owner, Mr W.R. Reid, in 1926.

Cramond Road South continues past the 18th-century lodges and gateway to Cramond House, and turns down to the village of CRAMOND at Glebe Road. The village was the site of a Roman fort of the 2nd and 20th Legions under Lollius Urbicus in the 2nd century AD, and its name is derived from *Caeravon* (fort on the river). Slight traces of the Roman fort can be discerned in the lower sections of the church walls, where Roman-dressed stones have been incorporated, and in the open grassed area alongside. A Roman bath-house was discovered during the construction of the car park (behind Cramond Inn) but it is at present covered over.

The church has a 15th-century tower; the remainder, cruciform, rubble-built and crowstepped, dates from 1656, but has been substantially altered since, with major renovations in 1912. There are vaults, a bell of 1619, and some fine tombs. The adjoining manse is of 1745. Nearby, the white-washed Old Schoolhouse, 2-storey L-plan, is late 18th-century. Cramond Inn dates from 1670, with 18th- and 19th-century additions.

Behind the inn are the remains of Cramond Tower, built by the bishops of Dunkeld in the late 15th century of rubble with a circular stair and vaulting on the ground and top floors. Nearby is Cramond House, now a community centre; the central part, dating from 1680, was built for Sir John Inglis of Cramond, the wings being added *c*. 1772. At the bottom of the hill the road opens out to Cramond Foreshore and the picturesque mouth of the RIVER ALMOND. Now a popular yacht haven, this was once a thriving industrial community of iron mills. On the east bank is a row of cottages built, 1780–90, to house the mill workers, and restored in 1961. The riverside path leads to the remains of a massively-built dock where the ore boats were drawn in to supply the late 18th-century Cockle Mill, which once produced most of Scotland's spades, and is now restored as a house. Its original owners, Cadell and Edington, set up the famous Carron Ironworks at Falkirk. A short distance upstream is the waterfall, dock and ruins of Fair-a-Far Mill.

At the mouth of the Almond a ferry gives access to the west bank and the grounds of the Dalmeny estate, through which there is a pleasant 4-mile walk to the Forth Bridges. A short distance along the path is the Eagle Rock, which bears a faded carving with a doubtful claim to be a Roman eagle scratched by a Cramond legionary. Further along is Barnbougle Castle, built by the 5th Earl of Rosebery in 1881, an approximate re-construction of a 17th-century keep which stood here and was accidentally blown up in 1820.

Back at Cramond village, the riverside path continues along the Almond through a wooded valley to old Cramond Brig, originally 15th century, rebuilt 1619, and repaired several times since. It has 3 pointed arches with heavy cutwaters. Brae-head House, in Braehead Park Road to the east of the bridge, is an L-plan 2-storey of *c.* 1700, crowstepped with alterations and additions of 1890; it has associations with the legend of Jock Howieson, who saved King James V from a band of ruffians near here in 1530.

From Cramond, Whitehouse Road leads back to Queensferry Road. In the road is Whitehouse, mainly mid 19th century, but incorporating a house of 1615. There are interesting relics in the garden, including an unusual sundial of 1752.

From the top of Whitehouse Road, Queensferry Road continues westwards to cross the Almond at Cramond Brig Hotel. On the left of the main road is the entrance to Craigiehall, an early Georgian style mansion designed (Sir William Bruce, 1699) for William Johnston, second Earl of Annandale, sited on the wooded banks of the Almond, now Army Headquarters for Scotland. In the grounds there is a 17th-century dovecot with 617 nest holes, and an 18th-century grotto with a picturesque rustic bridge.

On the north side of the road, stretching all the way from the Almond to South Queensferry, are the grounds of Dalmeny House, home of the Rosebery family. The house, hidden by trees and not normally open to public view, is a large Tudor style mansion (William Wilkins, 1814–17) with conspicuous turrets and crenellated parapets, built for Archibald Primrose, 4th Earl of Rosebery, whose grandson Archibald, the 5th Earl, was Prime Minister, 1894–5.

The village of DALMENY, reached by a side road from the Forth Bridge Approach, is a mainly 19th-century model village built by the Rosebery estate, but its chief glory is DALMENY CHURCH, the finest and most complete Norman church in Scotland. The 12th-century building originally consisted of a west tower (demolished), an aisleless nave, chancel and apse. There is a fine sculptured Norman doorway; the Rosebery aisle was added in 1671. The whole church was extensively restored in 1937 by the parishioners themselves, when a new west tower was added. The interior now has ribbed vaults in the apse and chancel, and open timber ceilings. In a vault beneath the church lie members of the Rosebery family.

From the Forth Bridge Approach, the old road turns off and descends a steep hill to the water's edge at South Queensferry. Between the two great bridges straddling the Queensferry Narrows lies the ancient and historic burgh of South Queensferry, which was incorporated into the City of Edinburgh District in 1975.

The FORTH RAILWAY BRIDGE is one of the largest in the world, a triumph of Victorian engineering. Earlier plans for crossing the Queensferry Narrows included suggestions for 15-foot road tunnels in 1805, and for an iron suspension bridge in 1818. In 1873 a consortium of Scottish and English railway companies was formed to build a bridge, and sought a design from Sir Thomas Bouch, who had lately won acclaim for his rail bridge over the River Tay. Bouch planned a twin suspension bridge, with a huge 550-foot central tower on Inchgarvie Island; the foundation stone was laid, and one of the brick piers on the island begun, still visible supporting a navigation light. But in 1879 Bouch's Tay Bridge collapsed, taking with it a train and 75 lives. Bouch was dismissed in favour of Sir Benjamin Baker and Sir John Fowler, who designed the present cantilever bridge. It was begun in 1882, a prodigious work which cost £3 million, employed 5,000 men, and claimed 56 lives. The last rivet was driven by the Prince of Wales on 4 March 1890 and the first train driven across by the Marchioness of Tweeddale on the same day.

The bridge contains 8 million rivets and almost as many statistics. It is 1 mile 972 yards long, including approach viaducts, and contains 50,958 tons 1 cwt of steel. The main towers are 330-feet high and 680-feet long, with 350-foot intermediate spans; the two main arches are 1,710-feet wide, and the rail track is 156 feet above high water. The largest tubular steel members are 12 feet in diameter, cross-braced inside, and the whole structure rests on granite and concrete piers sunk up to 89 feet into the bedrock. The ends of the bridge are mounted on rollers to allow for expansion.

A short distance upstream is the FORTH ROAD BRIDGE, opened by the Queen on 4 September 1964. It is just over 1½ miles long, with a central span of 3,300 feet, side spans of 1,340 feet, and 500-foot towers. It contains 39,000 tons of steel and 150,000 cubic yards of concrete, but has now lost its claim to be the longest suspension bridge in Europe, having been superseded by the Salazar Bridge in Lisbon, the Bosphorus Bridge in Istanbul, and the Humber Estuary Bridge which is due to open in 1979.

South Queensferry, an ancient settlement, was created a burgh of regality in 1577 and a full royal burgh by Charles I in 1636; much ancient building survives. Beneath the rail bridge by the old ferry pier, the Hawes Inn, mentioned in Scott's *Antiquary* and Stevenson's *Kidnapped*, is late 17th century with Victorian additions. There remain a number of 17th-century buildings in the High Street, including nos. 17 (Queensferry Arms) and 19, no. 36 (Forth Bridge Hotel) dated 1674 and 1683, but much altered, and nos. 38–40 (Black Castle), a restored traditional 2-storey house of 1626, with forestair at the rear and inscribed pediments. In West Terrace, the Tolbooth is 17th century, altered in 1720 and again in 1890, and incorporating a Queen Victoria Golden Jubilee clock of 1887. West, East and Mid Terraces have 18th-century housing.

Continuing through the town, Hopetoun Road contains Plewlands House, an L-plan 3-storey house of 1641 with turnpike stair tower and moulded doorway inscribed with the initials of the first owner, Samuel Wilson, and his wife Anna Ponton. It was restored in 1955 by the National Trust for Scotland; the inside is greatly altered, but retains some original moulded fireplaces. The nearby Church of St Mary of Mount Carmel contains remnants of a 15th-century Carmelite friary, most of which was long ago ruined but parts of which were incorporated in an 1890 restoration of the church. In the Vennel, the Old Parish Kirk, disused since 1962 and now an architect's office, is a Gothic survival of 1633, and it contains a Burgerhuys bell of 1635. Behind the town, off the Queensferry–Kirkliston road, Dundas Castle is an L-plan keep of c. 1425 with platform roofs, corbelled parapets, slit windows and barrel-vaulted interiors. The attached castellated mansion is by William Burn, 1818; in the grounds is an 18th-century cylindrical dovecot, and an unusual fountain and sundial of 1623, carrying the date and Latin inscriptions.

In the nearby village of KIRKLISTON is a Norman church containing remnants of the original, built c. 1200, notably a fine south doorway; there is a 17th-century burial aisle and belfry. In Kirkliston High Street, no. 25 (Castle House) is dated 1682, with carvings and the initials of the owner and his wife. Outside the village, towards Newbridge, Newliston is a Robert Adam Georgian mansion of 1789. In the grounds are relics of an earlier house on the site, including an 18th-century dovecot, one of the largest surviving in Scotland, with over 2,600 nest holes. Niddry Castle, to the west of the village towards Winchburgh, is an oblong keep of c. 1500, in which Mary Queen of Scots stayed in 1568 after her escape from Loch Leven Castle; it is now partly ruined.

The district contains several other antiquities of note, but being outside the city are strictly outside the scope of this book. Mention must be made, however, of HOPETOUN HOUSE, on the Forth shore west of South Queensferry, a huge Palladian mansion begun by Sir William Bruce in 1696 and completed by William Adam in 1751. Now owned by the Marquis of Linlithgow, it is one of the finest Adam works in Scotland, and is open to the public.

# CHAPTER 9

# The Glasgow Route

♣ ♣ ♣

*Shandwick Place – Haymarket – Donaldson's School –*
*Coltbridge – Roseburn House – Murrayfield – Belmont*
*House – Scottish National Zoological Park – Corstorphine*
*Church – Dovecot – Castle Gogar*

From the west end of Princes Street, Shandwick Place leads westwards to Haymarket, Murrayfield, Corstorphine and the main exit to Glasgow. On the north side is St George's West Church (David Bryce, 1869) in Renaissance style with giant Corinthian columns and a tall Venetian campanile with green copper spire added by Rowand Anderson, 1881. In the garden of Coates Crescent to the west is the city's memorial to W.E. Gladstone (Pittendrigh McGillivray, 1917), removed here from St Andrew Square in 1955. The street becomes West Maitland Street; the south side is by James Haldane, 1825, and the north by John Lessels, 1864. The clock at the junction at Haymarket is a memorial to members of the Heart of Midlothian Football Club who fell in two world wars.

Haymarket Station (John Miller, 1842) is early Victorian, with an Italian 2-storey frontage and Tuscan portico. This was the first main-line railway terminus in Edinburgh; the Edinburgh and Glasgow Railway, opened in 1842, finished here until the boring of the 1,000-yard Haymarket Tunnel took the line through Princes Street Gardens in 1846. The bay platform has interesting original ironwork of 1842.

The Glasgow road continues by Haymarket Terrace to DON-ALDSON'S SCHOOL, an outstanding quadrangular building in ornate Tudor Jacobean style (W.H. Playfair, 1854). The school specializes in the teaching of deaf children, and was built, at a cost of £100,000, with a bequest from James Donaldson, a wealthy printer. The 250-foot frontage has in the centre a 4-storey tower with 4 octagonal angle turrets rising to 120 feet, 3-storey square towers with square corner turrets at each end, and fine neo-Tudor detail, including buttresses, chimneys and tall mullioned windows.

Half a mile to the west, the main road crosses the Water of Leith by a bridge of 1841. Immediately to the north is the Old Colt Bridge, a late 18th-century rubble-built single segmental arch. By the bridge Roseburn Street leads to ROSEBURN HOUSE, a 16th-century tower with 17th- and 18th-century additions, built originally by Mungo Russell, an Edinburgh burgess. On the oldest part is an ornate door lintel, broken and barely legible, bearing the date 1562, a religious inscription in Latin and English, two badly defaced shields, and the Scottish lion rampant. Over an inner door is another lintel, also bearing the date 1562, the arms of the Roseburn family, and another religious motto. The lower storey of the old tower is massively vaulted. An unsupported tradition associates the house with Mary Queen of Scots and Bothwell, Bothwell having been seized by Mary's troops on the main road nearby. Another states that the house was occupied for one night by Oliver Cromwell, after his repulse on the land west of here by General Sir David Leslie's Scots army in 1650.

Beyond the bridge, on the north side in Murrayfield Avenue, is the Church of the Good Shepherd, an interesting work by Sir Robert Lorimer, 1899, in neo-Perpendicular style with some unusual details, including its low proportions and buttress dividing the west window. At the top of the same street is Murrayfield House, a fine 3-storey mansion of 1735 built for Archibald Murray, advocate.

To the west on the main road is Murrayfield Parish Church (A.H. Crawford, 1905) in curvilinear style with an unfinished south-west tower. Opposite is Murrayfield, the Scottish international rugby ground, opened in 1925 to replace an earlier pitch at Goldenacre in the north of the city, and the largest rugby stadium in the British Isles. Murrayfield Road has some sizeable dwellings, including Kinellan House (no. 33) a mansion of 1840 with pilastered frontage. In the adjoining Ellersly Road there are several more, including the Ellersly House Hotel

(Watherston and Craig, 1910), and Innerwick (1826) with elegant pilastered doorpiece and fanlight. At the western end is BELMONT, the grandest of all, a sumptuous Italian-style residence (W.H. Playfair, 1828) with notable interior work, built for Lord Mackenzie, one of the presiding judges at the trial of Burke and Hare.

On Corstorphine Road beyond Belmont Gardens, and hidden by trees, is the mansion of Beechwood, now a school, built *c.* 1780 as the home of General Alexander Leslie, a commander under Lord Cornwallis in the American War of Independence.

A short distance beyond is the entrance to the SCOTTISH NATIONAL ZOOLOGICAL PARK, one of the finest zoos in Britain, covering 80 acres on the southern slopes of Corstorphine Hill, rising to a summit of 510 feet through delightful parkland to give excellent views over Lothian and the Forth. The zoo gates are early 19th century taken from Falcon House, Morningside and erected here in 1926.

On the south side of the main Glasgow route is Kirk Loan, leading to the 15th-century village of CORSTORPHINE and its splendid church. The origin of the name is obscure, but is probably derived from 'Cross of Torphin', possibly a memorial to a son of Thor, which may have stood here. CORSTORPHINE CHURCH was founded in 1429 by Sir John Forrester, Lord High Chamberlain of Scotland, and much of the original remains, although the nave was largely rebuilt by William Burn in 1828, and again by George Henderson in 1905. The church has a squat 50-foot west tower with stone spire, heavy buttresses, perpendicular tracery and, its most striking feature, a roof of great stone slabs. Inside are notable tombs of the Forrester family, including one, an effigy of an armoured knight, of Sir Adam Forrester, who founded an even earlier chapel on this site in the late 14th century. In former days the land between Roseburn and here was a marsh, and the church has a lamp niche wherein a guiding light used to steer travellers.

In the High Street is the Dower House built *c.* 1660 by the Forresters, 3 storey with garret, rubble-built and harled, with crowstepped gables on the main block.

To the south in Dovecot Road, off Saughton Road North, is the only remaining fragment of CORSTORPHINE CASTLE, a large circular dovecot, probably 16th century, tapering towards its slate roof and with more than 1,000 pigeon holes, the finest example in the area.

At the Maybury roundabout, the A9 Stirling road leads to the City Airport at Turnhouse, while the main Glasgow Road continues past Ingliston, where the Royal Highland Showground is the site of Scotland's premier agricultural show. On the north side of the road is Castle Gogar (formerly Gogar House), built by John Cowper and with the date 1625 on a window gablet. There are 18th-century additions; the original house is 3-storey L-plan, rubble-built with crowstepped gables, semi-octagonal tower with balustraded parapet, round tower with conical roof, and corbelled angle turrets. The entrance from the main road has ornate 18th-century wrought iron gates, gatepiers and a bridge of 1672. The lands of Gogar were originally bestowed by Robert Bruce upon Sir Alexander Seton, one of the signatories to the Declaration of Arbroath of 1320.

# CHAPTER 10

# The Lanark Route

♣♣♣

*Haymarket Station — Caledonian Distillery — Dalry House —*
*Saughton Park — Stenhouse Mansion — Craiglockhart Dell*
*— Redhall Mill — Slateford — Hailes House — Spylaw —*
*Juniper Green — Currie — Balerno — Dalmahoy*

From Haymarket station Dalry Road strikes south-west, and
leads to the main exit routes to the south-west, to Kilmarnock
and Lanark. On the north side in Distillery Lane is the CAL-
EDONIAN DISTILLERY (1855), one of two in the city, producing
bulk grain whisky by the continuous patent-still process for
blending. When built it contained the largest whisky still in
Scotland. By the gate is a traditional farmhouse of 1740 recently restored as an architect's office. Off Dalry Road in
Orwell Place is DALRY HOUSE, a mid 17th-century mansion restored and somewhat altered in 1969 as an old people's day
centre. The house is an oblong 3-storey block with 2 semi-hexa-
gonal towers capped with ogee roofs; the one at the south-west
corner is a 19th-century addition. Inside is a notable 17th-cen-
tury ceiling. The house was built for the Chieslie family of
Dalry.

At the south end of Dalry Road the route divides and Gorgie
Road continues south-west as the A71 Kilmarnock road. A
short distance beyond, in Wheatfield Road, is the city's other
distillery, the North British, also producing bulk grain whisky
for blending. At the junction of Balgreen Road is SAUGHTON
PARK, containing an outstanding group of gardens, including
a rose garden of 15,000 blooms, an Italian garden, dahlia garden
and, for the benefit of the blind, a scented garden.

On the south side of Gorgie Road, in Stenhouse Mill Lane, is
STENHOUSE MANSION, a scheduled monument owned by the

National Trust for Scotland and used by the Department of the Environment as a restoration centre for other historic properties. The house is an oblong block with 2 projecting wings; the oldest part is the mid 16th-century north wing, but the majority of the house dates from 1623, and was built by Patrick Ellis, an Edinburgh merchant. Over the main door is a lintel with the arms and initials of Ellis, the date 1623, and the motto, 'Blisit be God for all giftis'. The present restoration dates from 1964, by Ian G. Lindsay.

We return to the end of Dalry Road, where Ardmillan Terrace leads to Slateford Road and the main route to the villages of Currie and Balerno, now within the extended City of Edinburgh District, and the main route to Lanark. At the corner of Newmarket Road are the city's principal grain and cattle markets, moved here in 1911 from the Grassmarket, where a weekly market had been held since 1477. Immediately beyond the canal bridge Craiglockhart Avenue runs east off the main road. Craiglockhart Parish Church on its north side is an interesting example of Scots Gothic by George Henderson, 1899. In Craiglockhart Dell Road is Craiglockhart House, an early 19th-century residence with some Tudor detail. Craiglockhart Drive South leads to Redhall House, by James Robertson, 1758, 2-storey with attics and basement, pedimented front and Ionic columned porch with balustraded balcony; the house was extensively altered in 1900. An earlier Redhall House on the same site was the property of Sir Adam Otterburn, Lord Advocate of Scotland under James V, and was the scene of a siege by 10 companies of Cromwell's troops in 1650, after Sir David Leslie's Scottish army had foiled them in their attempt to break the defences of Edinburgh.

South of Redhall, in Craiglockhart Park, no. 1 (Dunderach) is a private house by Lorimer, 1904, in Scots 17th-century style in snecked rubble with bell roof features.

Back on the main road is the entrance to CRAIGLOCKHART DELL and the start of a pleasant woodland walk which follows the Water of Leith through Colinton Dell, continues out of the city to the village of Balerno, and leads eventually into the Pentland Hills. The walk has been improved and extended by the conversion of an old railway trackbed, and includes a disused railway tunnel. The first stage of the path, from here to Colinton, passes the old grotto of Craiglockhart House, in early 19th-century Gothic. A short distance further on is the disused Redhall Mill, a mid 19th-century sawmill with Victorian water turbine and water-driven timber dressing machinery.

Opposite the path entrance on Lanark Road is Slateford Aqueduct, carrying the Union Canal over the Water of Leith on 8 arches, by Hugh Baird, 1822. Behind it is the railway viaduct (John Miller, 1842), carrying the former Caledonian Railway from Edinburgh to Carstairs on 14 segmental arches.

Opposite Inglis Green Road, the Cross Keys Inn is mid 19th century with railed forestair at the rear. The adjacent Slateford United Presbyterian Church (now premises of G. Laing and Co.), is *c.* 1783, renovated 1826, with a square corbelled bellcote with ogee cap and weathercock. The adjoining Old Manse is *c.* 1800. No. 53, Slateford House, now an architect's office, is 18th century.

In Redhall Bank Road, off the south side of Lanark Road, is an eccentric block of quarriers' cottages by Sir James Gowans, *c.* 1850, built, unusually for this area, of a type of Kentish Rag stone. Nearby in the same road is Millbank, an 18th-century house with pediment, roundel and stone stair.

Opposite Kingsknowe golf course on Lanark Road is Hailes Avenue, containing Hailes House (Sir James Clerk, *c.* 1767) a 2-storey house (now a hotel) with William and Mary detail including a decorative doorway with Gothic fanlight, corniced windows, scrolled chimneys and moulded eaves course.

A short distance beyond on the south side of Lanark Road are the streets of SPYLAW, containing several private houses by Lorimer. No. 3 Spylaw Avenue (Acharra) is of 1897, in English traditional style. No. 10 Spylaw Park (Hartfell) is of 1899, with additions of 1905–9 in a mixture of Scots and English traditional, decorated with a small angle tower. No. 47 Spylaw Bank Road (Glenlyon) is also in Scots-English traditional, with bow and loggia features, as is no. 49 (Almora). No. 52 is by A. Balfour Paul, 1899, built as the Sir William Fraser Homes, with extensive 17th-century Scots detail, including moulded door-pieces, crowsteps, angle towers, and open pavilions with ogee leaded roofs. No. 1 Spylaw Bank Road is 18th century. No. 1

Pentland Road (Lorimer, 1915) is English traditional with some fine detail.

Gillespie Road contains four more examples of Lorimer's domestic work, at nos. 14, 21, 26 and 32, built 1895–8.

At Juniper Green, where (at no. 547 Lanark Road) there is an 18th-century manse originally built as the dower house of Woodhall House nearby, the road crosses the old city boundary and enters the village of Currie, now part of City of Edinburgh District.

To the north of the main road here is Baberton House, a traditional Scots mansion of 1622 built for Sir James Murray, master of works to King James VI, and with the date and initials of Murray and his wife Katherine Weir on the pedimented dormers. Currie village has an attractive row of early 19th-century cottages in the main street adjoining the Riccarton Arms, and there is a Georgian style parish church of 1785. In the next village of Balerno is Malleny House, also built *c.* 1635, for Sir James Murray, later passing to the Scott family, and to the Earl of Rosebery in 1882. The house, in traditional Scots style with a Georgian addition, is now owned by the National Trust for Scotland; it is privately occupied, but its attractive formal gardens are open to the public.

Beyond Balerno, on the north side of the main A70 road, are the twin hills of Kaimes and Dalmahoy, each with the faint remains of an Iron Age hill-fort on its summit.

# CHAPTER 11

# The Colinton Route

♣♣♣

*Caledonian Hotel – St Cuthbert's Church – Castle Terrace –
Usher Hall – Royal Lyceum Theatre – Gardner's Crescent –
Tollcross – King's Theatre – Royal Blind Asylum – Barclay
Church – Bruntsfield Links – Merchiston Castle –
Glenlockhart Castle – Colinton Castle – The Drummond
Scrolls – Colinton Village – Bonaly Tower – Torphin –
Pentland Hills*

From the west end of Princes Street, Lothian Road strikes south
towards the districts of Tollcross, Morningside and Fairmilehead, and is the start of the A702 exit road to Biggar, Carlisle and north-west England.

At the Princes Street corner is the Caledonian Hotel, opened
in 1898 as part of a new terminus for the Caledonian Railway;
the station, opened in 1894, lay directly behind, and has been
demolished. The original terminus lay a few yards to the south
on the same side of Lothian Road opposite the Usher Hall, and
was opened in 1848; only a vestige of the Italianate building
remains, and a road now covers the trackbed of the old railway. Behind the hotel, Rutland Street and Square are by John
Tait, 1830–40. Lord Lister lived at no. 11 Rutland Street and Dr
John Brown, the 19th-century essayist, at no. 23.

On the east side of Lothian Road is ST CUTHBERT'S CHURCH,
standing on the oldest ecclesiastical site in the city. As early as
the 8th century there was a church here dedicated to Cuthbert,
Bishop of Durham, and mentioned in King David I's 12th-cen-
tury charter to Edinburgh. The present church is by Hippolyte
J. Blanc, 1892, in the Renaissance manner, but retaining the
spire of an earlier building dated 1789. Inside are some
examples of Tiffany glass, and a war memorial chapel (P.M.

Chalmers, 1921). Among those buried in the extensive church-yard are John Napier, inventor of logarithms, and the author Thomas de Quincey; there is also a notable memorial (John Flaxman, 1802) to 3 children who died in infancy. At the corner of the churchyard, by King's Stables Road, is a small watchtower (1827) erected to guard against bodysnatchers.

King's Stables Road, on the site of the 16th-century 'Barras' or jousting ground, leads to the Grassmarket. Beside it is Castle Terrace, designed by Thomas Hamilton and Robert Wright in 1826 as part of a new western approach road to the Old Town, but not completed until 1860. It incorporates St Mark's Uni-tarian Church (David Bryce, 1835), in an Italian style with Doric doorway and 2 elaborate pediments.

The eastern side of Lothian Road, mainly 1864, contains the Caley Cinema (Richardson and McKay, 1922), with its large Venetian arched frontage; the interior is in a simple art deco treatment, and was notable when opened for having lifts from the foyer to the auditorium. On the same side is the USHER HALL, the city's principal concert hall, built through the generosity of Andrew Usher, distiller and pioneer of the art of whisky blending, who gave £100,000 for its construction. In Renaissance style (J. Stockdale Harrison, 1914) it is built of chanelled ashlar with a polygonal frontage, semi-elliptical windows flanked by Doric columns, and a copper saucer dome. There are sculptures by Birnie Rhind and Crosland McLure on the front, and by H.S. Gamley on the Grindlay Street side. On the pavement in front is a chiming clock donated by another eminent distiller, Arthur Bell.

To the left of the hall, Cambridge Street (1863) continues Hamilton's Castle Terrace design. Immediately behind the Usher Hall is the ROYAL LYCEUM THEATRE (C.J.Phipps, 1883), in a rich Victorian Renaissance style, with a Corinthian columned and pedimented frontage and a fine interior with 3 tiers of gal-leries on cast-iron columns, a honeycomb pattern circular ceil-ing and ornate friezes on the gallery fronts. The original foyer with its chimney-piece is retained, and there is a matching tea-room on the first floor. Cornwall Street, which rejoins Castle Terrace, has an unusual block by Sir James Gowans (1870), a near-symmetrical composition with 5-storey octagonal bay-window towers in the centre and twin projections on the end blocks, with highly original details and elaborate crests.

On the west side of Lothian Road, Lothian Road Church, designed by William Burn and executed (1830) by David Bryce, is said to have been the latter's first commission, the start of a career which led him to become Scotland's greatest Victorian architect. Morrison Street contains further work by Burn at nos. 6–8 and 10–32. A short distance along on the south side is GARDNER'S CRESCENT, an isolated fragment of New Town development which was to have been the start of a large neo-Georgian scheme, but which was strangled at birth by being on the unfashionable side of town. By R. & R. Dickson, 1826, it has unusual fenestration, with the window divisions or astragals corresponding with the joints in the stonework. Grove Street, running parallel, has some plain town housing of 1822. At its southern end on the Fountainbridge corner is an ornate composition by F.T. Pilkington, 1864, 3-storey with an unusual attic (bell-cast mansard), a fanciful frontage with intricate decoration of flowers and leaves, and dormers flanked by twisted columns.

On the west side of Lothian Road beyond Morrison Street Lothian House, a large Government office block, stands on the former basin of the Union Canal, and the friezes on the front depict various canal activities. Opposite is Bread Street containing, on its south side, the buildings of St Cuthbert's Co-operative Society, an early example of fully glazed curtain walling (T.P. Marwick and Sons, 1937). The Society owns the leading workshop in the British Isles for the repair and renovation of horse-drawn carriages; its dairy still employs horse-drawn milk floats, and royal coaches from Buckingham Palace are sent here for restoration.

Lothian Road continues to TOLLCROSS, where much has been swept away by recent demolition. From the main road junction Brougham Street, leading to The Meadows, contains St Michael and All Saints' Church (Rowand Anderson, 1866–78), making an attractive early Gothic group with its adjoining parsonage and halls. Nearby, at the entrance to The Meadows, the road is flanked by the Masons' Pillars, built by Sir James Gowans for the Edinburgh Exhibition of 1886, and containing

specimen stones from many Scottish quarries, topped by unicorns.

From Tollcross the main road climbs by Home Street to the
KING'S THEATRE (J.D. Swanston and J. Davidson, 1906) with an
Edwardian baroque frontage in red ashlar. The interior is lavish
neo-rococo, originally with 3 tiers, now reduced to 2; there is
a fine marble staircase to the grand circle, and a foundation
stone laid by Andrew Carnegie.

At the King's Theatre the road divides into two alternative
routes to Colinton. The first strikes west along Gilmore Place,
an elegant residential street built mainly 1803–15, with some
later additions. Midway along it, the street Viewforth crosses
the Union Canal by a bridge (Hugh Baird, 1822) with the crests
of Edinburgh and Glasgow carved on the keystones.

The other route to Colinton continues past the King's
Theatre into Leven Street and Bruntsfield Place. On the west
side, in Gillespie Crescent, is the ROYAL BLIND ASYLUM (Robert
Burn, 1801), built as Gillespie's Hospital, a charitable institution for the elderly founded by James Gillespie, a wealthy
city snuff merchant; it later became a school. The frontage
incorporates 2 sculptures from the 14th-century mansion of
Wright's Houses, which stood on the site.

A short distance up Bruntsfield Place on the east side is BAR-
CLAY CHURCH, a bold and unusual treatment of the Second
Pointed style by F.T. Pilkington, 1864, full of eccentric detail,
with a 250-foot spire visible from across the Forth. There is an
interesting heart-and-trefoil-shaped interior with 2 tiers of galleries. Behind the church is the Golf Tavern, one of the city's
oldest inns, and a reminder that the adjoining BRUNTSFIELD
LINKS was one of the earliest homes of golf, where played two
of the world's first golf clubs, the Burghers (1735) and the
Honourable Company of Edinburgh Golfers (1744); the latter is
still in existence at Muirfield, East Lothian. The area was formerly the Burgh Muir, the town's common grazing ground, to
which victims of the plague outbreak of 1645 were banished.

In Bruntsfield Place beyond the Links is a classic group of late
Victorian tenements at nos. 131–151 (Sir G.W. Browne, 1887),
in early Renaissance style and retaining some original shop
fronts with sculptured panels. The adjoining block nos.

155–95 (H.J. Blanc, 1882) has attractive attic gables. On the north side nos. 208–26 form another fine block (Dunn and Findlay, 1902) extending into Merchiston Place, with arched doorway, ogee-roofed turrets and other Renaissance detail. On the south side, Bruntsfield Terrace leads to Greenhill Gardens, with a fine double row of spacious villas built mainly 1849–60, many with unusual detail. No. 42 (St Bennet's) is a baronial copy by John Henderson, 1859, with crowsteps and corner tower; the adjoining archiepiscopal chapel (R.W. Schultz, 1907) has a combination of Byzantine and Celtic motifs under a low-pitched copper roof with central domed Greek-style octagon. Greenhill Park has another stylish group of Victorian villas, mainly 1853–75, including a double pair by John Henderson at nos. 2–4 and 7–9; Henderson himself lived at the latter, 1859–62. In Chamberlain Road, which leads back to the main road, the adjoining graveyard wall has a door lintel inscribed 1645.

Chamberlain Road rejoins Bruntsfield Place at 'Holy Corner', so called because it is surrounded by churches. The finest is Christ Church (H.J. Blanc, 1878), in French Gothic with a wide aisleless nave under a hammerbeam roof. Opposite is Morningside Congregational Church (James Maclachlan, 1929), with its slim tower, in an early Christian round-arched style with open porches, and pantiled roof. Here our route leaves Morningside Road and strikes south-east along Colinton Road.

A short distance along on the north side is MERCHISTON CASTLE, birthplace (1550) of John Napier, discoverer of logarithms, now incorporated into the buildings of Napier College (Alison, Hutchinson, 1964). The L-plan castle is early 15th century remodelled in the 17th century, and was acquired by the Napier family in 1438. It is of 5 main storeys, with a corbelled parapet upon which Napier is said to have strolled while puzzling out his invention, and contains a fine ceiling of 1581 brought from a house at Prestongrange, Midlothian. Napier published his logarithm tables in 1614, and is also credited with the invention of 'Napier's Bones', an early calculating machine for multiplication and division.

Beside the college in Napier Road, no. 10 (Lammerburn) is an example of the eccentric style of Sir James Gowans (1860), based on his system of 2-foot squares, and angles of 22½, 45½ and 67½ degrees. On the south side of Colinton Road is George Watson's College, founded by the first accountant of the Bank of Scotland in 1723 and moved here in 1930; the music school has an early hyperbolic paraboloid roof by Michael Laird, 1964. In Lockharton Gardens nearby are several more idiosyncratic villas by Gowans.

Colinton Road then passes under Easter (519 feet) and Wester (575 feet) Craiglockhart Hill, occupied by a golf course and bisected by the rural Glenlockhart Road, in which is the ruined fragment of the 15th-century GLENLOCKHART CASTLE, a simple square rubble tower built by the Lockharts of Lee, of which little more than the vaulted ground floor remains, and about which little is known.

On the hillside facing Colinton Road is the huge Sacred Heart Convent, now Craiglockhart College of Education for the training of Roman Catholic teachers. Built as the Edinburgh Hydropathic (Peddie and Kinnear, 1880), it is in an Italian style with a 280-foot frontage; it was commandeered as a military hospital during the First World War, and assumed its present use in 1918. Adjoining is a chapel (Reginald Fairlie, 1933) with barrel-vaulted roof and marble-lined apse.

No. 302 Colinton Road (South Cottage), an 18th-century 1-storey house, was the home of Henry Mackenzie, Exchequer official, author of the sentimental novel, *The Man of Feeling*, and the first to review Burns' poetry in 1786. Patie's Road nearby gives access to the Colinton Dell footpath. Beyond Redford Barracks, where Colinton Road turns sharply to the west, a drive on the north side leads to the ruin of COLINTON CASTLE and Merchiston Castle School. The castle is 16th and 17th century, L-plan, now a ruin, with a circular stair tower in the angle and another stair projection on the south wall; the ground floor, now overgrown, is vaulted. The castle, a scheduled monument, was built by the Foulis family of Colinton. Beside it is a large 17th-century lean-to dovecot with crowsteps, also in ruins. Merchiston Castle School is by W.J. Walker Todd, 1930, with details borrowed from Sir Edwin Lutyens. It incorporates Colinton House, built, 1801–6, for Sir William Forbes of Pitsligo, an eminent city banker who financed much of the New Town building; it has an Ionic portico with decorated frieze, and some interesting interior work carried out by W.H. Playfair in 1840, for a later owner.

On the south side of Colinton Road, Redford Road runs east towards Oxgangs and Fairmilehead. On its north side is Redford House, the oldest parts of which date from 1712, when it replaced a 16th-century mansion belonging to Foulis of Colinton; the present house is mainly a low 2-storey block with wings projecting to form a forecourt, with an 18th-century octagonal tower and Victorian porch. By the entrance gateway is the curious lodge house known as THE DRUMMOND SCROLLS, built in 1880 by R.A. McFie, the then owner of Redford House and MP for Leith; the front wall incorporates pilasters and scrolls from William Adam's original Royal Infirmary of 1738, opened at the instigation of Lord Provost George Drummond near the present South Bridge. The lodge also incorporates pieces of the original North Bridge of 1769. A short distance along, near where Redford Road crosses the Braid Burn, is the Covenanters' Monument, also built by McFie in 1880 using Infirmary relics, notably the columns from its original façade.

Back on Colinton Road, a little way beyond Redford Road is Westgarth Avenue, containing a picturesque grouping of church and cottages. St Cuthberts Church (Rowand Anderson, 1888–97) is in a late Scots Gothic style, rubble-built under a tiled roof; nos. 1–7 Rustic Cottages (Robert Lorimer, 1901) are in English vernacular style with interesting dormer detail. Running parallel is Dreghorn Loan leading to Laverockdale House, another Lorimer work of 1914, in Scots 17th-century manner, 3-storey rubble, with matching stables and generator house.

The main road descends to COLINTON VILLAGE at Bridge Road, where on the south side, deep among the trees, is the house of Spylaw, the home of James Gillespie, snuff merchant. The original house is *c.* 1650, with a north front added 1773, most of which is occupied by a curved double stair; there is a pedimented centrepiece, and iron balcony at the first floor. From Bridge Road, Spylaw Street descends to cross the Water of Leith by a mid 19th-century single arch bridge. The village of Colinton is ancient; records show a church here being gifted to Dunfermline Abbey by Ethelred, son of Malcolm Canmore, c. 1100, and for centuries a string of mills prospered along the river here. The village was occupied on 18 August 1650 by ten companies of General Monck's Regiment (now the Coldstream Guards), part of Cromwell's forces attempting to take Edinburgh. The present church dates from 1771, although there are fragments of an earlier building, chiefly the tomb of Agnes Heriot, wife of one of the Foulis family of Colinton, dated 1593. The church is by Robert Weir and Walter Watters, rebuilt (1907) by Sydney Mitchell. Beside it is Colinton manse (1783), the holiday retreat of R.L. Stevenson whose maternal grandfather, Dr Lewis Balfour, was minister of Colinton in the 1850s. The scene has changed little since Stevenson described it in his *Pentland Essays*.

From the eastern end of Bridge Road, Woodhall Road strikes south-west towards the hills. In Barnshot Road, on its south side, no. 2. (Thirlestane) was built by Rowand Anderson for himself in 1884; the painter Erskine Nicol, RSA, was his tenant here. Bonaly Road rises steeply to the very edge of the city and the Pentland foothills. At the top is BONALY TOWER, home of Lord Cockburn, judge and antiquary, from 1811–54, now converted to flats; it was built by W.H. Playfair (1836) in Scots baronial style with turrets and crowstepped gables, and there is a later library wing by Mitchell and Wilson, 1889. The tower has a splendidly romantic setting on the wooded hillside, and is best seen from the public path which continues beyond it to the start of a number of Pentland walks, including one to the nearby Torduff Reservoir, and another to the Poet's Glen, where there is a memorial stone to an otherwise forgotten city bard, James Thomson.

In Fernielaw Road, which also leads to Torduff by a private water board road, is Fernielaw House, mid 18th century, much reconstructed in the 20th century, but retaining its crowsteps. In Woodhall Road, no. 1 is a villa of 1835, and no. 15 (Allermuir) was built by Rowand Anderson, also for his own use, in 1883, with rock-faced rubble, crowsteps, and a red tiled roof. Torphin Road leads to a city bus terminus and the start of more Pentland walks, while Woodhall Road continues to Woodhall

House, originally 17th century with a contemporary panel above the door, but rebuilt in 1815 as a castellated mansion, with 3-storey crenellated entrance tower, for the Foulis family of Ravelston.

# CHAPTER 12

# The Biggar Route

♣ ♣ ♣

*Bruntsfield House — St Margaret's Convent — Marchmont —*
*Church Hill — Grange Loan — Canaan Lane — Morningside*
*— Craig House — Hermitage of Braid — Braid Hills —*
*Mortonhall — Comiston Springs — Comiston House — Caiy*
*Stane — Hunter's Tryst — Swanston — Stevenson's Cottage —*
*Hillend*

The main route from the city centre to Morningside, Fairmilehead and the A702 road to Biggar and Carlisle begins at
Lothian Road, at the west end of Princes Street. The first part of
the route is the same as that to Colinton, described in Chapter
11. We pick it up again here at Bruntsfield Place by Bruntsfield
Links, a short distance before Colinton Road strikes away to
the west.

On the eastern side of the main road, off Bruntsfield Place, is
Whitehouse Loan, containing two historic mansions. BRUNTS-
FIELD HOUSE, one of the oldest mansions in the city, is incorporated in James Gillespie's Girls' School on the east side of
the road. Of late 16th century date, originally Z-plan, with additions in 1605, including the entrance gateway and garden
walls, it is of 3-storeys, rubble-built, with stair turrets and crowstepped gables. The house, which is reputed to have a ghost and
a secret chamber, was built for the Lauder family, but in the
18th century came into the hands of the Warrenders who occupied it until 1935.

On the same side of Whitehouse Loan, at the corner of
Strathearn Road, is ST MARGARET'S CONVENT, established in
1835 as the first Roman Catholic convent in Scotland since the
Reformation, named after the saintly 11th-century queen, and
belonging to the Ursuline order. The convent incorporates the

mansion of Whitehouse, built *c.* 1670, mainly 4-storey, with a square pend tower with ogee roof. It originally belonged to a family called Chrystie, but subsequently passed through several hands. It was in this house that Dr William Robertson, principal of the University, 1762–93, is said to have written his celebrated history of Charles V, and the playwright John Home his *Douglas*. The surrounding convent buildings include a Romanesque chapel by Gillespie Graham, 1835, and a sanctuary and apse in Second Pointed style by Archibald Macpherson, 1896. Also in Whitehouse Loan, no. 21 is a villa of 1835 in Italianate style, with balustraded stairways and low-pitched, broad-eaved roofs.

In Warrender Park Crescent off the north end of Whitehouse Loan, the Dean College, formerly James Gillespie's School, is in a free Renaissance style by J.A. Carfrae, 1914. In Marchmont Road, the former James Gillespie's Boys' School is by Robert Wilson, 1822, in Gothic style with decorated windows. At the eastern end of Warrender Park Road, Argyle Place and Sylvan Place form an attractive town house development of 1825. Sylvan Place has paired arched doorways with fanlights; Hugh Miller the Cromarty writer, geologist and stonemason, who came to Edinburgh in 1824, lived at no. 5. No. 13, Sylvan House, is late 18th century, originally known as 'William's Hutt'.

In Beaufort Road, at the southern end of Marchmont Road, the Grange Cemetery (David Bryce, 1847) contains the graves of the publisher Thomas Nelson; Hugh Miller; General Sir James Hope Grant, veteran of the Indian Mutiny of 1857; and Doctors Chalmers and Guthrie, pioneers of the Free Church.

Morningside Road climbs to the summit of CHURCH HILL, from where there is a fine view into the Pentlands. On the east side of the road is the Church Hill Theatre, converted from a disused church. A short distance beyond, on the east side, is the street of Church Hill, built mainly 1842–50, with nos. 1, 1a, 3, 5 and 7 by John Henderson, 1842–3. No. 4 is decorated with urns and iron balconies, no. 7 has an octagonal tower, and no. 14 has unusual late neo-classic detail. In no. 1 Dr Thomas Chalmers died in 1847.

Across Morningside Road no. 112 (Bank House) is late 18th

century, remodelled in the 19th but retaining its crowstepped gables. In it Cosmo Gordon Lang, Archbishop of Canterbury, 1928–45, spent part of his youth while his father was minister of the parish church opposite from 1868–73. Morningside Parish Church is by John Henderson, 1838, one of the first to be built in the expanding Victorian southern suburbs. In the outer wall is the Bore Stone, a boulder in which, according to a legend perpetuated by Scott in *Marmion*, the royal standard of Scotland was planted when James IV mustered his army on the Burgh Muir to march to Flodden in 1513. The stone was placed here in 1852.

Newbattle Terrace, on the east side of the main road, has substantial Victorian villas of 1848 at nos. 5 and 7, both with ornate doorpieces. In Clinton Road, to the north, stands East Morningside House, a 2-storey, steep-roofed mansion of *c.* 1730, with 19th century and modern additions, but retaining some original glazing. Beside it is an 18th-century small, rectangular lean-to dovecot. Newbattle Terrace leads to Grange Loan, where nos. 129 and 131 (Tyne Lodge) are a fine pair of Victorian villas by F.T. Pilkington, 1872, built as an exhibit for the Royal Scottish Academy.

North of Grange Loan, in Blackford Road, is another fine villa at no. 17 (The Limes), built by the architect Sir George Washington Browne for himself in 1899, in yellow-washed harl under a red tile roof, with an outside stair and finely panelled interior. On the south side of Newbattle Terrace, Falcon Avenue contains St Peter's Roman Catholic Church, an interesting Italianate group by Sir Robert Lorimer, 1908 (additions 1929), of early Christian inspiration with late Gothic details, surmounted by a squat tower. The church, hall and priest's house form a pleasant cloistered open court.

On the west side of the main road, Morningside Place is one of the earliest suburban streets in the area, by Robert Wright, 1824, with pilastered doorpieces and iron balconies. Morningside Park leads to the Royal Edinburgh Hospital for Mental Disorders, orginally built by Robert Reid, 1810, as the Royal Edinburgh Asylum, and extended by William Burn, 1840, a 3-storey, H-plan building in plain classic style. On the east side of Morningside Road is Canaan Lane, whose name, along with the adjacent Jordan Lane and Nile Grove, is obscure, but thought to have been bestowed on the district by gypsies. Nos. 40 and 42 Canaan Lane date from 1820, and no. 42 (Millburn House) has a pair of ornate little gatehouses to the street. The Astley Ainslie Hospital has a fine pair of wrought iron gates and gatehouses by Jamieson and Arnott, 1932, in Scots Renaissance style. The adjoining Woodburn nurses' home is a villa of 1820, with Roman Doric doorpiece and iron balcony.

To the south of Canaan Lane is Nile Grove. At its western end by Morningside Road is the unusual Braid Church (Sir George Washington Browne, 1886), octagonal in plan, under a tall roof with centre cupola, and a pedimented front with semi-circular portico of Ionic columns, and a Venetian window flanked by turrets.

Morningside Road reaches the main centre of MORNINGSIDE suburb at a large road junction, dominated on the east side at the corner of Cluny Gardens by St Matthew's Church of red rubble in Early Pointed style, by Hippolyte J. Blanc, 1890.

Here the southward route divides, the main route being by Comiston Road, which follows the Braid Burn valley past a fine public park with open air theatre and 19th-century gateway at the corner of Greenbank Crescent taken from Comiston House and erected here in 1937. From Morningside crossroads, Morningside Drive leads to Craighouse Road, and the historic CRAIG HOUSE, now incorporated in a branch of the Royal Edinburgh Hospital for Mental Disorders. The original house, which bears the date 1565 on the main door lintel, is rectangular, rubble-built, with a square crowstepped tower. The north-west wing, with an assortment of crowstepped gables, was added in 1746. The house, which is said to be haunted by a ghost known as 'the Green Lady', was built for the Sumsounes of Craighouse. In the 1870s Craig House was the home of John Hill Burton, the Aberdeen-born historian.

From Morningside crossroads Braid Road runs southwards parallel to the main Comiston Road, but higher up the Braid hillside. A short distance up, by the Braid Burn, is the entrance to the HERMITAGE OF BRAID, and the start of several walks among the Braid and Blackford Hills. The path is the old drive to the Hermitage of Braid (Robert Burn, 1785), in a Roman castellated style in the Adam manner, of 2 storeys with pep-perpot turrets at the corners. The house was built for Charles Gordon of Cluny, father of the Countess of Stair. Its last private owner gave it to the city in 1937, and it is now used as a Scout hostel. Adjoining the house is the 18th-century ice house, with entrance passage and arched ceiling, and a large double lean-to dovecot, its back wall decorated with stone urns. The path continues along the Braid Burn, and a left fork leads round the western edge of Blackford Hill where, according to Scott, Marmion surveyed the army of James IV gathering for Flodden. Another path follows the burn past Blackford Quarry; near here a portion of fenced-in rock denotes where the Swiss naturalist J.L.R. Agassiz (1807–73) observed the score marks of glaciers from the end of the last Ice Age. Opposite the quarry, another path leads south across Braid Hills golf course and back to Braid Road, while the main path joins Blackford Glen Road, leading to a bus route at Mayfield Road.

Further up Braid Road, Braid Hills Road leads to BRAID HILLS GOLF COURSE, opened in 1889 and one of the finest public courses in the world, with its excellent springy turf and views over the city. A second 18-hole course was opened alongside in 1922. On Sundays, when no golf is allowed, the course becomes a popular walking ground.

South along Braid Road, past the entrance to Mortonhall golf course, a long winding path leads, in well over a mile, to Mortonhall House. It was built by John Baxter, 1769, for the Trotter family, merchants in the city, but was somewhat altered in 1835. The house is 3 storey, of square plan, pedimented with a circular window in the tympanum on the north side, and a fluted Doric doorway; there is some fine interior work.

From the west side of Comiston Road, Comiston View leads to COMISTON SPRINGS, the source of Edinburgh's first piped water supply in 1681. Off Oxgangs Loan is the original water house, built in 1676, and still containing its original lead cisterns. Nearby, at Comiston Springs Avenue, are the small stone buildings over the four original springs, named Hare, Fox, Teu-chat (Lapwing) and Swan.

A short way south, in Camus Avenue, COMISTON HOUSE (now the Pentland Hills Hotel), was built in 1815 for Sir James

Forrest, in classical style, with pedimented front, giant Ionic pilasters, Ionic doorpiece with fanlight, and semicircular bay at the back. In the grounds is a late 16th-century dovecot.

At the crossroads of Fairmilehead, Oxgangs Road strikes west towards Colinton. A short distance along in Caiystane View is the CAIY STANE, a rugged monolith, now owned by the National Trust for Scotland, of uncertain history, but traditionally supposed to mark the site of some prehistoric battle. A short distance further west, by the entrance to a private Army road to Dreghorn, is HUNTER'S TRYST, a late 18th-century inn of whitewashed rubble which, during the early 19th century, was a favourite venue for meetings of the Six Foot Club, a social and athletic body whose leading members were Sir Walter Scott, James Hogg, 'The Ettrick Shepherd', and Professor John Wilson. The present premises are an extensive modern restoration.

From Oxgangs Road, Swanston Road leads due south to the restored hamlet of SWANSTON, directly under the Pentland peaks of Allermuir and Caerketton, once the summer retreat of R.L. Stevenson and the setting for part of his novel, *St Ives*. The views from here in good weather are magnificent, from Ben Lomond in the north to the Lammermuirs in the south, with the whole panorama of Edinburgh immediately beneath. On the right of the road, before the village proper, SWANSTON COTTAGE (up the farm track in private grounds) was the summer home of Stevenson, 1867–80. It was built by the town council in 1761 in connection with the waterworks here, but has been much altered since, including additions by Sir Robert Lorimer, 1908. At the gate below is Swanston Water House, built at the same time and inscribed, 'George Lind, Lord Provost, 1761', standing over a spring which once supplied some of the city's water. From the car park, a path leads uphill to the village, an 18th-century community, its whitewashed rubble cottages restored by the city in 1962, and displaying the only examples of thatched roofs in the area. No. 16, the White House, is the 18th-century village schoolhouse. From the village, a path returns due east by the side of Lothianburn golf course to Biggar Road, and another strikes into the hills between Lothianburn and Swanston courses.

Back at the main Fairmilehead junction, Frogston Road West strikes east to skirt the southern fringes of the city. On its north side is the Princess Margaret Rose Orthopaedic Hospital (1932). On the south side Winton Drive leads to Morton House, a mansion of 1702, but chiefly late 18th century in its present form. The house has a pedimented front and Doric columned doorpiece with fanlight. By the gateway at Winton Loan are 2 ogee-roofed pavilions, formerly a coach house and dovecot.

From Fairmilehead, Biggar Road leads south out of the city. A short distance out on the east side is Bowbridge, a whitewashed 2-storey 18th-century house mentioned by Stevenson, and on the west side in HILLEND PARK, is the largest artificial ski slope in Britain, open all year round, a quarter of a mile long and equipped with a chairlift.

# CHAPTER 13

# The Liberton Route

♣ ♣♣

*Causewayside – Sciennes Hill House – Scott and Burns –
Grange – University King's Buildings – Blackford Hill –
Royal Observatory – Liberton Village – Liberton Tower –
St Katherine's Balm Well*

From Buccleuch Street, Causewayside runs south as one of two
main routes to Liberton and exits from the city to Peebles,
Galashiels and the Border country. Immediately beyond the
Royal Dick Veterinary College, Summerhall Place is an elegant
tenement block of 1832. Sciennes Road, to the west, contains
the Royal Hospital for Sick Children. 'Sciennes' derives from a
Dominican nunnery of St Catherine of Siena, founded on this
site in the 16th century.

On the west of Causewayside, in Sciennes House Place,
nos. 3–7 form SCIENNES HILL HOUSE, the original 18th-century
frontage of which now forms the rear. It was here, the home of
Professor Adam Ferguson, that in 1786 the young Walter
Scott, then a youth of 15, met Robert Burns, and earned a word
of praise from the bard for being able to identify some lines of
verse on a print.

Also on the west side is Grange Road, principal street of the
opulent Victorian suburb of THE GRANGE. The earliest houses,
all pre-1852, are nos. 30, 32, 34, 40 and 46. Lauder Road has
another good villa of the period (1845) at no. 13; the adjoining
Mansionhouse Road has single storey villas of 1845. In Dick
Place, parallel to Grange Road, no. 38 (Egremont House),
was built, 1869, by the architect F.T. Pilkington for himself in
an idiosyncratic Romanesque style, with fine interior work.
Nos. 48 and 50 are also by Pilkington, in rogue Gothic with
curious porches and chimney gables. Opposite the eastern end

of Grange Road, Salisbury Place has a block of 1810 at its corner with South Gray Street, and contains, on its north side, the Longmore Hospital for Incurables (1877).

Causewayside continues as Ratcliffe Terrace; nos. 27–43, 2-storey pantiled, are late 18th century forming a small court to the street. To the west, in Grange Loan at its corner with Blackford Avenue, is West Grange House, originally 18th century but with extensive later alterations and additions, including a north-east wing by Reginald Fairlie, 1931. Across Blackford Avenue is Oswald Road where, at no. 14, is a finely detailed house by John Kinross, 1907, in 17th-century Scots traditional style, 2-storey rubble-built with corbelled bays. Adjacent in Mortonhall Road are three more by Kinross in the same style (nos. 31, 33 and 35), each with matching walls and gates. In West Savile Terrace is the Reid Memorial Church, by L.G. Macdougall, 1933, after the style of Lorimer.

South along Mayfield Road, at the junction of West Mains Road, are the KING'S BUILDINGS, housing the principal science departments of the University. The 115-acre site was acquired in 1920, and the foundation stone of the first building, the department of chemistry (Balfour Paul, 1924) was laid by King George V. In front is a statue, by William Brodie, of Sir David Brewster, the physicist who discovered the refraction and polarization of light and who was principal of the University, 1859–68. Next came the departments of zoology and engineering, both by Sir Robert Lorimer and John F. Matthew (1929), followed by genetics (1930) and geology (1932) by the same architects. At the south end of the site is the Edinburgh and East of Scotland College of Agriculture (1959). In recent years there has been a major expansion of this campus to house new departments and rehouse old ones moved from the city. The department of botany (Gardner Medwin, 1965), was followed by the Darwin Building (1966) housing forestry and molecular biology. Largest of all is the James Clerk Maxwell Building, named after the Edinburgh-born 19th-century physicist, designed by Hardie Glover and housing mathematics, physics and the Edinburgh regional computing centre. The Cumming Fountain in the gardens originally stood in the quadrangle of Old College.

West Mains Road strikes west towards BLACKFORD HILL, reached by Observatory Road, under a memorial arch to Sir George Harrison (1812–85) a former Lord Provost. Near the summit is the ROYAL OBSERVATORY (W.W. Robertson, 1896) with its distinctive green copper cupolas. The observatory, under the control of the Astronomer Royal for Scotland, is an establishment of the Science Research Council, specializing in the application of automation to astronomy and in the design and building of advanced instrumentation; it is also an important seismic station, capable of recording earthquakes and thermonuclear tests throughout the world. There are 4 telescopes and outstations in Peeblesshire and in Italy; and the observatory has built the world's most advanced infra-red telescope in Hawaii. Beyond the observatory the road continues to the 539-foot summit, where a viewfinder identifies distant hills.

Mayfield Road continues to Liberton Dams, where it joins the alternative route from the city by Minto Street. Nearby is an unusual police station, by Morris and Steedman, 1963.

The main road continues south as Liberton Brae, and enters the old village of LIBERTON where, in 1143, King David I granted to the monks of Holyrood the ancient chapel and its surrounding lands. The name is thought to be a corruption of Lepertoun, from an ancient lepers' hospital which once stood here. Liberton Drive runs west across the Braid Hills. On its south side is Liberton House, an L-plan, well restored mansion of *c.* 1675, with 2 storeys and attic, crowstepped gables, a sundial of 1683, and a lean-to dovecot. On the north side is Liberton Tower, a 15th-century keep built by the Dalmahoys of Liberton, oblong, of 4 storeys with a stone-slabbed roof, and vaults. Adjoining is an early 18th-century farm steading bearing the date 1701.

Back in Liberton Village, Kirkgate contains the parish church, by Gillespie Graham, 1815, replacing a much earlier building, neo-perpendicular with crenellated and pinnacled tower, galleried interior, and bell of 1747.

From the eastern end of Kirkgate, Lasswade Road runs south out of the city. Nos. 37 and 39 are late 18th century. Nearby Gracemount, now part of a school, is a house of *c.* 1800, incorporating some earlier work of *c.* 1770, and with considerable Victorian additions.

From Liberton village the main road continues as Liberton Gardens. On the west side is the entrance to Mortonhall Crematorium, by Sir Basil Spence, 1967. Nos. 65–7 and 77–9 Howdenhall Road are 18th-century cottages, with an old smithy attached to the south end of the latter.

Opposite the crematorium entrance, in the grounds of St Katherine's Home (John Simpson, 1806) is the historic ST KATH-ERINE'S BALM WELL in a small vaulted well house built by order of James VI in 1617 and incorporating a lintel of 1563. The well was destroyed by Cromwellian troops in 1650, but later restored. Tradition states that a St Katherine was despatched by Queen Margaret, wife of Malcolm Canmore, about the year 1080 to fetch a quantity of holy oil from Mount Sinai; on her return, within sight of home, she spilled some here, and a well of miraculous curative properties immediately appeared. Unfortunately none of the real St Katherines of history was alive at this time. The film of bitumen from the coal deposits below which floats on the surface of the water was believed to be the secret of its healing. Its existence was noted as early as 1526 by the writer Hector Boece.

Burdiehouse Road continues south out of the city. On its east side, near Burdiehouse Mains Farm, is a group of 3 18th-century limekilns.

# CHAPTER 14

# The Gilmerton Route

♣ ♣ ♣

*Newington – Minto Street – Nether Liberton – Inch House*
*– Ellen's Glen – Gilmerton Village – Drum House*

From the east end of Princes Street, North and South Bridge form the beginning of the A7 road through the Borders to Galashiels and Carlisle. The first section is covered by Chapter 7, and we pick it up here at South Clerk Street, by Hope Park Terrace in the district of NEWINGTON.

A short distance south from the Hope Park junction, on the east side of South Clerk Street, is the former Newington and St Leonard's Church (Robert Brown, 1823), surmounted by a steeple, with an Ionic peristyle, a fine pointed dome, and decorative cast-iron railings and gates at the front. The building is enjoying new life as a concert and rehearsal hall. To the right of the church, Lutton Place contains St Peter's Episcopal Church (William Slater, 1857–67), in early geometric style with a fine pulpit inside, but its spire has recently been removed.

At the far end of East Preston Street, Newington Old Burial Ground (1820) contains a circular watch tower, a reminder of the days of the resurrectionists. From the corner of East Preston Street southwards along Newington Road is a tenement block of 1825; the block from East Newington Place to Salisbury Road is earlier, c. 1811. On the opposite side no. 10, West Newington House (1805), with a Doric porch and decoration on the façade, was the home of William Nelson, publisher. Nos. 52 and 58–68 are by Thomas Brown, 1825. Salisbury Road has elegant rows of 2-storey villas, mainly c. 1815, several with decorative doorways, fanlights and cast-iron balconies. No. 2 was the home, 1815–30, of William Blackwood, founder of *Blackwood's Magazine*.

Here the main road becomes MINTO STREET, an avenue of elegant villas, built 1808–30. No. 3 (Newington Grange) has more refined detail than the rest. A short distance down on the east side are the gatepiers leading to Blacket Avenue and Blacket Place, among the most elegant late Georgian and early Victorian residential streets. Blacket Place has another set of gatepiers at its other end at Dalkeith Road, and in mid Victorian times the gates were manned by uniformed attendants and closed at night. The street was planned by Gillespie Graham, and consists mainly of large 2-storey villas with heavy columned porches, built mainly 1825–60. Nos. 23–5 are by Sir James Gowans, 1860.

On the west side of Minto Street is Duncan Street, containing the Edinburgh Geographical Institute, home of the world-renowned map makers, John Bartholomew. The building (H.R. Taylor, 1910) has a Corinthian pilastered and pedimented front, with an early 19th-century portico and entrance hall taken from the demolished Falcon Hall at Morningside. Upper Gray Street, leading from Duncan Street, has villas of mainly 1810–50; its continuation, South Gray Street, is mainly 1815–30. Middleby Street, off South Gray Street, has a curious row of apparently 1-storey villas of great solidity which, because of a sloping site, conceal another floor below street level. Nos. 2–12 (1827) form a symmetrical block with balustraded parapets and Greek Doric doors. The rest of the street is *c.* 1817, with fanlights and windows set in arched recesses.

The main road continues as Craigmillar Park, on the east side of which is Edinburgh University's Suffolk Road Halls of Residence (A.K. Robertson and Frank Wood, 1914–25), a campus in the English arts and crafts style with details borrowed from Lorimer. At Nether Liberton the road divides (for Liberton route see Chapter 13) and we follow Gilmerton Road, branching off to the south-east. At the corner Liberton Bank House, 1-storey in whitewashed rubble, is 18th century. Beyond the junction, on the north side of Gilmerton Road, is Old Mill Lane, by the Braid Burn, the site of a mill in the 12th century which, along with the church and lands of Liberton, was bestowed on the monks of Holyrood by David I. Here now is Nether Liberton House, an 18th-century L-plan building, originally a coaching inn, with 19th-century alterations, whitewashed and with octagonal chimneys. The adjoining outbuildings are of similar date, as are the single-storey White House nearby, whitewashed and pantiled, and Liberton Green House. A vestige of the mill (although an 18th century one, not the original) survives at no. 7 (Old Mill Cottage).

A short distance along on the same side is the gateway to INCH HOUSE, a 17th-century mansion whose grounds are now a public park. The house, built in 1617 for George Winram of Liberton, is 3-storey L-plan, with ogee-roofed stair tower, stone dormers, crowsteps, and a vaulted ground floor. The north-east wing has sculptured dormer heads of 1634. There are extensive and ungainly later additions, particularly at the south-west (1891), with an elaborate porch and bay window.

Kingston Avenue leads to the entrance to Liberton Golf Club and Kingston Grange, originally a Robert Adam house of 1785, in a simple late Georgian style with a centre bow, but greatly altered. On the north side of the road, the Kingston Clinic is a florid Second Pointed creation by Pilkington and Bell, 1869.

From the south side of Gilmerton Road, Ellen's Glen Road leads to the 18th-century hamlet of ELLEN'S GLEN, hidden among trees in the valley of the Burdiehouse Burn, and once a small milling community. The old mill house still exists as nos. 1, 3 and 5 Ellen's Glen Loan. There are 18th-century cottages on Gilmerton Road at nos. 360 and 362, and a restored 18th-century house, harled and pantiled, at no. 338. Hudson Cottage, also 18th century, has a sundial over the gateway on an arched iron lampholder.

At the crossroads of Ferniehill Drive the road enters GILMERTON VILLAGE as Drum Street, containing a number of 18th-century houses, notably nos. 16–18, 53–5, and no. 36 (Mitchell's Bar) an 18th-century inn. At the premises of James Watt, Plumber (no. 20), is a most curious dwelling. In 1720 George Paterson, a blacksmith, excavated at the end of his garden a complete subterranean house from the soft sandstone, containing a smithy, dining room, parlour, kitchen, bedroom, cellar and washhouse, each lit by skylight windows, and finished with an inscription above the door. Paterson lived in his cave for 11 years, and was the object of much curiosity.

Ravenscroft Street contains more 18th-century houses; no. 47, Wayside Cottage, is restored.

At the far end of Drum Street a private road leads to Drum House, a fine 18th-century mansion built by William Adam, 1726–34, for the Somerville family, whose crest appears on the façade. William de Somerville came to Scotland with William the Conqueror, and the family inherited the lands of Drum in the time of Robert Bruce. The 15th Lord Somerville introduced the Merino sheep into Britain in the late 18th century. The elegant façade is fronted by a curved 2-flight staircase, and topped by balustraded parapets and urns. The 3-bay, 3-window main front is flanked by lower linking blocks, decorated with niches, joining the wings. The east wing was not built, but the west wing contains portions of an earlier 17th-century house. The interior has some splendid plasterwork by Samuel Calderwood and Thomas Clayton. The grounds contain several items of interest; there is a replica of the old Mercat Cross which stood in the High Street of Edinburgh, removed here in 1756, and returned to the city in 1886 to form part of the existing Mercat Cross in Parliament Square. Nearby is a 17th-century sundial, and over the garden gate is a tablet carved with the arms of Hugh, 6th Lord Somerville, and dated 1524, erected here 1694.

# CHAPTER 15

# The Dalkeith Route

♣♣♣

*Royal Commonwealth Pool – Salisbury Green – Prestonfield
House – Peffermill House – Niddrie – Craigmillar Castle –
Little France*

From the Cowgate in the heart of the Old Town, the Pleasance
runs south to begin the main A68 exit route to Dalkeith, Jed-
burgh and north-east England. The first section is covered in
Chapter 7, and we join it here at East Preston Street, where the
route becomes Dalkeith Road.

Opposite East Preston Street, at the corner of Holyrood Park
Road, is the headquarters of the Scottish Widows' Fund (Sir Basil
Spence, Glover and Ferguson, 1976) clad in copper-tinted glass,
designed to blend with Arthur's Seat behind. On the other
corner of Park Road is the ROYAL COMMONWEALTH POOL (Alan
Reiach, 1970), of Olympic standard, built for the Commonwealth Games. Park Road is one of the main entrances to
Holyrood Park; just before the entrance the road crosses the
now-disused St Leonard's Tunnel of the Edinburgh and Dalkeith Railway.

South of the pool is the large campus of Edinburgh University's Pollock Halls of Residence, built around the mansions
erected for the brothers Thomas and William Nelson, sons of
the founder of the printing and publishing business. Salisbury
Green (John Lessels, 1867) was William's home, in Scottish
baronial style and incorporating, on the roof, a replica of the
18th-century cottage in which his father was born at Throsk,
Stirlingshire, in 1780. The adjacent St Leonard's Hall (Lessels,
1870) in a similar style, was the home of Thomas.

On the west side of Dalkeith Road, no. 58 is a mansion of
1812; no. 60 (Arthur Lodge) is an elegant neo-Greek villa of

1830, reputedly by Thomas Hamilton, of unusual plan and interesting detail. Beside it, no. 62 was formerly the gatehouse to the exclusive residential development of Blacket Place; there is another at no. 74, and yet another, the one-time gatehouse to the private Mayfield Terrace, at no. 122.

On the east side of the main street, Priestfield Road leads to PRESTONFIELD HOUSE, now a hotel, built in 1687, probably by Sir William Bruce, to replace an earlier house burnt down in 1681. The frontage is symmetrical, with twin curvilinear gables and a Doric columned porte-cochère. The interior is notable, with fine 17th-century wood and plaster work, similar in details to that at Holyroodhouse, which is also by Bruce. The porch and bowed extension to the side are additions of 1820; the door and window pediments they replaced, dated 1687, are in the garden nearby, along with an 18th-century sundial. The lands of Prestonfield originally belonged to the Hamiltons, one of whom, Thomas Hamilton, fell at Flodden. They were bought by Sir James Dick, who built the first house in 1676. His grandson Sir Alexander Dick, President of the Royal College of Physicians of Edinburgh, entertained Boswell and Johnson here for several days during their Scottish tour of 1773. Off Priestfield Road in Marchhall Crescent is Abden House, a large neo-Jacobean suburban mansion (T. Davies, 1855) used by the University for entertaining important guests.

At the road junction of Cameron Toll, Peffermill Road strikes north-east towards Craigmillar. On the left a short distance along is Cameron House Avenue, containing Cameron House, a mansion of 1770 built, like Prestonfield, for the Dick family. Nearby, at Cameron Bank (nos. 2 and 4 Peffermill Road), there is a picturesque group of late 18th-century houses with outbuildings and pigeon loft. Farther up Peffermill Road, beyond the University sports ground on the north side, a short drive leads to PEFFERMILL HOUSE, an L-plan, 3-storey house dated 1636, with circular stair tower in the angle and crow-stepped gables, but of no notable history. Peffermill Road continues to Craigmillar and Niddrie, sites of large city housing estates. Beyond Craigmillar, where the road becomes Niddrie Mains Road, in Greendykes Road on the south side are the few remaining fragments of Niddrie Marischal House, the now-demolished seat of the Wauchope family. The tombhouse, off Niddrie Marischal Terrace, is 18th century, built on the site of a chapel founded in 1502, and incorporating fragments of the original building. The adjacent burial ground was used by the Wauchope family from 1685.

Also in Greendykes Road is the Thistle Foundation Settlement (1950), a village of 100 houses for gravely disabled ex-servicemen. Niddrie Mains Road continues to the mining village of Newcraighall; on the main road through the village at Whitehill Street is a row of 18th-century miners' cottages, pantiled, though much altered in later years, and a cast-iron drinking fountain made at the Lion Foundry, Kirkintilloch, in 1907.

Returning to Old Dalkeith Road, it passes on the south side beyond Peffermill Road the entrance to Inch House (see Chapter 14) and reaches, about 1 mile from Cameron Toll, Craigmillar Castle Road, which leads to the largest and most important antiquity in outer Edinburgh, CRAIGMILLAR CASTLE. Its name is a derivation of the Gaelic *craig moil ard* (the high bare rock). It is a noble ruin, fairly complete except for its roof, and is one of the finest examples in Scotland of a fortified baronial residence.

The central and oldest part of the castle is an L-plan tower, with walls 9-feet thick, built by Sir Simon Preston in 1374 and containing, on the first floor, a great hall 36 feet by 22 feet, with an 11-foot-wide fireplace at one end. Adjoining it is a smaller apartment believed to have been the room of Queen Mary when she stayed here. Most of the roof of the tower, originally of stone slabs, has been restored in concrete. Over the entrance door of the tower are the arms of Sir Simon Preston, 3 unicorns' heads.

The next stage of construction, in 1427, was to erect a fortification of towers and curtain walls, amply equipped for the siting of cannon, around the original keep; these form what is now the inner courtyard, and above their main entrance the Preston arms are repeated, together with the inscription 'Craigmyllor' and the lion rampant of Scotland. The courtyard was then filled with buildings on its east and west sides, turning the original keep into a large, U-plan, substantially fortified mansion. Despite its defences, the castle was captured and burned by the Earl of Hertford in 1544. The courtyard buildings were destroyed; the present range on the east side was rebuilt shortly afterwards, while the west range was rebuilt by Sir John Gilmour, President of the Court of Session and by then owner of the castle, in 1661.

During the restoration after 1544, a second defensive wall was added, enclosing an area of well over 1 acre and including extensive gardens and a chapel. At the north-east corner is a round tower built as a dovecot but well supplied with gun-loops.

Craigmillar has many historical associations. In 1479 King James III imprisoned his younger brother John, Earl of Mar, here, for allegedly plotting against him; Mar died in captivity. In 1517 the young King James V was moved here from Edinburgh Castle to escape the plague, and he resided here frequently in later years. In 1566 Queen Mary, deeply grieved at the murder of Rizzio, withdrew here from Holyrood; it was here that Bothwell, Huntly, Argyll and others drew up the 'bond of blood' pledging themselves to the murder of her husband, Henry Darnley. Craigmillar Castle came into the possession of Sir John Gilmour in 1660, and his descendants owned it until 1946, when it was given to the nation.

A short distance along Old Dalkeith Road is the district known as LITTLE FRANCE, so named from Mary's large French retinue quartered here while she was resident at Craigmillar. A large plane tree behind the wall on the north side of the road is said to have been planted by Mary.

On the north side of Old Dalkeith Road opposite Ferniehill Drive, a drive leads up to the site of the now demolished Edmondstone House through an 18th-century gateway decorated with rosettes and crowned with lampholders. It was here that the Scots army assembled before their defeat by the English at the Battle of Pinkie in 1547.

CHAPTER 16

# The Musselburgh Route

♣ ♣ ♣

*Holyrood Park – Arthur's Seat – St Margaret's Well –*
*St Anthony's Chapel – Muschat's Cairn – Queen's Drive –*
*Salisbury Crags – Samson's Ribs – Duddingston Village –*
*Duddingston House – Brunstane House*

Towering over the palace of Holyrood, guarding the old city like a crouching lion, is the 822-foot mass of ARTHUR'S SEAT, the weathered stump of a volcano of the Carboniferous period. The hill is of sandstone with intrusions of basaltic lavas, of which the most prominent is the great dolerite sill on the west side, its overlayer of sandstone weathered away, which forms the red wall of Salisbury Crags. The hill is a geologist's paradise, demonstrating as it does the spread of volcanic lava, the subsequent weathering by ice sheets, and the deposits of haematite, steatite, green fibrous iron ore, calcareous spar, talc and amethyst quartz. The core of the hill is strongly magnetic. The origin of the name is lost to history, but it is unlikely to have had any connection with King Arthur of Camelot; it may come from the Gaelic *ard-na-said* (height of arrows), suggesting a former use as a practice ground for archery. Certainly the name is old, and is referred to in writings of 1508.

Arthur's Seat itself is one of two principal vents of the volcano which was active some 300 million years ago; the other is the smaller and flatter hill immediately to the south-east, known as the Lion's Haunch. From the south-west of the summit, a great gash runs down the hillside to the road below; this is the Gutted Haddie, formed by a violent waterspout in 1744. To the west is the steeply rising top of the lava sheet which ends in Salisbury Crags; the overlaying sandstone has long since been removed by the action of weather and ice, and on numerous parts of the hill the striations of the passing ice sheets can be seen in the rock. On the summit of Arthur's Seat there is an indicator which identifies many landmarks, some a surprising distance away in the Highlands.

Holyrood Park is girded by a motor road, the Queen's Drive, which alternates between seemingly remote glens and broad panoramas of the city and the country beyond. There are entrances at Dalkeith Road and Meadowbank, but the principal one is that by the gates of Holyroodhouse, at the north-western corner of the park. Turning left to make the obligatory clockwise circuit of the park, the road comes almost immediately upon St Margaret's Well under the slopes of the hill. The well, in the form of a miniature hexagon, rib vaulted with a central pillar, is 15th century, moved here from Restalrig and restored in 1860. Immediately above the road, on a small knoll named Haggis Knowe, is the ruin of St Anthony's Chapel and hermitage, probably early 16th century. It is a small, 3-bay vaulted chapel, with the remains of a 2-storey dwelling above; a few yards to the south-west are the remains of the hermitage, partly formed of the rock. The chapel is thought to have belonged to the Knights Hospitallers of St Anthony at Leith, from where they could watch for the arrival of ships, and from whose tower they may have hung a guiding light. It also had some connection with the spring of St Anthony's Well, which rises from a boulder on the slopes below.

From the well a path climbs towards the summit, overlooking Hunter's Bog immediately to its west, long used as a rifle range. Above the east side of the path is the 584-foot Whinny Hill, on which at least 14 lava flows can be recognized. There is an easier ascent of Arthur's Seat from Dunsapie, further round the Queen's Drive.

The drive continues past the artificial St Margaret's Loch, where it divides, with the park exit to London Road ahead, and the circular drive climbing to the right. At the exit is Muschat's Cairn, which figures in Scott's *Heart of Midlothian*, erected near the spot where Nicol Muschat of Boghall, a surgeon, murdered his wife by cutting her throat in 1720, after efforts at divorce and poisoning had failed.

The Queen's Drive now climbs steeply round the eastern

flank of Whinny Hill, and affords fine views over the eastern side of the city and surrounding country. From the car park by the artificial Dunsapie Loch, sheltered by the adjoining Dunsapie Hill to its east, the easiest climb to the summit begins, but it is still a steep path ascending through 500 feet.

From Dunsapie Loch the Queen's Drive continues round beneath the Lion's Haunch and through a rocky cutting to the beginning of Salisbury Crags high above on the right. From the road a path climbs to the base of the crags and follows them round to the Holyrood gateway. This is the Radical Road, built in 1820 at the instigation of Sir Walter Scott, to provide work in a period of high unemployment after the Napoleonic wars; Scott and others were concerned at the increase of militant radicalism among the workers, and sought to dissipate their energies in public works.

From the Radical Road the stratification of the Arthur's Seat rocks can be seen clearly, with the volcanic dolerite overlaying the sedimentary sandstone. It was here that James Hutton (1726–97), the Scottish-born founder of modern geology, observed that some of the earth's rocks were igneous in origin, an epoch-making discovery which he presented to the Royal Society of Edinburgh in 1785 under the title *Theory of the Earth*. In some parts of the crags there is evidence of quarrying carried out by the Earl of Haddington, the last private owner of the park, to pave the streets of London in the early 19th century.

The Queen's Drive continues round beneath the Crags and returns to the Holyroodhouse gate, providing yet more fine views towards the old town. But we take the previous junction near the beginning of the crags, and double back eastwards along the lower and older road towards Duddingston. This route almost immediately passes under SAMSON'S RIBS, a fine formation of pentagonal basaltic columns 60-feet long and 5 feet in diameter, similar in formation to the Giant's Causeway on the Ulster coast. The road then passes through a rocky canyon known as Windy Goule, and emerges on the shores of Duddingston Loch, a delightful reed-edged bird sanctuary. On the hill slopes above can be seen the outlines of prehistoric cultivation terraces; a number of bronze arms and artefacts have at times been discovered in the loch.

Duddingston Loch was once much larger than it is now, fed by springs at the Wells O'Wearie, hidden in a corner of Prestonfield golf course. It has been a bird sanctuary since 1925, and among the 100 or more species seen regularly there are great crested grebe, willow-warbler, pochard duck, bullfinch and chiff-chaff.

DUDDINGSTON VILLAGE has been continuously settled at least since the 12th century when its fine Norman church just outside the park gates was begun; a richly carved Norman door and chancel arch survive from the church's earliest period. The north aisle is an addition of 1631. There are considerable 18th-century alterations, and the present building is largely the work of Rowand Anderson, who remodelled it in 1889 in 17th-century style. The adjoining octagonal watch tower is by Robert Brown, 1824. By the gate are a set of 'jougs', a 17th-century iron collar used to fasten up scolding women, and beside it a 17th-century 'loupin-on stane' with 4 steps, by which corpulent or elderly parishioners mounted their horses. The adjoining manse of 1805 was the home of John Thomson, landscape painter, who was minister here, 1806–40, and 3 of whose works hang in the National Gallery of Scotland. Both J.M.W. Turner and Sir Walter Scott were occasional visitors here, Scott writing part of *Heart of Midlothian* at the manse and becoming an elder of the kirk in 1806. The remaining houses in Old Church Lane are chiefly 1815–20.

Behind Old Church Lane to the north is The Causeway; no. 8, an 18th-century 2-storey restored house, is said to have been that in which Prince Charles Edward slept on the night before the Battle of Prestonpans, 1745, while his army gathered on the slopes of Arthur's Seat. Nearby Ian's Hill House is also 18th century, and the rest of the street is mainly early 19th century. The Sheep's Heid Inn is of ancient foundation, a public house having stood on this site from at least the 16th century, although the present building is mainly mid 19th century; there is an old bowed stair and skittle alley at the back. Nearby Bella Vista is an unusual house, with a late Victorian curiosity attached as a studio, originally built as a billiard room, with giant balusters of Jacobean style. Duddingston was in the late 18th and early 19th centuries a busy weaving village, with up to 40

looms producing a coarse linen cloth called 'Duddingston hard-
ings'.

Duddingston Road West runs north to join the main A1
route at Willowbrae Road. A short distance back towards the
city on Willowbrae Road is a group of large early 19th century
suburban villas, including Nairne Lodge (now Lady Nairne
Hotel) built in 1805 for Lady Carolina Nairne (1766–1845)
writer of many popular Scots songs, including *Caller Herrin'*.
On the opposite corner is Mayfield (R.S. Reid, 1912), a copy of a
17th-century Scottish house with crowstepped gables and stair
tower.

From the Duddingston Road West junction, the main route
continues to the eastern boundary of the city and Musselburgh
as Milton Road.

A short distance along Milton Road West, on the south side,
is the gateway to DUDDINGSTON HOUSE, the former manor
house of the village and now a hotel, and a scheduled monument. Duddingston estate was sold in 1745 by the Duke of
Argyll to the 8th Earl of Abercorn, who built the present house
1763–8 to the design of Sir William Chambers. Duddingston,
regarded as his finest villa, is of 2 storeys, with a 5-window
main front dominated by a fluted tetrastyle Corinthian portico.
The main house contains few of the usual facilities of a home,
most of the private apartments being in a separate 2-storey
block, with pedimented front and cupola, attached at the side.
There is fine interior work, notably the entrance hall and staircase with branching flights. The surrounding parkland, now
Duddingston golf course, was originally laid out by 'Capa-
bility' Brown, and contains an ornamental Doric temple, under
a central dome (Chambers, 1768). King Edward VII considered
buying it as a royal residence, but chose Sandringham instead.

Further along Milton Road, on the south side, Brunstane Road
South leads by a picturesque rubble-built single arch bridge
once thought to be Roman, but probably 18th century (since
rebuilt) to the mansion of BRUNSTANE HOUSE, dating from 1639
but incorporating traces of an earlier building. The house, built
for the 2nd Earl of Lauderdale, was originally L-plan, and was
extended in 1673 by Sir William Bruce, architect of Holyroodhouse, with octagonal stair turrets in the angles and

square angle towers on the south front. The house was occupied 1747–66 by Andrew Fletcher, Lord Justice Clerk and
nephew of Andrew Fletcher of Saltoun, the Scottish patriot
who led the opposition to the 1707 Treaty of Union.

# CHAPTER 17

# The Portobello Route

♣ ♣ ♣

*London Road – Marionville House – Lochend Castle –*
*Craigentinny House – St Triduana's Aisle – Meadowbank*
*Stadium – Craigentinny Marbles – Portobello High Street –*
*The Shore – Joppa*

From the east end of Princes Street, Leith Street descends to
Leith Walk and the start of London Road, the principal exit to
Berwick-on-Tweed and the north-east of England.

London Road drives through the district of Abbeyhill; on its
north side, Marionville Road leads to Lochend and Restalrig.
Marionville House, a short distance down, was built in the mid
18th century by two local spinster shopkeepers, the Misses
Ramsey. The house is a plain rectangle, 3-storeys of coursed
rubble, with a curious off-centre bow-fronted dormer in the
roof. Nearby St Triduana's Church is by Sir Giles Gilbert Scott,
1933, in Scots Gothic, and is unfinished.

In Lochend Park, on the north side of Marionville Road, is
LOCHEND CASTLE, partly 16th century and occupied by the
Logans of Restalrig, but consisting mainly of an early 19th-
century addition. Most of the original house was demolished in
the 16th century but the remaining part has an interesting
massive chimney at its north end. To the north is its 16th-
century dovecot, circular and sharply tapered, said to have
been used during the plague of 1645 for the burning of infected
clothing and belongings.

At the eastern end of Marionville Road, in Loaning Road, is
CRAIGENTINNY HOUSE, mainly 16th and 17th century, built for
the Nisbets of Craigentinny. Originally a plain rectangular
block with small turrets at each corner, it was considerably

embellished 1849–50 by David Rhind, an architect with a passion for turrets.

Nearby, in Restalrig Road South, is the ancient Restalrig Parish Church and the adjoining ST TRIDUANA'S AISLE, a 15th-century relic. The church is originally 15th century, restored by William Burn in 1836, when most of the north and south walls were rebuilt and the tracery replaced to the original design. The style is late Scots Gothic, with heavy buttresses. The west porch is an addition of 1884, and the modern vestry (1962) is built on the site of the old sacristy. The adjoining aisle was once thought to be a well, but is now seen to be part of the ancient church, begun before 1477 and completed in 1486, a rib-vaulted hexagon 35-feet across, with a central column. A chapel which stood above it has disappeared except for a few fragments; a new roof and buttresses were added in 1907. Also in Restalrig Road South is part of the 16th-century wall of the priory which adjoined the church, its doorway and windows long since blocked up. Nearby, no. 62 Restalrig Road South is a house of 1678, with a moulded and dated doorway.

We return to London Road, which continues east past MEA-DOWBANK STADIUM, built for the Commonwealth Games of 1970, and including a main stadium of 15,000 seats, 400-metre athletics track, 3 large indoor sports halls, and a 250-metre velodrome. On the south side of London Road, Meadowbank Terrace leads to the northern entrance to Holyrood Park; behind, in Considine Terrace off Queen's Park Avenue, is Parson's Green House, a good late 18th-century town mansion now neglected.

At Jock's Lodge, named after a hamlet which once stood here, London Road divides, Willowbrae Road striking south-east to form the direct exit route, and Portobello Road continuing eastwards to Portobello.

Halfway down Portobello Road on the north side, in Craigentinny Crescent, is a remarkable tomb known as the CRAIGENTINNY MARBLES built by David Rhind, 1848–56, in the form of a Roman mausoleum with two large marble bas-reliefs by Alfred Gatley. The tomb is that of William Miller, one-time MP for Newcastle-under-Lyme and a wealthy and eccentric bibliophile, whose father was the owner of Craigentinny

House, and who begat this son when he was 89, and his wife 49. The grave inside is 40-feet deep, as specified in Miller's will.

At the foot of Portobello Road we enter the suburb of PORTO-BELLO proper, founded by a sailor named George Hamilton who had fought under Admiral Vernon at Puerto Bello in 1739. Hamilton built himself a house on what was then a desolate and windy spot. It was in 1765 that Portobello attracted some importance with the discovery of valuable clay deposits on the site of the present open-air swimming pool. The manufacturing of bricks, bottles and pottery became important industries, and the last pottery did not close down until 1972. While William Jameson, regarded as the father of Portobello, was exploiting the clay beds, others were promoting the village as a seaside resort, with horse racing on the Figgate Whins, and bathing machines on the beach, introduced in 1795. During the 19th century Portobello became an elegant resort, as its streets of fashionable houses still testify. As a holiday resort it is now in decline and the area between the High Street and the sea is becoming dilapidated. Portobello, made a burgh in 1833 under the Burgh Reform Act, was amalgamated with Edinburgh in 1896.

At the bottom of Portobello Road is the red brick bulk of Portobello Power Station. King's Road beside it is so called because here, on his state visit to Edinburgh in 1822, King George IV came to review a large body of Highland troops drawn up on the sands. Rosebank Lane, on the other side, leads to the site of the old Marine Gardens, now obliterated by industrial buildings. Portobello's open-air swimming pool (1939), built by the mouth of the Figgate Burn which drains Duddingston Loch, has a wave-making machine, underwater illumination, and can accommodate 3,000 bathers. A large covered swimming bath adjoins it. In Bridge Street, beside the pool, no. 3, now derelict, was the birthplace (1870) and childhood home of Sir Harry Lauder.

Pipe Street, a short distance beyond, leads to Harbour Road, and a remnant of the pottery industry. The Thistle Pottery was the last to close, in 1972, and beside its late 18th-century buildings, 2 bottle ovens, dated 1906 and 1909, are preserved.

On the north side of the main street, Figgate Street (formerly

Tower Street) was built mainly 1810–35. It was in a house here that Hugh Miller, the eminent geologist and writer, shot himself in 1856. At the seaward end of the street is a curiosity formed of an 18th-century tower and a 19th-century mansion. The octagonal tower was built in 1785 by James Cunningham, an Edinburgh lawyer, using for the lintels and cornice stones taken from old High Street houses demolished to make way for South Bridge. It remained unfinished for many years, until in 1864 it was restored, and the adjoining castellated mansion added, by Hugh Paton.

On the south side of the main road, Rosefield Avenue and the adjoining Rosefield Place form an attractive development of mainly single-storey villas developed by John Baxter, a local landowner, in 1822. The High Street itself has developments of similar age. Nos. 90–98 are of 1825, with a bow corner to Figgate Street, and no. 283 is *c.* 1820. The blocks on either side of the Bath Street corner, nos. 164–72 and 174–84, date from 1818, the former built as the town's assembly rooms. Bath Street itself consists largely of superior seaside villas built 1805–25, now dilapidated. Bath Place, at the seaward end, has 1-storey cottages of 1815–20, some with coloured doorpieces; no. 2 has a decorative frieze. In Bath Street, nos. 29–39 is a later intrusion, *c.* 1865, with some idiosyncratic detail.

Opposite Bath Street is Brighton Place, another stylish villa development by John Baxter, begun in 1820 and grander than that at Rosefield Avenue. East and West Brighton Crescents, which cross it, are part of the same development. In Brighton Place, at the corner of Sandford Gardens, St John's Roman Catholic Church (J.T. Walford, 1906) bears the stamp of the art nouveau school on its basically Gothic style, with tall louvred belfry windows in its south-west tower, and an octagonal spirelet. Inside is a waggon roof and fine alabaster altarpiece. Beside it, in Brighton Park, is an 18th-century sundial originally situated at the Tower, the curious folly in Figgate Street. Sandford Gardens is also part of Baxter's scheme, built 1825–6, with an iron balcony at nos. 3–6.

Back in Portobello High Street, nos. 186–96 date from *c.* 1810, nos. 198–208 from 1820, and nos. 210–40 from 1823. On the north side, Regent Street is by Lewis A. Wallace, 1815–30;

no. 48 is finely detailed, with Ionic columns and Tudor window tracery. Most of the 2-storey houses are mid-Victorian additions of 1860–70. Marlborough Street and Straiton Place are also part of Wallace's scheme. All the streets lead down to the Promenade, built by the Portobello town council in the 1860s; there were villas facing the sea long before its construction, and nos. 16, 17 and 18 date from 1815. At the foot of Marlborough Street is a fountain, presented by Alexander Paterson, Portobello town clerk, to commemorate several visits made here by Edward VII, then Prince of Wales, in 1860. Here in 1871 was built a 1,250-foot long iron pier jutting into the sea, with an observatory and restaurant at the far end, but it has long since been dismantled.

On the south side of the High Street east of Brighton Place, the Baptist church is said to stand on the site of Portobello's first house built by the sailor Hamilton. Windsor Place, a short distance along, was begun in 1825 on land originally belonging to William Jameson, developer of the town's clay industry. No. 9 is one of the earliest, a typical 1-storey villa, and no. 7 is a 2-storey house of the same date, as is Windsor Place Lodge, a grander residence altogether with an Ionic columned porch, pediment, and 1-storey wings. Nos. 15–17 is of 1840, with Gothic bay windows and elaborate wood tracery. Nos. 35–45 is of similar date, with iron balconies, and a more elaborate house in the centre with a parapet. In St Mark's Place, rejoining the main road, St Mark's Episcopal Church, built privately by Lt-Col Robert Halyburton in 1828 (altered 1892), has a semi-circular front with Doric peristyle and dome.

Back on the north side of the High Street, Bellfield Street and the adjoining Pittville Street are by Robert Brown, 1810–17. No. 37 Bellfield Street was the holiday home of J.G. Lockhart, Sir Walter Scott's son-in-law and biographer, for a short time in 1827, and Scott, who was fond of riding on the sands, frequently visited him here.

Here the main road becomes Abercorn Terrace, and the developments of the early 19th century give way to a predominantly Victorian suburb. There is an attractive square, *c.* 1860, around Abercorn Park, and most of Abercorn Terrace itself is of the same period. The last remnants of an earlier age are in John Street, a mixture of 1820–30 and early Victorian. At the foot of Brunstane Road North, on the Promenade, nos. 75, 76 and 77 are opulent villas by J.C. Walker, 1867–8. No. 75 has unusual details and fine Victorian cast-iron railings. The nearby Hamilton Lodge Hotel is an Italianate villa of *c.* 1840.

In Abercorn Terrace, St Philip's Parish Church (John Honeyman, 1875) is in Early Decorated style with fine stone spire. Here the main road becomes Joppa Road, and the district becomes Joppa which, being the ancient name for Jaffa in Israel, was apparently christened by another retired seadog. The village is of early 19th-century foundation, but the salt pans by the shore were making coarse salt long before that.

# CHAPTER 18

# Leith and the Shore

♣♣♣

*Leith Walk – Gayfield Square – Transport Museum – Pilrig House – Leith – Leith Links – Kirkgate – Trinity House – Constitution Street – Bernard Street – Shore – Lamb's House – Old Docks – Leith Citadel – Leith Fort – Bonnington Mills – Newhaven – Granton – Muirhouse*

From the bottom of Leith Street, Leith Walk forms the main route between Edinburgh and its ancient seaport of Leith, following the line of a breastwork built to defend the city against Cromwell's attack in 1650.

At the beginning of LEITH WALK, by its junction with Picardy Place, the blocks of Union Place and Antigua Street are *c.* 1800, the former being part of a scheme by Robert Burn. On the same side, Gayfield Square is a pre-New Town private development in the grounds of Gayfield House, mostly by James Begg. The earliest block is no. 33, continued as a near-symmetrical frontage in Gayfield Place, and built 1791. The remainder, in a plain but pleasing classic style, is mainly 1795–1808. Opposite, in Elm Row, the corner block to London Road is part of W.H. Playfair's New Town extension scheme of 1821. On the west side, Haddington Place is by Robert Brown, 1825, with Ionic column doorways, and matching columns on the circled corners of nos. 7 and 8; the scheme is continued in Annandale Street and Hopetoun Crescent, named after Major John Hope, on whose estate it was built.

A short distance down the Walk is Edinburgh's TRANSPORT MUSEUM, with a display of preserved tramcars and buses, scale models, uniforms, and other mementoes. On the west side, Middlefield contains a large 18th-century L-plan traditional Scots house, built by Robert McMillan in 1793 with ashlar-dressed front, and stair tower at the rear. Between here and Pilrig Street junction, nos. 372–6 Leith Walk are of 1810, with some original iron lamp brackets remaining.

Pilrig Street marked the old boundary between Edinburgh and Leith. Pilrig Church, dominating the corner, is by Peddie and Kinnear, 1862, in a rogue Gothic style with a rose window, and 2 large windows in the Pilrig Street gables, all with elaborate tracery. Nos. 2–6 Pilrig Street are of 1810; the rest is chiefly 1821–30. On the north side of the street the public park contains PILRIG HOUSE, a once attractive but now abandoned small mansion, built by Gilbert Kirkwood in 1638, occupied for most of its life by the Balfour family. The house is L-plan, with a circular stair tower with square top, and a symmetrical 2-storey front, a later 17th-century addition, with curvilinear gables and Roman Doric doorpiece. It was closed up in 1969. Further down the Walk, on the east side, is Smith's Place, built 1824 and incorporating a late 18th-century house, classically styled with a centre pediment and urn finials.

On Leith Walk itself, the lower end at Leith is mainly of 1820, with a row of 3-storey houses from no. 12 to no. 62; no. 12 has a doorpiece with Adam-style pilasters and ornamented frieze. The street ends at a major road junction dominated by a bronze statue of Queen Victoria by John Rhind, 1907, with bas-reliefs on the plinth. Here we reach the old town of Leith proper, contained chiefly within the triangle of Constitution Street, Great Junction Street, and the shore.

For centuries the port of LEITH was confined to a small but busy harbour at the mouth of the Water of Leith, and the earliest building was in the area of the Shore and Tolbooth Wynd; a few remnants of the old Leith survive here, but the former main street of the town, Kirkgate, has been rebuilt as a pedestrian shopping precinct. It was a sizeable and prosperous town by 1493 when Robert Ballantyne, Abbot of Holyrood, built the first stone bridge across the Water of Leith. But it became prey to attack, notably by the Earl of Hertford in 1544. Three years later, after the Scottish rout at the Battle of Pinkie, Leith was pillaged again, and little from that time survives. Immediately afterwards Leith was taken over by Mary of Lorraine, the Roman Catholic Queen-Regent of Scotland, who filled it with French troops to help her defend Scotland against the rising tide of the Reformation, and the town was fortified with a substantial system of earthworks and bastions, no trace of which survives. In 1560 the Protestant Lords of the Congregation, assisted by English troops, besieged Leith for 2 months, and at one stage had 12,000 men surrounding the earthwork. But the town did not succumb, and in June 1560 peace negotiations began, leading to the Treaty of Edinburgh, and the withdrawal of all forces.

In 1645 Leith, like Edinburgh, was swept by the plague, and some 2,300 inhabitants, half the entire population, were wiped out. Sufferers were banished to huts on Leith Links, and hundreds of casualties were buried there. In 1650 Cromwell occupied Edinburgh and Leith after his victory at the Battle of Dunbar. General Monck, left in charge by Cromwell, set up his headquarters in Leith, and in 1656 erected a citadel and barracks, the gate of which is preserved. Monck induced a number of prominent English merchants to settle in Leith, reinforcing its position as a major trading port. Leith's final brush with battle was during the first Jacobite rising of 1715, when a Highland force under Brigadier Mackintosh of Borlum entered the town, occupied the Citadel, and released a number of Jacobite prisoners. In 1710 the first stone pier was built, and the first dock erected in front of the present Customs House in 1720.

In 1777 the harbour was widened and deepened, and a new west pier was built; but it remained hopelessly crowded, and in 1799 the engineer John Rennie was called in to advise on improvements. He suggested an extensive range of enclosed docks as the only means of achieving a greater draught of water, and in 1801 the foundation stone of the first Leith Docks proper was laid; the old range of docks, running parallel to the shore along the line of Commercial Street, and completed in 1817, is now filled in, and the present range of docks, Edinburgh, Imperial, Victoria and Albert, were built mainly 1852–81. Victoria, the smallest, was first, and the remainder were built after the reclamation of 84 acres of land and the building of the 3,400-foot eastern breakwater, 1862–9. The last major work to improve the docks was the building of a deep-water lock across the harbour entrance in 1968.

We return to the foot of Leith Walk and turn first to the east along Duke Street, leading to South Leith. On the corner, the disused Leith Central station (1903) has typical Edwardian detail, with decorative tiles and elaborate woodwork. In Wellington Place are a range of 4-storey houses *c.* 1817, and 2 large warehouses; the further, by John's Place, is by J.A. Hamilton, 1862, 5-storeys high, a simple design of immense strength, with rope-moulded doorways.

Across the road is the open space of LEITH LINKS, one of the earliest homes of the game of golf, which was played here regularly at least from the early 17th century. Charles I, a passionate golfer, was playing here in 1642 when news was brought to him of the Irish rebellion. John Paterson, an Edinburgh shoemaker, played a celebrated game here with the future James II and built a handsome house in the Canongate on the proceeds. In 1744 Edinburgh Town Council gave a silver club to be played for annually on the Links, and one of the world's first golfing societies, the Honourable Company of Edinburgh Golfers, was founded in the same year. At the western end of the Links are two mounds, known locally as the Giant's Brae and Lady Fyfe's Brae, which held the batteries of Lords Somerset and Pelham during the 1560 siege.

Along the southern edge of the Links, Vanburgh Place is by William Lamb, 1826, with Ionic columns and pilasters with unusual tasselled necking. Hermitage Place, adjoining, is by Thomas Bonnar, 1817–25; Claremont Park, skirting the eastern end of the Links, is particularly grand, probably by Thomas Hamilton, 1827–30. In Seafield Place, at the eastern end, nos. 1–3 are by John Paterson, 1813, the former Seafield Baths, with portico and dome, a fashionable and well-equipped baths and hotel in its day.

From the foot of Leith Walk, Constitution Street runs north towards the docks and the shore. Behind it to the west is the remains of the KIRKGATE, containing St Mary's Church, built by Thomas Hamilton, 1848, to replace a 15th-century chapel which had been the parish church of South Leith since 1609. The present church is in late Second Pointed style, with a balustraded square tower and hammerbeam roof. Vestiges of the original chapel remain in the west piers of the crossing inside,

Leith and the Shore

at the east end. In the churchyard are interesting arched burial arcades containing the remains of the Bartons, great Leith sailors of the 15th century; the Balfours of Pilrig House, ancestors of R.L. Stevenson; Captain Gibson, leader of the ill-fated Darien expedition; and the Rev. John Home, author of the verse tragedy, *Douglas*.

Opposite is TRINITY HOUSE, the headquarters of a company of senior mariners founded in 1380 to run a seamen's hospital, and still in existence. The hospital, which stood on this site, is no more, but two stones from it, dated 1555 and 1570, are set into the St Anthony's Place wall. The present building, by Thomas Brown, 1816, is 2-storey classical, with a fluted Greek Doric column porch, Ionic columns and pilasters at the first floor, pediment, 1-storey wings, and cast-iron gates in front.

CONSTITUTION STREET passes behind St Mary's Church. St James' Church, a short distance along on the east side is an Early Pointed structure with prominent spire, now partly demolished, by Sir George Gilbert Scott, 1863, with a fine reredos and waggon roof inside. Almost opposite is the Catholic Church of St Mary Star of the Sea, by E.W. Pugin and J.A. Hansom, 1854, in Second Pointed style but without a tower; there are mural paintings in the chancel.

At the corner of Queen Charlotte Street is the old Leith Town Hall (R. & R. Dickson, 1828), in an unusual neo-classical style, with an Ionic columned façade to Constitution Street and a Doric portico round the corner. Its council chamber contains a huge painting by Alexander Carse of King George IV landing at Leith in 1822. The Queen Charlotte Street side has a Georgian-style addition of 1903. At the corner of Mitchell Street is the Leith Post Office (Robert Matheson, 1875) in an Italian style with bracketed cornice. The remainder of Constitution Street is mainly early 19th century. At its foot, on the east side, are the Exchange Buildings, by Thomas Brown, 1809. They include, at the north end, the original Leith Assembly Rooms, built in 1783 as a meeting place for merchants. The later building is 3-storey classical, with a central tetrastyle Ionic column and pediment feature; in its original days it had assembly rooms, library, and the old Leith post office, a 2-storey section built slightly earlier than the rest. The Exchange is now used as offices and warehouses.

To the west runs Bernard Street, with a fine array of 19th-century commercial architecture. At the junction is Leith's statue to Robert Burns, a bronze by D.W. Stevenson, 1898, with bronze reliefs on the red stone plinth. At no. 1, on the corner, is Waterloo Buildings, a 5-storey block of 1815–16, with pilastered ground floor and Ionic columns at the bow corner. The block adjoining, nos. 15–23, is by Thomas Beattie, 1815, with arched windows and a recessed centre.

Adjoining is an attractive and unusual Royal Bank branch, built for the Leith Bank (John Paterson, 1806) and modelled on a now-demolished house at Montgomerie, Ayrshire. It is 2-storey classical, its façade decorated with Ionic columns and pilasters, and its bowed front surmounted by a dome. Maritime Street, running from the south side, has unusual warehouse buildings at no. 8 (James Simpson, 1893) with pedimented panel and sculptured crest, built for Bertrams Ltd., and at nos. 11–14 (James Simpson, 1898) in free Renaissance style with cupola and vine sculpture. No. 29 was the birthplace of the Rev. John Home, author of *Douglas*. On the north side of Bernard Street, the Royal Bank of Scotland at the Constitution Street corner is in Italian style by Peddie and Kinnear, 1871, while nos. 22–4 is a double bow-fronted late 18th-century creation with later top storey. At no. 28, by the corner of Timber Bush, the Bank of Scotland is another Italian imitation by James Simpson, 1871, built originally for the Union Bank. Back on the south side, the Scottish Baronial office block of 1865 at no. 37, with its moulded doorpiece, stands on the site of the old White Horse Inn and the King's Wark. The Wark was a large and ancient building, part palace and part arsenal rebuilt by James VI in 1618 and put in the charge of Bernard Lindsay, a groom in the royal household, who opened an inn in part of the premises. The innkeeper gave his name to the street, but no trace of the Wark survives. The last block, nos. 50–58, is a rogue baronial creation by J.A. Hamilton, 1865, with extravagant detail. The corner block on the south side, also built on the site of the King's Wark, is a restored early 18th-century house, harled with scroll skews; the southern end has been demolished except for a finely detailed doorway.

Crossing the western end of Bernard Street is the street

known as The Shore, one of the oldest localities in the port. Here Mary Queen of Scots stepped ashore from France in 1561, and King George IV landed on his state visit of 1822, the latter event recorded by a plaque on the quayside. At no. 28 is the Old Ship Hotel, of 16th century origin, although the present building is 17th century; above the doorway an ancient ship is carved in bold relief. Nearby at no. 20 was another historic tavern, the New Ship Inn, of 17th century origin, but now gone except for its heavily moulded doorway. The taverns were frequented by Burns and Robert Ferguson, both of whom made mention of the good cheer and food. Behind The Shore here, Timber Bush contains a group of 18th-century warehouses. Near the seaward end of The Shore is Leith Signal Tower, built by Robert Mylne in 1685 as a windmill for the grinding of rape oil. The battlements and public house are much later additions. Opposite here, on the west bank of the Water of Leith, are the remains of the entrance to the old LEITH DOCKS (John Rennie, 1801–6), with the original iron swing bridge, 2 sets of decayed lock gates, lock keeper's house, and some old bollards and winches. The modern docks lie chiefly to the east of the river; near the modern harbour entrance on the eastern breakwater is a half-buried Martello Tower built in 1809.

From Bernard Street The Shore continues south along the river bank, following the line of the ancient street. No. 57 is a deserted 18th-century warehouse. Behind it, in Water Lane, is one of the finest surviving antiquities of the area, ANDRO LAMB'S HOUSE, a much-restored early 17th-century merchant's house, combining dwelling and warehouse. Of 4-storeys, harled and pantiled, it has large crowstepped chimneys, projecting stair tower, and half-shuttered windows. Inside are huge fireplaces and ogee-arched sinks on the stairs. In an earlier house on this site, Mary Queen of Scots rested for an hour when she came ashore on 19 August 1561 before proceeding to Holyrood. The house, now owned and restored by the National Trust for Scotland, serves as an old people's day centre.

The line of the ancient main street is continued along Coal Hill and Sheriff Brae, but all has been swept away. The bridge at Sandport Place is on the site of the first bridge across the Water of Leith built by Abbot Ballantyne in the 15th century.

At the top of Sheriff Brae St Thomas' Parish Church (John Henderson, 1840) was built by Sir John Gladstone, father of Prime Minister W.E. Gladstone, as part of a scheme of church, asylum, school and manse round a court. Sir John was born in Coal Hill nearby, the son of a local flour and barley merchant. The church is in a simple Romanesque style, with an elaborate neo-Norman doorway. Off Coal Hill, Parliament Street leads to Giles Street, where, at no. 87, are the Black Vaults, a 4-storey building probably early 17th century, rubble-built and pantiled, with vaults excavated from the natural sand, and originally a large dwelling, with a few fragments of interior work remaining, and a draw-well in the courtyard.

Returning to The Shore, Bernard Street crosses the Water of Leith and continues westwards as Commercial Street. Immediately across the bridge is the Customs House (Robert Reid, 1812) in Greek Doric with a centre pediment over a heavy recessed portico. Next to the Customs House is Dock Place, which contains the gateway to John Rennie's original Leith Docks, with octagonal gatepiers and ball finials. Beside are some of the old warehouses, built 1817–25, timber-framed and with brick vaulted ground floors. On the south side behind Dock Street, Coburg Street contains North Leith Burial Ground, which has been in use as a cemetery since 1664 and has interesting old memorials of ancient mariners. Dock Street itself has the only remaining fragment of LEITH CITADEL, built by John Mylne in 1656, to house Cromwell's troops, at a cost of £100,000. It was a large fort, 400-feet by 250-feet within its massively thick walls, with a central courtyard. It had a short life and demolition began within 10 years of its construction. The long, low pend or vaulted passage which remains was its main entrance.

From the west end of Commercial Street, North and Great Junction Street complete the triangle of Leith and return to the foot of Leith Walk. Great Junction Street contains Junction Road Church (William Bell, 1824) and, by the junction of Henderson Street, Kirkgate Church (Shiells and Thomson, 1885) in Italian Romanesque style with some elaborate detail, including arched doorways with heavily sculptured tympanum and pilasters and a wheel window.

From the southern end of North Junction Street, Ferry Road

strikes west through the district of North Leith. A short distance along on the north side, by the modern Leith Town Hall now used as a theatre, Madeira Street contains North Leith Parish Church (William Burn, 1816), with an ornate front of tetrastyle Ionic portico with a 3-stage tower and octagonal steeple above. The interior has a coved ceiling and gallery on Ionic columns, and the churchyard has ornate Grecian style graves.

North Fort Street leads to the site of the old LEITH FORT, now almost obliterated by modern housing. Only part of the boundary wall and gateway, with the guardroom and adjutant's office, survive. The fort was built in 1779 by James Craig, architect of the New Town, to defend the port with a battery of 9 guns, and housed French prisoners during the Napoleonic wars when it was enlarged.

Ferry Road is crossed by Newhaven Road whose southern half crosses the Water of Leith at BONNINGTON MILLS. A mill has existed on this site since the 15th century but the existing buildings are mainly 18th century, consisting of an iron framed corn mill, 3-storey granary, mill house and office, and a row of 17th-century cottages. The mill was converted to electric power in the 1940s, and ceased operation in 1967, but the 14-foot diameter mill wheel still exists, in ruins. Beside is Bonnyhaugh House, a plain 3-storey dwelling of 1621, which was the home of Robert Keith, Bishop of Orkney and the Isles and Scots church historian, until his death in 1757. North of Ferry Road, Newhaven Road contains Victoria Park House, a small 2-storey mansion of 1789 with a stair bow at the back; the pedimented wings are later additions. The park has a bronze statue of King Edward VII, by John Rhind, 1910.

We return to the dockside at Leith and, from the west end of Commercial Street, follow the shoreline to Newhaven and Granton.

A chapel appears to have existed at NEWHAVEN in the 15th century, but the development of the village really began in 1506, when King James IV erected a shipyard for the construction of the biggest vessel ever built at that time, a gigantic wooden warship the *Great Michael*, launched in 1511. For centuries afterwards the village grew and prospered at the fishing, and the city's fish market is still sited here although the harbour is now used only by pleasure craft. Newhaven became famous for its oysters, and by mid 19th century it was landing up to 6 million a year.

Annfield branches off the shore road and leads to Newhaven Main Street, where some attractive 18th-century heavily restored fishermen's cottages survive, some with rebuilt outside stairs. The Peacock and the former Marine Hotel at nos. 1–5 Main Street (1825) were famous for their fish dinners in the heyday of Newhaven's fishing. From Main Street Fishmarket Square leads towards the harbour, and contains more 18th-century survivals as does Pier Place, fronting the harbour.

In Laverockbank Road, running up from the shore, no. 46 (Strathavon Lodge), a villa of *c.* 1817, was the home of Sir James Young Simpson, pioneer of anaesthesia, 1854–70. York Road, running parallel, is *c.* 1820, with a curious crenellated and pinnacled Gothic villa at no. 24, and other notable villas of the period at nos. 22 and 30. On the shore here a 500-foot long chain pier was built out into the estuary in 1821, and had a brief career serving small steamers which plied to Queensferry and Stirling. Trinity Road, running south from the shore, has a house of 1789 at no. 70, with extensive Victorian additions, formerly owned by the Ballantynes, Sir Walter Scott's printers, and called by them 'Harmony Hall'. No. 102 is in the style of Sir James Gowans by J.C. Walker, 1863. Lennox Row, adjoining, has a neo-Greek villa with fine detail at no. 6 (Grecian Cottage).

Lower Granton Road continues along the shore behind a railway embankment. Boswall Road, behind and above the Wardie Hotel, has an impressive group of large 2-storey villas of 1830, all with Doric porches and notable wrought-iron railings. Lower Granton Road leads into Granton Square, built by John Henderson in 1838.

GRANTON HARBOUR was built by the 5th Duke of Buccleuch, on his own land and largely at his own expense, an act which earned him a statue outside St Giles' Cathedral. It was opened on 28 June 1838, Queen Victoria's Coronation Day, and became an important ferry port on the east coast rail route before the opening of the Forth Bridge. On 7 February 1850 the world's first train ferry began operation from here to

Burntisland in Fife, the coaches being loaded on to the paddle steamer *Leviathan* by a complex arrangement of moving platforms on ramps, designed to cope with a spring tidal difference of 20 feet. They were the invention of Sir Thomas Bouch, an engineer of shadowy qualifications but great imagination, who went on to build the first ill-fated Tay Bridge. The train ferry ceased with the opening of the Forth Bridge in 1890, but a passenger ferry continued to run until the 1950s. Granton is now the base of a trawler fleet, and its eastern harbour is the home of the Royal Forth Yacht Club.

On the south side of West Shore Road, a short distance before the gasworks, is Caroline Park House, with the remains of its 1696 gateway by the roadside. The house is of 1685, 2-storey quadrangular, with ogival-roofed pavilions, and a façade with Doric porch with a wrought iron balcony, and an ogee roof above; some good interior work is preserved. It was built by George Mackenzie, first Earl of Cromarty and Justice-General for Scotland under Charles II, and passed to the Dukes of Buccleuch in the 18th century. It is now occupied as commercial premises by a printing ink manufacturer. To its west is a 17th-century lean-to dovecot, the only survival of Granton Castle, demolished in the 1920s. Towards the west end of West Shore Road is Craigroyston House, a castellated mansion of *c.* 1800, with alterations by Lorimer, 1908. In Marine Drive, the final stretch of the shore road, is Muirhouse, a Tudor-style mansion of 1832, built by the Davidson family, Scots merchants at Rotterdam, with notable frescoes in the drawing room. Marine Drive ends at Silverknowes, but a promenade from West Shore Road, by the gasworks, continues by the shore to Cramond.

# Glossary of Architectural Terms

❧ ❧❧

*Architrave*: In classical architecture, the beam which rests on top of the columns. Also, the moulded frame round a door or window.

*Astragal*: A small semicircular moulding in stonework, also applied to the bars between panes of a window.

*Ashlar*: Masonry of squared stones laid in regular courses, as distinct from *rubble*.

*Bartizan*: A small turret at the corner of a tower or parapet.

*Bellcote*: An open framework on a roof in which bells are hung.

*Corbel*: A block of stone projecting from a wall to support a beam, parapet or turret. Also a series of stepped stonework, each course projecting further than the one below, acting as a bracket beneath a turret.

*Corinthian*: The latest of the three Orders of classical architecture. In all the Orders, the proportions and decorations of the columns and *entablature* are precisely laid down. This Order originated in the 5th century BC, and is identified by the intricate leaf decorations at the top of the columns.

*Cornice*: The top portion of a wall before the roof, often moulded or decorated.

*Crowstep*: A gable whose top edges are stepped rather than straight. A common feature in Scotland and the Low Countries.

*Cruciform*: In the shape of a cross, referring to the plan of a church.

*Curtain Wall*: A wall which does not support a building, but acts merely as a screen. Almost universal in modern high-rise building, but also applied to the outer defensive wall of a castle.

*Doric*: One of the three Orders of classical architecture, and the oldest and simplest. Doric is most easily identified by the plain, undecorated tops of the columns. Greek and Roman Doric are similar, except that the Roman columns have a base, while the Greek rise straight from the floor.

*Dormer*: A window projecting from a sloping roof, usually of an attic room.

*Dovecot*: Known in Scots as *Doocot*. A structure in which pigeons, once a valuable source of food, lived and nested. Found in the grounds of almost all large houses up to the early 18th century.

*Entablature*: In classical architecture, the structure which rests on top of a row of columns, consisting of *architrave*, frieze and *cornice*.

*Fanlight*: The window directly above a door, usually semi-circular with radiating bars suggesting a fan. Also refers to the upper, opening section of modern metal-framed windows.

*Finial*: The ornament on top of a pillar, gatepost, gable or similar feature, often in the shape of an urn, pyramid, ball or fleur-de-lis.

*Freestone*: Any building stone which cuts easily in all directions, which in Edinburgh is invariably fine-grained sandstone.

*Gothic*: The pointed style of architecture prevalent in Western Europe from the 13th century to the dawn of the 16th century Renaissance. Seen in many great cathedrals of Britain, France and Germany, and still the commonest style of church architecure.

*Hammerbeam*: A *Gothic* style of timber roof without direct cross-ties, and with the main beams resting on stone brackets in the wall.

*Harl*: The Scots equivalent to the term *roughcast*, a roughly textured coating of cement over masonry, often with the addition of small pebbles.

*Hexastyle*: In classical architecture, a *portico* of six columns.

*Ionic*: The middle of the three Orders of classical architecture, originating in Asia Minor in the 6th century BC, and identified by the scroll decorations at the top of the columns.

*Lunette*: a small semicircular window.

*Mansard*: A roof with a steep lower slope and a flatter upper portion.

*Ogee*: A roof shaped from a convex and a concave curve; also applied to arches of similar shape.

*Octostyle*: A *portico* of eight columns.

*Pediment*: In classical architecture, the triangular portion of wall above the *entablature*, which supports the roof. Also applied in later buildings to any triangular gable.

*Pend*: A long, low arch, usually an entrance to a courtyard.

*Peripteral*: Surrounded by a single row of columns, as in many ancient Greek temples.

*Peristyle:* In classical architecture, a row of columns.

*Pilaster*: A decorative feature in the shape of a half-column projecting from a wall. A row of pilasters is a *pilastrade*.

*Porte-Cochère*: An open porch large enough for a carriage to drive through.

*Portico*: An entrance or vestibule supported on columns.

*Reredos*: The screen behind the altar of a church, often elaborately decorated.

*Roundel*: A circular feature in stonework, often containing a crest or inscription.

*Rubble*: Masonry built from irregular stones, as distinct from *ashlar*. Random rubble is of stones taken straight from the quarry; snecked rubble is of roughly squared stones built in an interlocking pattern.

*Rustication*: Masonry in which the joints are emphasized by deeply-cut bevelling, usually employed to give a bold and solid effect to the lower part of a wall.

*Sarking*: The wooden boarding in a roof on which the tiles or slates lie.

*Skew*: The sloping upper edge of a gable, usually raised above the level of the adjoining roof.

*Spandrel*: The triangular space enclosed by the curve of an arch.

*Tetrastyle*: A *portico* of four columns.

*Turnpike*: A spiral stair.

*Tympanum*: The triangular space enclosed by a *pediment*, often decorated with sculpture.

*Volute*: The scroll decoration at the top of a column.

# Index

♣♣♣

## Index

Edinburgh Castle, 25–40, 43, 51, 56–60
Edinburgh Co-operative Building Co., 114
Edinburgh and Dalkeith Railway, 138, 186
Edinburgh and Glasgow Railway, 154
Edinburgh International Festival, 49, 54, 103–4
Edinburgh Merchant Company, 75, 104, 146
Edinburgh University, 36, 134–7, 140–42, 179, 183, 186–7
Edward VII, King, 85, 194, 200, 210
Eglinton, Countess of, 73–4
Elizabeth II, Queen, 59, 68, 88, 152
Ellen's Glen, 184
Elliot, Archibald, 118–19, 122–3
*Encyclopaedia Britannica*, 73, 101, 111, 114
Ensign Ewart, 61, 63
Erskine, Henry, 77, 135
Erskine, Mary, 147
Erskine, Thomas, 77
Eugénie, Empress of France, 106
Ewbank, John, 114

Fairfax, Admiral, 110
Ferguson, Adam, 45, 135, 178
Fergusson, Robert, 82, 133, 208
Ferrier, Susan, 105
Fettes, Sir William, 102, 146
Findlay, J.R., 107, 145
Fleming, Ian, 146
Fletcher of Saltoun, Andrew, 195
Flodden Wall, 34, 40, 44, 92, 132–3, 140–41
Floral Clock, 99
Forbes of Culloden, Duncan, 132
Forbes, Edward, 145
Forbes of Pitsligo, Sir William, 167
Forrester, Sir Adam, 156
Forth Bridges, 53–4, 150–52
Fowler, Sir John, 151
Franklin, Benjamin, 104

Freemasons, 65, 74, 80, 103

Gayfield House, 117, 202
Geddes, Sir Patrick, 61–4
General Post Office, 93–4
George IV, King, 46–7, 88, 104, 198, 206, 208
George V, King, 60, 88, 179
George VI, King, 88
George Square, 135–6
George Street, 102–5
Georgian House Museum, 54
Gillespie, James, 73, 165, 168, 171–2
Gladstone, William Ewart, 63, 71, 121, 154, 209
Gladstone's Land, 63–4
Glenlockhart Castle, 167
Goethe, 104
Gogar, Castle, 157
Goldsmith, Oliver, 74
Gowans, Sir James, 139, 160 ,163–4, 166–7, 183, 211
Graham, Gillespie, 62, 74, 109, 112, 115–16, 120, 127, 133, 138, 148, 172, 180, 183
Grahame, Kenneth, 103
Grant, General Sir James Hope, 172
Grant, President Ulysses S., 139
Granton Castle, 212
*Great Michael*, The, 33, 210
Greyfriars Bobby, 130
Greyfriars Kirk, 132
Guthrie, Dr Thomas, 61–2, 89, 100, 172

Haig, Earl, 60, 102
Hailes House, 160
Haldane, Viscount, 102
Hamilton, George, 198, 200
Hamilton, Thomas, 52, 62, 91, 107, 119, 123, 126, 130, 145, 163, 187, 205
Hamilton, Sir William, 111
Heart of Midlothian Football Club, 22, 154
Heriot, George, 74, 131, 133
Heriot-Watt University, 130–31

# Index

# Index